ALSO BY DAVID OWEN

High School
None of the Above
The Man Who Invented Saturday Morning

THE
WALLS
AROUND US

THE WALLS AROUND US

The Thinking Person's Guide to How a House Works

David Owen

Illustrations by Polly Roberts Swain

VILLARD BOOKS
NEW YORK · 1991

Villard Books is a registered trademark of Random House, Inc.

Two chapters of this work appeared in
slightly different form in *The Atlantic.*

LIBRARY OF CONGRESS CATALOGING-IN-PUBLICATION DATA
Owen, David, 1955–
The walls around us: the thinking person's guide to how a house
works/by David Owen.—1st ed.
p. cm.
Includes bibliographical references and index.
ISBN 0-394-57824-4
1. Dwellings—Maintenance and repair. 2. Dwellings—Remodeling.
I. Title.
TH4817.O89 1991   91-50064
643'.7—dc20

Book Design by Anne Scatto
Manufactured in the United States of America
9 8 7 6 5 4 3

For my favorite helpers,
Laura and John

Contents

THE WALLS AROUND US

Chapter 1

Home Improvement for Its Own Sake

I love buying expensive power tools and using them to wreck various parts of my house. This hasn't always been possible. For the first seven years of my postcollegiate adulthood, I lived on the fourteenth floor of an icky modern apartment building on Second Avenue in New York. The only power tool I owned, not counting the vacuum cleaner, was a single-speed nonreversible Black & Decker electric drill, a gift from my father-in-law. Occasionally, I would use this instrument to bore a small hole in one of the walls, creating a pile of dust so tiny I could wipe it up with a Kleenex.

For seven years I glumly punctured the inner surface of my rented dwelling and dreamed of two things: cooking hamburgers on a charcoal grill and owning a real house in which I could make full-scale, messy, time-consuming improvements. These dreams were fulfilled when my wife and I abandoned our apartment and the nearby playground, where our tiny daughter had cheerfully frolicked under the narrowed gaze of drug dealers,

3

and moved into an old house on a dirt road in the country. Because the house was not thrust a hundred feet above a busy city street, I could cook hamburgers. Even better, the house was filled with rooms that cried out for the systematic application of power tools.

I began timidly at first, nailing down a loose board here, painstakingly ruining some old molding there. Each completed task, no matter how amateurishly executed, inflamed my appetite for harder and scarier projects. As my confidence grew, I repaired old windows, installed electrical outlets, hung wallboard, replaced leaky pipes, built furniture, framed partitions, shored up sagging floors, and used a fancy tool called a reciprocating saw to cut a big hole in a wall between two rooms. What would I think of next? That is what my wife wanted to know.

When the results of my projects were unsatisfying, I took solace in my ownership of the sleek new tools that the projects had compelled me to buy. These tools, unlike my projects, were superbly engineered and almost erotically beautiful. I loved them for themselves. Displaying my ugly projects in my house was simply the price I had to pay for the privilege of possessing the breathtaking, costly equipment I used to build them.

I didn't do all the jobs myself. Particularly in the early stages, and for all the truly frightening jobs, my wife and I hired people who knew what they were doing. These people drove their trucks into our yard and became, for the time it took them to complete their work, oddly important characters in our lives. When they were gone, we missed them as we would have missed departed relatives. When they were here, we orbited around them. Instead of rushing upstairs to my office to earn the money I would need to pay them, I generally stood around and watched them work. Some years before, my father had retired from business and embarked on a new career that consists to a great extent of watching people fix the things that break in his house. Drawn by a force I didn't completely understand, I found myself following in the old man's footsteps for hours at a time. Occasionally I was allowed to help.

As the hired workers and I gradually took apart my house and put it back together, I began to think deep, philosophical thoughts about remodeling. An improved home, it occurred to me, is the only major creative work most of us will leave behind when we step into the void. How will future generations judge us? What will they think of the new medicine cabinet in the upstairs bathroom? Will they wonder—in the same way modern scholars attempt to sleuth out Michelangelo's thoughts about chiaroscuro—why we didn't buy a more expensive model?

My house was a canvas on which other people had been painting (or, more recently, wallpapering) for more than two hundred years. The responsibility for nursing this flame of creativity had now fallen to me. I began to feel the burden of both the future and the past and to contemplate my role in the great conversation of mankind—home improvement for its own sake.

ARE HOUSES EVIL?

Every house is a work in progress. It begins in the imaginations of the people who build it and is gradually transformed, for better and for worse, by the people who occupy it down through the years, decades, centuries. To tinker with a house is to commune with the people who have lived in it before and to leave messages for those who will live in it later. Every house is a living museum of habitation, and a monument to all the lives and aspirations that have flickered within it.

Also, of course, it eats money.

Shortly after we moved in, several big things broke. The drier dried two or three loads, then stopped working. It would make a sound that was not unlike the sound of a functioning drier, but the drum would not spin and the clothes would not become dry. Through trial and error I discovered that the appliance would resume normal operation if I pressed my hand against certain spots on its front panel. Doing this made me think of acupuncture. The location of the pressure points shifted from load to load, and sometimes from moment to moment. After a few days, the drier stopped even sounding like a drier, and we re-placed it.

The washing machine, meanwhile, developed the habit of continuing to fill itself with water long after its tub had become full. The extra water, frothy with soapsuds, poured onto the floor while the lid of the machine clanged up and down, as in various scenes from *I Love Lucy.* This water ran under the radia-tor and dripped into the basement. We tried to work around the problem by laundering miniature loads, but the flooding re-turned at random intervals. We summoned a repairman, who came and tinkered with a valve. Then we did a big load. Water poured onto the floor. So we replaced the washing machine.

Not long afterward, a contractor who was doing some work upstairs went down into the basement with me to look at some-thing that needed to be repaired. While we were talking, some-one upstairs happened to flush the toilet in the bathroom on the first floor. We heard water pouring onto the ground. The con-tractor shined his flashlight into the spooky crawl space beneath the bathroom, from which the sound was coming. Water was streaming through the floor above. The toilet, it turned out, was not bolted to the floor. Little more than inertia had ever kept it positioned over the waste pipe. A proper flange was installed and a portion of the decaying subfloor was replaced.

And there were other worrisome discoveries, too numerous to mention. (For example, there was the time I casually asked a plumber to give me a rough idea of how much longer our rusty water tank might last, and he guessed, "Two weeks?") Back when we had lived in our apartment in New York, I had fretted that the money we paid in rent each month was money down the drain. A Twilight-Zonishly huge check on the first day of every month, and no equity to show for it! If we had a house, I brooded, we would pay about the same amount each month but, bit by bit, we would become the owners of a small piece of the same kind of stuff that had built many of the great fortunes in America.

Now that we had the house, we were rapidly becoming the opposite of rich. Mortgage in hand, I realized that there was more than one way to pour money down the drain. In a rented apartment, a broken toilet was fixed, for free, by the superintendent. Now I stood at the receiving end of a seemingly endless procession of unexpected bills.

Then, after six months or so, the flood of catastrophic expenses slowed to a manageable stream. Things still went wrong, and we still had to pay for them, but ten things didn't go wrong all at once.

What had happened? I now believe that when a new family moves into a house, the house suffers something like a nervous breakdown. A few days after the deal is closed, water begins to drip from the chandelier in the dining room, a heating pipe bursts, and the oven stops working. The house is accustomed to being handled in certain ways. Then, suddenly, strangers barge in. They take longer showers, flush the toilets more forcefully, turn on the trash compactor with the right hand instead of the left, and open windows at night. Familiar domestic rhythms are destroyed. While the house struggles to adjust, many expensive items—including, perhaps, the furnace—unexpectedly self-destruct. Then, gradually, new rhythms are established, the house resigns itself to the change of ownership, and a normal pace of deterioration is restored.

There is another possible explanation. It may be that it simply takes several months for a new homeowner to become numb to the cost of maintaining what is essentially a huge box filled with complicated things that want to break—a box that sits outside, day and night, in the rain and snow, surrounded by creatures that would like to eat it.

It was partly in the hope of saving money that I undertook a number of my do-it-myself projects. As is well known, however, doing the work oneself often turns out to be a surprisingly expensive way to economize. In a typical scenario, the eager homeowner buys a hundred dollars' worth of new tools in order to repair a leaky faucet, then spends half a day turning the trickle into both the Canadian and the American sides of Niagara Falls, then discovers that the water cutoff valve under the sink is corroded and doesn't work, then shuts off the water at the main and calls a dozen plumbers, any of whom could have repaired the original leak in a few minutes but all of whom are now busy, then spends Memorial Day weekend unable to flush the toilet, then finally finds an expensive plumber who grudgingly agrees to spend two or three hours installing an exotic new fixture.

The unfortunate thing about being an amateur is that the knowledge one gains in the course of doing something is usually the knowledge one ought to have had before trying it in the first place. Now that I have spent an afternoon wrestling with a reciprocating saw, I have a pretty good idea of how to cut a hole in a wall between two rooms. But when will I get a chance to use my experience? The hole is already in the wall. Filling it up just to cut it properly would be absurd. I could cut a big hole in another wall, but I can't think of one that isn't better off as it is.

Still, many jobs around the house, including ones that initially seem to cry out for professional intervention, can be handled by amateurs. I used to be afraid of getting in over my head. Now there's almost nothing I won't try. When I built myself an office in an old guest room on the third floor, I did everything myself, including the electrical work. Almost everyone is scared of electricity, and generally speaking this is a good thing. But most of the wiring in an ordinary house is logical and straightforward. Many jobs can be done safely and well by people who are not electricians. (To make certain that one hasn't made a dumb mistake, one can have an electrician inspect one's work when it's finished, as I did.)

On some jobs, a well-prepared amateur can actually achieve better results than most pros. Few professional house painters can afford to paint only when the weather is exactly right for painting. To make a living, they have to compromise. They have to paint when it's too hot, too wet, too humid, too cold, too sunny. A house down the road from mine was painted, in part, in pouring rain. Painting in the rain is a terrible idea. When my neighbor's house begins to peel, he'll wonder what happened. The painter will probably blame the paint.

Even if one never lifts a finger around one's house, understanding how the thing works can be extremely useful when hiring someone else to work on it. Most people have no choice but to throw themselves on the mercy of their contractors. Often they have difficulty even envisioning what they want. How can a homeowner weigh the merits of different materials or different techniques if the homeowner has no understanding of what is being proposed?

Actually, I love reading about people who hire someone to repair their doorbell and end up with water in their attic and a bill for $400,000. There's nothing like the misfortune of others to make one feel cheerful and optimistic. But most such horror stories can be avoided. A homeowner who has at least a vague idea of what is being done is more likely to notice when the job begins to go awry.

Even more important, there is a powerful feeling of tranquillity that comes from knowing how one's house is put together and how its systems are supposed to function. My childhood would have been somewhat less anxiety-ridden had I realized that because of the way a house is framed, there was no way for pirates to crawl through the floor from the laundry chute to the space beneath my bed and stab me through my mattress with their long pirate swords.

When my wife and I first moved into our house, few things upset me more than the sight of water coming through the ceiling. Unfortunately, I had a number of opportunities to view this sight. Now, though, the leaks have been repaired and I have learned how they came to exist in the first place. If I see water coming through a ceiling again, I'll feel no more panicky than I ought to feel, and I'll know what to do or whom to call to put things back to rights.

Before I began to develop a sense of how my house works, the things that went wrong with it seemed cruelly whimsical. Now I realize that every effect has a cause and that the causes can be discovered and understood. A gurgle in my baseboard radiators means that there is air in the pipes and that I need to bleed them, which I now know how to do. A wet spot in one corner of my basement means that pine needles have clogged a gutter again. A clicking sound in the control panel of my well pump means that I need to call the plumber. I no longer feel as though I'm being held hostage by the box in which I live.

David Owen

PLAYING

When I was a boy, my favorite places to play were construction sites. Every so often, a new house would go up in my neighborhood. My friends and I would hang around, watching the workmen work. Then, when the workmen left, we would take possession. We would have nail fights. We would throw rocks at the bulldozer. We would climb among the rafters and dream of becoming builders ourselves. I can still remember the envy I felt, at the age of ten or so, as I gazed at a group of carpenters assembling a house across the street. Occasionally, my friends and I would steal a few lumber scraps and try to construct something real-looking, such as a clubhouse or a machine-gun nest.

Then I became an adult and grew wistful whenever I thought of those golden afternoons. My youth is gone forever, I would moan as I trudged through the grown-up world, paying bills and registering to vote. No more hanging around the old construction site. No more shooting at Nazis from the top of a pile of dirt in a vacant lot on my block.

Then, around the time I turned thirty, I made an astonishing discovery: if you set your mind to it, being a grown-up can be even better than being a kid, because you have more money and a car. Grown-ups don't have to steal tiny bits of plywood from a building site. They can drive to the lumberyard and buy entire sheets. When I decided, a couple of years ago, that it might be fun to divide my basement into a bunch of different areas, I didn't have to ask my mother. I just filled my car with two-by-fours and did it. Grown-ups, furthermore, are allowed to use dangerous electric saws.

Working on my house, or helping friends to work on their houses, has provided some of my happiest moments over the last few years. Not infrequently I have found myself lost in that time-collapsing absorption familiar to artists, crazy people, and children. Thomas Jefferson, who spent fifty-seven years happily working on Monticello, viewed building as a kind of play. It didn't matter to him that his house was never finished. (In 1802, when Monticello had been under construction for more than thirty years, Jefferson still hadn't gotten around to putting a floor in the entrance hall. Visitors had to tiptoe over boards laid loosely on the joists.) What Jefferson enjoyed was thinking about the design, and figuring out ways to improve it, and making bricks with his slaves.

Remodeling, as I've come to view it, is not a means to a particular end but, rather, a continuing process of creation and discovery. I tinker with my house in order to make it less mysterious to me. I also do it in order to add my own voice to the voices that whisper within its walls.

THE VOICES IN THE WALLS

My house was built in 1790 or so by people whose names I do not know. It was a boxy, rectangular house of the type now known—in its case, almost accurately—as Colonial. There were four rooms downstairs and four or five rooms upstairs. Each floor was bisected, from front to back, by a hall. The roof was steeply pitched. There were two chimneys and eight fireplaces. In one corner of my daughter's bedroom you can see black marks on the floorboards where, more than a hundred years ago, embers must have fallen from the hearth and smoldered. The original chimneys and fireplaces are now gone.

At some point in the mid-1800s, the house was bought by the man who ran the local general store, which stood next door. The storekeeper's name was Erastus Hurlburt; his wife's name was Emmeline; their son's name was Egbert Erastus. Egbert died before his second birthday. All three are buried in the local graveyard. Eerily, Erastus and I have the same birthday.

Well, not really. But it's still kind of creepy to look at those graves. When I take my children and dog to play among the tombstones, I sometimes stand before the Hurlburts' little plot and marvel that these people once lived, breathed, and lost their keys in rooms I now think of as mine.

I own two old maps of our town, both published in the 1850s,

11

on which the house and store are clearly marked. Above the store was a big room where (according to some old notices I found at the library) productions of *Uncle Tom's Cabin* and *Neighbor Jackwood* were staged. Singing lessons were also given there. A big barn abutted the store, and there were several other outbuildings. The ground in front was littered with corks from bottles of ginger pop, which were sold inside. Boys at the nearby school would sometimes gather these corks and throw them at one another. Today the store, the barn, and the outbuildings are all gone.

Plump with profits from the sale of ginger pop, the Hurlburts undertook a major remodeling project. New yellow pine floors were laid in the rooms on the first floor. New plaster walls were built right over the old walls in what are now the living room and dining room. New plaster walls were built upstairs as well. All the windows and most of the doors were replaced and, in the main public rooms, embellished with paneling and fancy moldings. Three rooms were added at the rear. A carpet was installed in the room that is now the dining room. It was held in place by pins attached to tiny brass fittings embedded in the floor. The carpet is gone now, but the tiny brass fittings remain.

When Erastus died, at the turn of the century, the house was bought by a rich New York industrialist named Van Ingen. Several years before, on land he owned near a bend in the river, Van Ingen had built a vacation hotel, called Holiday House, for poor shopgirls from New York City. The girls would take a train up from the city and spend a few days at Holiday House for next to nothing. Today the train and Holiday House are both gone.

Van Ingen bought Erastus Hurlburt's house not because he wanted to live in it—a shopkeeper's house was much too modest for a man of his wealth—but because he wanted to keep it out of the hands of the Catholics, who were looking for property near the village green on which to build a church. Van Ingen was a fierce antipapist. Every time a house on the green was put up for sale, he snapped it up. (Much to his dismay, the Catholics did finally succeed in buying a piece of land, about a quarter mile below the green, where they built a very nice church.)

Shortly after buying the house, Van Ingen leased it for a token sum to a local group that was forming a social club for residents of the town. The Hurlburts' home became a clubhouse. On August 1, 1903, the governors of the club voted to install a telephone, on the condition that it not cost more than three dollars per month. Other improvements were made as well. One hundred and thirty dollars was spent on painting and wallpapering. A piano was rented for ten dollars. A janitor was hired. Tipping was banned.

In time, a tennis court was built behind and below the house. I have seen photographs of people with large mustaches striking humorous poses on this court, which no longer exists. Attached to the back of the house was a wooden deck that overlooked the court; it, too, is gone. Children who are now old ladies took dancing lessons in the living room. Ladies who were already old played cards. Then, over the years, the club outgrew the house. A new club hall, with a large stage for dramatic productions, was built next door. The stage lasted until 1990, when it was torn down as part of a general renovation. The club, though, still exists.

In 1945 the house was sold to a local boys' boarding school, whose campus it adjoined. The school had been founded nearly a hundred years before by an educational pioneer who, in the late 1800s, disciplined unruly boys by making them sit for extended periods on each other's laps. He would also send troublemakers outside to hug trees for an hour. The house became a dormitory, called Hurlburt. When I tore apart the carpenter-ant-infested front steps of my house, I discovered a small painted sign that had hung beside the front door in those days. The sign said HURLBURT. It now hangs above a door in our kitchen.

Every now and then I meet a man who lived in Hurlburt as a boy. One man I know, a local carpenter, remembers tumbling down the stairs and putting his knee through one of the walls. Another man I know remembers going into Hurlburt as a young boy to gaze at members of the Yale football team, who held a summer practice camp at the boarding school. When I was pulling down a crumbling wall in the room that is now my office, I came across a large mouse nest crammed into the cavity

13

between two wall studs. The nest had been abandoned many years before. It was made of leaves, bits of wood, dust, string, and a tattered piece of cloth. The piece of cloth turned out to be the remains of a boy's undershirt. A name tag was still sewn into what was left of the collar: McDonald. The boy probably never noticed the disappearance of his shirt. But what an achievement for the mouse! Tiptoeing across the darkened room, dragging a human-sized expanse of cloth behind the radiator, pulling it backward through a chink in the plaster—and all for the sake of home improvement.

In converting the house from a club to a dormitory, the school made a number of alterations. A second-floor bedroom became a huge bathroom, complete with urinals and a large walk-in shower. Institutional green-gray paint was spread on the yellow pine and chestnut floors. Most of the walls were painted light green or light blue. The third floor was enlarged through the addition of six dormers, three in the front and three in the back. An illuminated exit sign was installed at the head of the stairs.

The house served as a dormitory for twenty-five years. Then, in 1969, the school decided to replace it with something new and modern. Like much of the world's most depressing campus architecture, the new building would be designed by an alumnus. To make room for it, Hurlburt would have to be torn down.

GHOSTS

In 1969, its final year of service as a dormitory, Hurlburt was inhabited by adolescent boys named Addicks, Allen, Bowen, Brown, Bucciarelli, Buckley, Farley, Forster, Labas, Newhouse, and St. Clair. I know their names because someone inscribed them in black ink on the walls of what is now my daughter's bedroom. We found them when we removed the wallpaper. The names are spaced out around the room in eleven numbered areas marked off on the walls. My wife and I initially hypothesized that these areas had something to do with the arrangement of beds, but the room is too small to have housed eleven teenagers. Could it have been a study hall? No, Addicks's and St. Clair's areas meet at a corner; their desks would have had to sit one on top of the other. The same fact rules out the room's having been used for storage.

We finally decided that the walls had been parceled out simply so that the boys could cover them with graffiti. The house was going to be demolished at the end of the year; why not divvy it up and make a mess before the wreckers arrived? A dormitory can be an oppressively anonymous structure. Now its impending destruction gave these boys the opportunity to give it, if only for a moment, a comforting human face. Because most of the decoration is in Forster's area, I assume that this was his idea.

Forster in 1969 was a young man with a great deal on his mind. "Why was I not made of stone like you?" he wrote beneath a window—perhaps looking meaningfully over his shoulder at Bucciarelli, whose assigned area remained undefiled. Up near the ceiling Forster painted a pink-and-red television set and filled its screen with pictures clipped from newspapers and magazines. On the wall above and beside it he wrote, "You love to watch it: the show." Since the clippings came off with the wallpaper, we can only guess what Forster's housemates saw when they looked at the screen. Soldiers in Vietnam, a peace sign, and a naked girl at Woodstock? Richard Nixon, a mushroom cloud, and a policeman frisking a hippie? (In the adjoining area Labas wrote, "I've got you in the sights of my gun" and "Love and death—are they man made and fake too?")

Below the television set and headed "Something to Live For" is a long, unpunctuated outburst. "Strike for the eight demands," Forster wrote angrily in dripping black and red paint,

    strike be
    cause you hate cops
    strike because your
    roommate was clubbed
    strike to stop expansion
    strike to seize control
    of your life strike to
    become more human

strike to return Paine Hall
scholarships strike be
cause there's no poetry
in your lectures
strike because classes
are a bore strike for
power strike to smash the
corporation strike to make
yourself free strike to
abolish ROTC strike because
they are trying to squeeze
the life out of you

Forster's proclamation is not indigenous; it was borrowed from another civilization (Harvard). There is only one full-time cop in this town, and no one, so far as we know, hates him. The thought of him trudging up the hill from his desk in the basement of the town hall to clobber a ninth-grader is intriguing but improbable. Nor is there an entity nearby that in seriousness could be called a corporation, much less "the" corporation. The local economy is based on groceries and hardware.

But Forster doubtless did not intend his demands to be interpreted literally or dissected coldly by historians. Thumbing through the newspaper one morning, perhaps, he stumbled upon a statement that seemed to echo his very own thoughts, but ne'er so well express'd, and wrote it on the wall. "To become more human," he repeated, thinking, perhaps, of his history teacher. Nor is his statement less authentic for having been pinched. Very likely he did feel that his classes were boring and that the life was being squeezed out of him. A lot of people Forster's age feel that way.

My wife and I were roughly Forster's age in 1969, and we looked at the world in just about the same way he did. Neither of us ever wrote a list of demands on a bedroom wall, but either of us might have. I'm just as glad I never did. One of history's cruelest tricks is to take words that sounded pretty good at the time and make them seem stupid. In Forster's case, history's trick was a last-minute reprieve for Hurlburt.

Just before the house was to be demolished, a history teacher offered to buy it and move it somewhere else. The school agreed.

The price was one dollar. Today there's a hot market for old houses. People buy them, dismantle them, move them across the country, put them back together, and sell them for a lot of money. But in 1969 an old house was often just an eyesore and an impediment to progress.

In January of 1970, the history teacher used an electric saw to separate Erastus Hurlburt's addition from the main part of the house. Then, on the coldest day of the year, a house-moving crew from a nearby town jacked it off the ground and rolled a big truck underneath it. There was a brick chimney on one side of the house. The movers said they thought they could move it right along with the house. When the house rolled down the road, the chimney went with it. It bowed out several inches, but it snapped back at the end of the ride. Much of the town turned out to watch the move. Power lines along the route had to be taken down so that the truck could pass. When the main part of the house was in place, the truck went back for the addition. You can still see the scar where the two parts were put back together. The rejoined floorboards are misaligned by half an inch.

After the two parts had been joined back together, the history teacher set about turning Hurlburt back into a house. He got rid of the urinals and the enormous shower. He tore down some walls that the school had put in. He turned a bedroom into a kitchen. He turned the third floor into an apartment. And, most of all, he covered the walls with wallpaper.

Wallpaper was the history teacher's answer to every aesthetic question. He pasted it in closets; he spread it out in cabinets; he even stretched it over the bare studs alongside the stairway to the basement. For the history teacher, wallpaper was a way of imposing harmony on a house that spoke with many voices. Wallpaper covered Forster's demands. It covered the boarding school's light blue paint, which covered the social club's paint and wallpaper, which covered Erastus Hurlburt's brand-new walls, which covered the walls of the people whose names we do not know.

When my wife and I spent our first night in our new house, I walked from room to room looking at the history teacher's wallpaper and thinking, Now it's my turn.

Chapter 2

The Best Paint in the World

If you are painting your house with a traditional oil paint, be sure to keep cows out of your yard. A cow will walk up to a freshly oil-painted house and lick it. A cow will also drink oil paint from a can. Power companies sometimes have to deal with angry farmers whose cows have become sick from licking freshly painted electrical-transmission towers. If a cow dies after licking paint from one of these towers, it will typically turn out to have been the farmer's prize cow.

Cows like traditional oil paint because the oil in it—linseed oil—is made from flaxseed, which for cows is food. The species of flax plant from which linseed oil is made has slender stems and pretty blue flowers. Linseed oil is useful as a paint ingredient because it hardens when exposed to oxygen. (It performs the same function in linoleum, which is named for it and which was invented in 1863. The other ingredients of linoleum are rosin, powdered cork, pigment, and canvas or burlap.) There are several other natural oils that harden when they oxidize. One of them is tung oil, which is made from the seeds of a tree that grows in Asia and which is sometimes used in furniture finishes. (Did anyone ever try to make tungoleum?) But most oils just sit there no matter how much oxygen they're exposed to. A paint made out of corn oil, for example, would be a terrible paint, although it might be of interest to a cow.

I learned about cows and linseed oil from Henry Long, who at the time I talked to him was the chairman of Keeler & Long, Inc., a small paint manufacturer whose headquarters are in Watertown, Connecticut. (He has since retired.) I had heard about Keeler & Long a couple of years before from a man whose business was selling antique building materials. This man had told me that he had discovered the best paint in the world. He said that this paint was very expensive, and that it wasn't sold in stores, but that it was worth tracking down because it would last for twenty years or more. Twenty years is at least two or three times as long as ordinary house paint usually lasts. The man said that he had used this paint on the several barnlike buildings in which he kept his antique building materials. I went outside and looked at these buildings. They did not appear to be in need of repainting.

Shortly after my conversation with the man, I forgot the name of the company that made the remarkable paint. I thought about calling the man, but I didn't get around to doing it. Then the man died. My house had needed painting for several years, but now it *really* needed painting. I called the dead man's business number. The person who answered the phone gave me the name and number of someone else, who gave me the name and number of someone else. Finally I was able to reach a man who was able to give me the information I needed. Watertown is less than an hour from where I live. I made an appointment to meet with Henry Long.

On my way to Watertown, I thought about how interesting it was that the best paint in the world was made virtually in my own backyard. Maybe I ought to paint my car with this paint, I thought. Or how about my driveway? Perhaps I would open a paint store and become a leading distributor. I got a little lost as I was having these thoughts, and I had to call Henry Long from a pay phone to ask for more directions. Finally I found his company's headquarters, a big low building on a hill.

On a wall in Henry Long's office was a broken golf club that had been twisted into a shape that was something like the shape of a flugelhorn. The rest of the office looked like just a normal office. Long himself had gray hair and looked old enough to be someone's grandfather, though not my grandfather. He ran Keeler & Long with the help of his two brothers, who now run the company by themselves. Keeler & Long had been founded, in 1928, by their father and a man named Keeler. Keeler left the company in the early 1930s. His name was retained because everyone felt that *Long* didn't have enough syllables.

I told Long about the dead man who had put me on his trail and asked him to explain the secret of his company's twenty-year house paint. The secret, Long said, is that Keeler & Long doesn't make a twenty-year house paint. Ninety-five percent of the company's business, he said, is making paints for industrial applications. Some of these industrial paints do last for twenty years or more, but they are not house paints. The company's biggest customers are electric utilities, which use Keeler & Long paints on transmission structures, substations, transformers, and power plants. Hence Long's familiarity with the appetites of cows. The company does produce house paints in small quantities, he said, but this is little more than a sideline.

Well, that just about used up all my questions. Instead of being in law school the next time I had to paint my house, my children would be in junior high. I looked around Long's office and noticed that virtually nothing in it was painted. I wondered for a moment whether the dead man who had sold antique building materials was playing some kind of terrible joke from beyond the grave. Then I asked Long if there was anything else that we could talk about.

"Well," he said, "we do make paint for nuclear power plants."

THREE MILE ISLAND AND YOUR HOUSE

"Paint and Nuclear Power: Partnership for Prosperity" is not one of Keeler & Long's slogans. But nuclear power plants do need paint, and they can't use regular kinds. The reason for this is safety. Nuclear power plants are protected, in part, by sprinkler systems. If a plant catches on fire or undergoes some other kind of high-temperature accident, its sprinklers spray water all over the place in an effort to cool things down. Since this water immediately becomes contaminated, it can't be allowed to run out the door and into nearby elementary schools. Instead it is collected and pumped back through the sprinklers. Because the water is continuously recirculated, it has to be kept free of anything that would clog the pumps. Such as peeling paint.

During the famous accident at Three Mile Island, which happened in 1979, a lot of things went wrong, but one of them wasn't the paint. When those guys dressed in space suits went into the building later to see what had happened, they found paint that was firm and smooth and not hanging down in big droopy curls the way it is on some parts of my house. The paint at Three Mile Island was made by Keeler & Long.

Keeler & Long's nuclear paint (as people at the company sometimes refer to it) is based on an epoxy resin. You have probably used an epoxy glue to mend something around your house. I once used an epoxy glue to play a practical joke on my father. He and I have a standing five-dollar bet on a college football game, and we have a tradition of paying off this bet in ways that don't do the winner any good. One year, when my team had lost, I had an athletic-supply company make me a trophy consisting of a wooden base with a desk pen mounted on one side and a little metal football-trophy guy mounted on the other. In the space between the pen and the guy, I used epoxy glue to cement five dollars' worth of quarters. The quarters looked like an ordinary pile of change, but the epoxy glue bonded them to one another and to the base so powerfully that they might as well have been welded. I gave this trophy to my father in payment of our bet.

Epoxy glues have two components, which come in separate tubes. When these components are combined, they undergo a chemical transformation that causes them to become very hard and very strong. Keeler & Long's nuclear paint works the same way. It has two separate components, which come in two separate cans. When the contents of the two cans are combined, they form a paint that, when dry, can withstand the heat of a nuclear accident.

As Long was telling me this, I began to think that I might want to use some of this nuclear paint on my house. Why not? It would probably be expensive, but it would last practically forever. Using it might even turn out to be a pretty good move, in the event of nuclear war.

"If epoxy paints are so good for nuclear reactors," Long said, "you may be wondering if they would be good for a house." I chuckled at this thought and let my eyebrows dart up, as in delighted surprise. "Well, they wouldn't," Long said. "One thing we've never been able to overcome in epoxies is their tendency to deteriorate in sunlight. When you expose an epoxy paint to the sun, it chalks rapidly. That is, the surface becomes powdery, like chalk dust, and it erodes very quickly."

All house paints eventually chalk to some extent. Some are even designed to chalk, because chalking keeps paint looking new and clean. As each layer of chalky pigment rinses off in the rain, it takes surface dirt with it. This makes the paint that's left look better. But for the most part chalking is a disadvantage. In the business district of my town there is a brick building that has long white streaks on its facade near the lower corners of its windows. These streaks were caused by paint chalking from the shutters. An epoxy-painted house would always look clean, because the surface would constantly be washing away, but the coating wouldn't last very long. You'd also have to spend a lot of time washing pigment off your windows and your grass.

Another problem with epoxy paints, from the homeowner's point of view, is that they are impervious to moisture. You might think that imperviousness to moisture would be a great quality in a house paint. Who wants a lot of rain getting into the house? But in fact most house paints have less trouble dealing with rain than they have dealing with moisture arising inside the house.

Cooking, taking showers, mopping floors, doing laundry, raising house plants, running humidifiers, breathing, and many other ordinary domestic activities produce enormous quantities of water vapor. Moisture also rises up into a house from the ground beneath it. A good house paint has to be permeable enough to let this vapor pass through to the outside, which is usually where it wants to go.

Sometimes the water vapor inside a house will overwhelm the paint on the outside. There's a house up the road from mine that has a lot of peeling paint on one section of one exterior wall. The cause of this peeling is the kitchen, which is on the other side of the wall. Kitchens produce a huge amount of water vapor. In this case, so much vapor is being produced that it is pushing the paint right off the outside of the house. One relatively simple solution to this problem might be to install an exhaust fan in the kitchen, or to make more use of the one that's already there. A solution would *not* be to use epoxy paint on the outside. Moisture migrating from the kitchen would cause the epoxy coating to pop right off.

Another way to prevent household moisture from causing exterior paint problems is to prevent excessive amounts of moisture from passing through the walls in the first place. Most new houses are constructed with so-called vapor retarders inside their exterior walls. These are relatively impermeable barriers, usually made of either polyethylene or aluminum foil, that are installed between the back of the wallboard and the insulation. (Polyethylene vapor retarders are installed between the studs and the wallboard. Aluminum-foil vapor retarders are almost always an integral part of either the wallboard or the insulation.) Vapor barriers don't eliminate water vapor. They simply impede the passage of moisture-laden air through walls and ceilings, forcing it to find other outlets, such as open windows, exhaust fans in kitchens and bathrooms, attic vents, and dehumidifiers. Builders have to be careful to provide these other outlets, so that interior water vapor doesn't build up inside the house or force its way out through the inevitable gaps, causing localized paint peeling outside or condensing on the cold exterior surface of the insulation inside the walls.

Of course, not all paint-peeling problems are caused by moisture originating *inside* the house. There's a house not far from mine that has a band of peeling paint on its southern side at the level of the second floor. The house was painted just a couple of years ago. The cause of the peeling is a strip of faulty flashing about six feet above the peeling area. (Flashing, which is usually made of sheet metal, is a barrier that is used to weatherproof joints in a roof or gaps between dissimilar building materials.) Rainwater gets behind the flashing and leaks into the wall cavity, where it soaks the back of the siding. When the sun heats the southern side of the house, the moisture in the siding evaporates and is drawn to the outside, pushing the paint ahead of it.

After listening to Long for a while, I realized that it simply wouldn't make sense to use nuclear paint on the outside of a house. But what about the inside? If the stuff is impermeable to moisture, using it as a wall paint would prevent internal water vapor from leaking out and making mischief with the paint on the outside of the house.

"I suppose you could do that," Long said after a moment. "The epoxy would seal the inside of the house very well. But epoxies are made with very strong solvents. If you used an epoxy paint inside your house, the whole place would smell just terrible for at least a week."

Keeler & Long's nuclear paints are also too inelastic to be useful on or in a house. In a nuclear power plant the surfaces requiring paint are mostly made of concrete or steel. These materials are very stable. They don't expand and contract in response to changes in humidity. Wood, in contrast, changes dimension constantly. In damp weather it takes on moisture and expands; in dry weather it releases moisture and shrinks. There are doors in my house that close only in certain seasons of the year. If I put epoxy paint on one of those doors—or on any other wood surface in my house—the paint would crack. In fact, it would probably pop right off. Paints that are used on wood have to be flexible enough to move with the weather.

If I couldn't use nuclear paint on the wood parts of my house, I thought, maybe I could use it on my basement floor, which is a concrete slab. Or maybe I could use another Keeler & Long epoxy paint, a self-leveling floor paint that is so thick it has to be applied with a notched trowel. Once it's troweled on, the paint spreads out into a smooth, shiny coating that, when dry, looks almost like vinyl-sheet flooring. This paint is intended for heavy industrial applications, such as covering the floors of chemical plants. I asked Long how either of these epoxy paints would work in my basement. He said that they would look great, and that I would be able to do things like spill uranium on them, but that water vapor rising from under the concrete slab would probably either make the paint peel or push it right off the floor in a big sheet, like a rug.

In other words, it would be dumb. So I pretty much gave up on the idea of trying to paint any part of my house with the kind of paint used at Three Mile Island.

THE HISTORY OF PAINT

In the olden days, of course, there was no such thing as nuclear paint. The first paints used by early American settlers consisted simply of linseed oil and pigment. The drying properties of linseed oil had been known and exploited for many centuries. People way back before the birth of Christ had rubbed it onto wood in the hope of making the wood look better and last longer. This worked, to some extent. In fact, many people still do it. When my wife and I had a screened porch added to our house a few years ago, a local carpenter suggested that we paint the wood floor with plain linseed oil. We didn't follow his advice. This was lucky, since cows aren't the only things that love to eat linseed oil. Fungi do too. Wood treated with linseed oil has a tendency to develop spectacular colonies of mildew, among other things. People will sometimes put linseed oil on their outdoor furniture and then watch it turn black.

Linseed oil has another interesting property: the ability to make things burst spontaneously into flames. When linseed oil oxidizes under certain conditions, it gives off so much heat that it can cause combustible materials to combust. One night a couple of years ago, my wife was awakened by the smell of smoke. Usually when we smell smoke it's just the dog's water bowl being incinerated by the heating coil in the bottom of the dishwasher, but this time it wasn't. We rounded up the kids and called the volunteer fire department. Then I ran around frantically trying to find the source of the smell. I found it in the basement, where a thin plume of smoke was rising from a garbage bag in a big plastic trash barrel. I tore open the bag and blasted its smoldering contents with a fire extinguisher.

The bag had been filled with, among other things, scrap paper and some old rags that I had been using to rub linseed oil onto a piece of wood the day before. The proverbial oily rags! I called the fire department again and told the chief I'd found the fire and put it out. He said he'd always heard about oily rags causing fires, but he'd never personally seen it happen. He also said he would swing by anyway, just to be sure I'd really taken care of the trouble. About a week before, he said, the fire department had found flames leaping through the roof of the house of a man who had just called back to say he'd found the fire and put it out. I went back down into the basement to look around again and to eliminate a few conspicuous fire hazards that I would have been ashamed to let the fire chief see. The next day I went to the hardware store and bought fourteen smoke detectors.

Paint came into being when someone had the bright idea of adding something to linseed oil that would give it body and color.* This something was pigment. For much of paint's history, the most highly regarded pigment was white lead, or lead carbonate. White lead is highly opaque, and when finely ground it mixes well with linseed oil. One popular method of making it

---

*Not all old paints contained oil. Whitewash, an inexpensive, short-lived paint used both inside and outside, consisted of lime (calcium oxide) and water, sometimes in combination with glue or other additives. Recipes for whitewash could be quite elaborate. Here's one for a tinted variety from the early part of this century: "To a peck of lime, add before slaking three-quarters of strong salt brine and two pounds tallow and color with such dry earth colors as yellow ocher, raw or burnt sienna, Venetian red or umber. Remember, however, that the material will dry out three or four shades lighter. Slake the lime with the required color in, let cool, and apply with whitewash brushes. The tallow will make the wash waterproof and the salt hardens it." Cost-conscious painters also sometimes used so-called cold-water paint, which consisted of water, glue, and pigment.

involved dangling pieces of lead over pots of vinegar kept warm by decomposing horse manure. A colonial painter would sometimes spend more than a day rolling an iron ball back and forth over a new batch of white lead, grinding it into a fine powder. He knew the lead was ready when he could rub it between his fingers without detecting lumps.

Rubbing lead carbonate between the fingers is not a good idea, since people's fingers tend to end up in their mouths, and lead is a powerful poison. Ingesting lead can cause, among other things, kidney damage, miscarriages, and mental retardation. To make matters worse, lead's effect on health is cumulative; once it settles in the body, it usually stays there. Young children are especially vulnerable, both because of their small size and because of the fact that lead is taken up by any part of the body that also takes up calcium, such as growing bones and brains.

The dangers of lead-based paints have been known for a long time. Early in this century, *Painters Magazine* offered the following advice: "A man who is a painter doesn't want to eat much breakfast, but he ought not to go to work on an empty stomach, as that is a good way to get painter's colic. If painters would only be more careful and not eat till they have washed their hands and not take a chew of tobacco with painty hands, there would be little danger of colic."

"Painter's colic" is still with us. The manufacture of household paints containing lead wasn't restricted until 1973, and it wasn't fully banned until 1978.* The Environmental Protection Agency has estimated that more than forty million American houses have at least some paint in or on them that contains lead. Now that the government has for the most part prohibited the use of lead in gasoline (in which it inhibits the engine malady known as "knock" by slightly reducing the combustibility of the fuel), the main source of lead in the blood of Americans is old paint. Contrary to the popular conception, you don't have to eat paint chips to be poisoned by lead paint. When paint chalks (a

---

*The use of lead is still permitted in paints intended for certain industrial applications, and lead is still included in government specifications for various coatings. Lead is also an ingredient in many inks, including inks used on some kinds of food packaging.

process described earlier in this chapter), the "chalk" is pigment; in lead paint, the pigment is lead carbonate. A child who rubs his hands on a chalking surface and then puts his hands in his mouth will in all likelihood absorb more lead than a child who swallows a bit of peeling paint.

There is no entirely safe way to remove lead paint. All new official guidelines recommend hiring professionals certified to perform lead abatement, but there are so few such people that this is almost never an option. The worst way to remove lead paint is to sand it, since this creates a cloud of lead-filled dust that is easily inhaled and settles on fingers, clothes, and sandwiches. A couple of years ago, a neighbor of mine had all the paint stripped from the outside of his nineteenth-century house by a man who used a handheld disk sander. There are still thick drifts of paint dust in the plantings around the foundation. Given the age of the house, this dust probably contains a fair amount of lead. The same may also be true of the man who operated the disk sander. Sanding is even more dangerous indoors, where dust can settle into cracks and corners and pose a threat for years.

The next worst way to remove lead paint is to burn it off with an open flame, such as that produced by a propane torch, since doing this vaporizes the lead. Electric heat guns (essentially, industrial-strength hairdriers) and heat plates (electric resistance coils with handles) are much safer, since they operate at lower temperatures and don't produce dust. Dry scraping leaves virtually all of the lead safely bound in the paint, but it still produces some dust, as does the demolition or removal of lead-painted surfaces. Chemical paint removers produce no dust but leave the user with lots of toxic crud.

I had the paint stripped from the outside of my house a couple of years ago. Most of the work was done by a young man who used a heat plate and a scraper. At the time, this was the method recommended in every source I had read; indeed, it is still the method recommended by many people involved in the restoration and renovation of old houses, and it may be the best method within the reach of an amateur. Still, it isn't perfect. Disturbing lead paint in any way is asking for trouble.

Since lead is dangerous only if it is in a condition in which it can be inhaled or consumed, the best way to deal with lead-based paint in many cases may simply be to bury it under something else, such as non-lead-based paint, wallpaper, or vinyl siding. Doing this won't get rid of the lead, of course. But it will arrest the chalking of lead compounds (by binding loose pigments and blocking the sunlight that is the main cause of chalking) and place a temporary barrier between them and people.

THE MODERN ERA

Beginning around the time of the Second World War, lead carbonate began to be replaced as a paint ingredient by titanium dioxide. This change had little or nothing to do with anyone's concern about anyone else's health. It was just that titanium dioxide is a vastly superior white pigment. It has much better hiding power than lead carbonate; a single coat of a modern paint is better at covering up what's underneath it than as many as three coats of old-fashioned lead-based paint. Titanium dioxide is now probably the single most important paint ingredient in most paints used by most people. When the world's supply of titanium dioxide dips, the price of paint rises. So do the prices of vinyl siding, some kinds of plastic, and the fake-sounding gemstone called titania.

Until well into this century, painters often mixed their own paints from scratch. Ready-mixed paints first became available in the 1860s, but they weren't universally used until much later. One recipe called for slowly stirring a gallon of linseed oil into a hundred pounds of white lead. This produced a thick white paste from which paint was made by adding more oil and additional pigments. (The same thick white paste was used as a putty for filling nail holes.)

House paints in the colonial era were extremely difficult to apply, especially with the crude hog-bristle brushes used at the time—like spreading tar with a broom. Viewed from closer than the next hill, a freshly painted house often looked blotchy, lumpy, mottled, and wet (early paints took an eternity to dry). Old paints also had performance records that to a modern homeowner would be distinctly disappointing. As late as the 1940s, it wasn't uncommon to have to repaint a house every two or three years. An exterior paint job that lasted six years was something to brag about. After four or five years, there was often little left of the original coating—early paints chalked heavily—and what was left was often crumbling or peeling.

The performance of early paints was improved substantially by the addition of turpentine, a natural solvent made by distilling resins collected from openings cut in the sides of certain kinds of pine trees—a process not entirely unlike the one for making maple syrup.* Linseed oil dissolves in turpentine. Adding turpentine to paint made the paint less thick and much easier to work. Turpentine also made paint dry more evenly, by permitting it to be spread in fairly uniform layers. Today turpentine has been supplanted by mineral spirits, also known as paint thinner, a relatively inexpensive petroleum distillate with essentially identical properties. A gallon of paint thinner at my local hardware store costs just a few dollars; a gallon of turpentine costs almost as much as a gallon of maple syrup.

Turpentine and paint thinner aren't the only substances in which oil paint will dissolve. Other hydrocarbons work too. If you spill oil paint on your skin you can clean it up with salad oil, Vaseline, or the grease from a handful of french fries, among other things. When I paint with oil paint I clean my hands (but never my brush) with a mixture of corn oil and dishwashing detergent. The detergent makes the corn oil cut through the paint faster. Cleaning up with salad dressing isn't as fast as cleaning up with paint thinner, but the corn oil doesn't irritate my skin.

Paints underwent a vast transformation around the time of the Second World War. One of the most important changes was the development of synthetic resins, called alkyds, to replace or

---

*Turpentine's first industrial use was in shipbuilding, where it was used to thin the pitch and tar that were used to protect wood and to caulk seams. Pitch and tar were also made from pine resins.

supplement linseed oil. Alkyds, in the words of Joseph W. Prane, an industrial coatings consultant, are "the reaction products of a polyhydric alcohol (such as glycerine), a polybasic acid (such as phthalic anhydride), and fatty acids derived from vegetable oils (such as linseed, soya, cottonseed)." Prane could just be making this up, for all I know. Still, there is no doubt that at some point scientists discovered that by modifying natural oils (including linseed oil) in certain complicated ways, they could produce better ingredients for paints.

The new alkyd paints were clearly superior to unmodified linseed-oil paints in virtually all applications. They dried faster, lasted longer, chalked less, tolerated sunlight better, and were more resistant to mildew. When people talk about oil paint today, what they almost always mean is alkyd paint. Referring to alkyd paints as oil paints is perfectly acceptable, though. Almost everyone does it, including people who manufacture and sell paint.

Alkyds haven't entirely displaced plain old linseed oil, however. Some paints (such as the paint Keeler & Long manufactures for use on electrical-transmission towers) are still based on linseed oil. Some other paints contain linseed oil in addition to alkyd resins. For example, the paint used in the recent restoration of the exterior of the White House—a project that was completed in the early 1980s—contained a cattle-friendly combination of linseed oil, tung oil, and an alkyd resin made from soybeans.

Not long after the development of alkyd resins, an ultimately more important transformation took place. This was the development of latex paints. In a latex paint, the resins that form the paint film (which are different from the resins in alkyd paints) are not dissolved in turpentine or mineral spirits. Instead they are emulsified, or suspended, in water. In fact, latex paints are sometimes called emulsion paints. They are also sometimes called water-borne paints, and oil paints are sometimes called solvent-borne.

Unlike solvent-borne paints, water-borne paints don't undergo a chemical transformation as they dry. Instead, they simply dry. As the water in them evaporates, the emulsified resin particles—each of which is as little as $\frac{1}{250,000}$ inch in diameter—draw tightly together and stick to one another. This creates a strong, thin, flexible film. Although this film is thinner than the film formed by an oil-based paint, it is more durable and erodes less rapidly.

Latex paints require a different kind of brush from that traditionally used with oil paint. The best brushes for oil paint and other solvent-borne finishes are so-called natural (or China) bristle brushes, which are made from the hair of badgers, hogs, oxen, and other animals. Natural bristles are porous (the best ones for painting also have split ends), which makes them capable of holding a great deal of oil paint and laying it down very smoothly. This same porousness is a disadvantage with latex paints, though. Natural bristles can pull the water right out of latex paints. A much better choice for these paints is a brush made of an entirely impermeable material, such as nylon or polyester. (Synthetic brushes can also be used with oil paints, although purists turn up their noses.)

The earliest latex paints were fairly crude. In particular, they were ill-suited to use outdoors. One of their main ingredients deteriorated in sunlight, causing the coating to turn yellow and fall off. These were not qualities that most people were looking for when they shopped for paint. Soon, though, these problems were solved, and numerous other improvements were made. As a result, modern latex paints have many of the same advantages over alkyd paints that alkyd paints have over linseed-oil paints: they dry faster, tolerate sunlight better, and are more resistant to mildew (latex paints contain almost nothing that fungi like to eat). They also hold their color better, resist blistering and peeling, don't become brittle as they age, are much easier to apply, give off virtually no toxic fumes as they dry, can be applied to damp surfaces, and can be cleaned up with soap and water. This last advantage is probably the most important one in the minds of most consumers.

Latex paints do have some disadvantages. The main one is that they are less tolerant of poor surface preparation than oil paints are. Latex paints tend to "float" on top of dirty, chalking, or deteriorated surfaces. A paint film still forms, but it isn't anchored to anything. This can cause the film to peel off in big sheets, like Elmer's glue from the palms of second-graders. As a result, experts often recommend using an oil primer on wood siding, even if the finish coat is going to be latex. (Primers are paints that are specially designed to be used as first coats, usually on previously unpainted surfaces.) Like all oil paints, oil primers have a certain ability to incorporate impurities into themselves. This helps to create a solid foundation for the latex finish coats.

Latex paints also have an appearance problem, in my opinion. Most oil paints dry so slowly that brush marks have time to level out and disappear. This doesn't happen with latex, which dries very rapidly. No matter how careful the painter is, the brush marks remain visible. This isn't a problem outdoors—who cares about brush marks on siding?—but it can be quite annoying indoors, especially on nice woodwork. Glossy latex paints also dry to a rubbery sheen that I find unappealing.

Another disadvantage of latex paints is that when wet, they are less tolerant of cold than oil paints are. As the temperature drops below sixty degrees or so, latex paints become increasingly difficult to apply. Brushing latex paint onto a cold surface can be a little like trying to spread water on a freshly waxed car. And if latex paints are exposed to freezing temperatures before they have dried thoroughly (or while they are still in the can), they can permanently lose their ability to adhere. In my part of the country—New England—exterior latex paints start becoming tricky to apply around the middle of September.

Oil paints can be applied in chillier weather, although the ideal temperature for most oil paints is about the same as that for latex. As the mercury falls below room temperature, oil paint becomes sluggish. It also takes longer to dry, because low temperatures inhibit the oxidation of the resins in the paint. Slower drying makes the paint more likely to sag, wrinkle, and develop a crust of stuck bugs, pine needles, and dirt. Painters will often add thinner to oil paint when working in cool weather. This makes the paint easier to apply, but it also reduces the thickness of the film and increases the likelihood of surface problems.

It is possible to take advantage of the effect of cold on oil paint by storing wet brushes in the freezer overnight. The cold prevents the oil paint from drying and eliminates the need for daily cleanup. This doesn't work with latex paints, however, because of the destructive effect that cold temperatures have on them. But cleaning latex brushes is so easy that few people think of it as a nuisance. (An even easier way to store a wet oil-paint brush overnight is to stick it in a can filled with water. The water prevents oxygen from reaching the paint, so the paint doesn't dry. And oil and water don't mix, so the paint isn't harmed or thinned. All you need to do the next day is wipe the bristles with a rag and resume painting.)

On balance, latex paints have most of the advantages. They're generally the best choice outdoors, and they're almost always the best choice for interior walls. They are also ecologically sound, relatively speaking. When a gallon of standard oil paint dries, roughly half a gallon of toxic petrochemical solvent evaporates and adds itself to our increasingly unpleasant atmosphere. (New oil paints are being devised that contain less solvent, or even no solvent, but virtually all of them still contain quite a bit.) When a painter uses paint thinner to clean a paintbrush, more solvent goes down the drain and into either the ground or a public water supply. These solvents are known as volatile organic compounds, or VOCs. In recent years a growing number of states, led by California, have passed laws limiting the use of VOCs in paint manufacturing. Most experts believe that in a few years, solvent-borne paints and finishes will essentially be a thing of the past.

Some people, including some people who work in paint stores, are upset about VOC laws because they believe that latex paint is for amateurs and sissies—the light beer of paint. I can sympathize with this feeling. When I go down to my local hardware store and ask for a can of latex paint, I sometimes feel as though I ought to make an excuse. ("It's for my wife!") But no one should be afraid to ask for a latex paint, if a latex paint is what the job demands. In fact, there are times when using latex paint can be a downright macho thing to do.

THE BASIC RECIPE

After we had talked for a while, Henry Long offered to give me a tour of his factory. We left his office, crossed through a big room filled with secretaries, and walked past a lot of shelves with small labeled cans on them. Every time Keeler & Long mixes a batch of paint, someone takes a sample and puts it in a little can. If a problem arises later, or if a color needs to be matched, the proper can is consulted. Or at least looked for.

Long and I climbed some stairs and went into a big room above the factory. Stacked on the floor of the room were a lot of bags and barrels, most of which contained pigments. There was aluminum paste, powdered zinc, mica, barium metaborate, magnesium silicate, titanium dioxide, and a lot of other stuff. Most of it was in the kind of bag that fertilizer and dog food come in. The rest was in fifty-five-gallon drums.

Virtually all paint recipes can be broken down into four broad categories of ingredients. The first category is pigments. These are almost always finely ground solid compounds, like the ones in the bags and barrels at Keeler & Long. Pigments are usually dispersed in paint rather than dissolved in it. This means that they have a tendency to settle out of the paint and form a thick layer of gunk on the bottom of the can. This is especially true of solvent-borne paints. As a result, you usually have to stir or shake paint thoroughly before using it. (One of the best ways to mix paint is to pour it back and forth between two buckets. Just be sure to scrape up and mix in any pigments that may have settled to the bottom. Another way to mix paint is to put the cans upside down in the trunk of your car and drive them around with you for a few days before you paint.)

Pigments perform a number of functions in addition to providing color. They may hide the surface being painted, inhibit corrosion, block ultraviolet light, or help determine the degree of gloss in the final finish. (Paint that doesn't have pigment in it is called varnish.) Inexpensive paints often contain silica, clay, or other pigmentlike materials that function not as pigments but as fillers or extenders, providing a little illusory heft to the finished product.

The second category of paint ingredient is vehicles or binders. The binder's job is to hold the pigments together and, usually, to make everything stick to the surface of whatever is being painted—like glue. In a linseed-oil paint the binder is linseed oil. In an alkyd paint the binder is an alkyd resin. In a latex paint the binder is a synthetic resin, such as vinyl acrylic or acrylic latex, or even a linseed-alkyd-modified synthetic resin. In nuclear paint the binder is an epoxy resin. Some paints contain more than one binder.

It is primarily the ratio between pigment and binder that determines how glossy a particular paint will be once it has dried. Paints with glossy finishes have proportionately more binder and less pigment than flat paints do. Paints with so-called eggshell finishes have a binder-to-pigment ratio that is somewhat higher than that of flat paints but considerably lower than that of glossy paints. Glossy house paints tend to become flat house paints after a couple of years, as ultraviolet light attacks the exposed binder.

The third category is additives. Among the most important additives are driers (metallic compounds that speed up drying), mildewcides, insecticides (to deter bugs from nose-diving into still-wet paint jobs), ultraviolet absorbers (like the stuff in sunscreen), and a large number of chemical compounds that affect such properties as viscosity and flow. Additives can also be used to control the degree of gloss.

The final category is solvents. In oil paints the solvent is mineral spirits or, occasionally, turpentine. In latex paints the solvent—although it doesn't really function as a solvent—is water. In shellac varnish the solvent is alcohol. (Shellac is made from lac, which is a resinous substance secreted by a beetle that lives in southern Asia.) A few paints, such as Keeler & Long's troweled-on, self-leveling floor paint, contain no solvent at all. Such paints are said to be "100 percent solids," which is another way of saying that they contain no ingredients that evaporate. Old-fashioned linseed-oil-and-lead paints were also 100 percent solids. That's why they were so hard to spread.

The properties of any paint are determined in large measure by how ingredients from these four categories are mixed. Adding more of one element leaves less room for other elements. This means that enhancing one desirable quality usually involves diminishing another. Improving adhesion may reduce longevity. Durability may come at the cost of flexibility. A formulation appropriate for use on one kind of material may not be appropriate for use on another. Every can of paint is a mixture of compromises.

The nature of these compromises can be seen in the difference between primers and finish paints used on interior and exterior wood. Like finish paints, primers consist of pigments, binders, additives, and solvents, but the proportions are different. Primers contain relatively less pigment and relatively more binder than finish paints do. The extra binder makes primers stick to wood better, providing a firm foundation for the finish paint. (The extra binder also makes primers a good choice as a first coat for previously painted surfaces whose old paint has deteriorated. The primer seeps into cracks and crevices and actually helps to glue down the old paint.)* Increasing the amount of binder leaves less room for pigment, though. This makes primers less opaque than finish paints and leaves them vulnerable to sunlight and other environmental forces. As a result, primers are unsuitable for use as finish coatings.

People will sometimes prime new exterior wood and then wait a year or longer before applying a finish coat. This is not a good idea. With relatively little pigment to protect it, the primer's exposed binder can deteriorate rapidly, making repainting difficult. For similar reasons, finish paints should not be used on raw surfaces (unless the manufacturer's instructions say otherwise). Their relatively high pigment-to-binder ratio can reduce their ability to stick to bare wood.

Painters sometimes claim that a finish coat of house paint should be applied as soon as the primer is dry to the touch (or

---

*Priming old paint before recoating can help make the new paint stick better, especially if the old paint is chalky or dirty. Primers are usually thinner than finish paints and thus better at working their way into small cracks. A coat of primer can actually work its way under failing old paint and help to glue it down. It also forms an ideal substrate for a subsequent finish coat.

that a second finish coat should be applied as soon as the first is dry to the touch). By applying a new coat before the first has dried completely, the theory goes, the two coats will blend together and create a stronger film. This isn't true. Latex paints can usually be recoated safely after just a few hours, but oil paints need to dry thoroughly. Recoating too quickly can trap solvent in the original coat and prevent oxygen from reaching the binder. This can substantially prolong drying time and cause the entire coating to wrinkle or sag. Even when the instructions say that a second coat can be applied the next day, it's usually a good idea to let oil primers and paints dry for longer. This is especially true in cool or damp weather, when oil paints can stay wet for days.

Many people believe they can eliminate problems they associate with ordinary house paint (peeling, blistering, fading) by using so-called exterior stains instead. These products have become very popular in recent years. People like them because they have a reputation for being maintenance-free and because stains seem sort of classy, like fine old cognac. But so-called exterior stains aren't really stains. They're just paints in which the proportion of pigments has been decreased and the proportion of solvents has been increased. (If they were called thin watery paints instead of semitransparent exterior stains, would they be as popular?) It's true that exterior stains are less likely to peel than true house paints are, but this is only because they don't form much of a film. Less film means less protection. Stains don't repel water as well as paints do, and they aren't as good at blocking ultraviolet light, which is the main enemy of wood. Stains also need to be renewed much more frequently than true paints do. On parts of a house that get lots of direct sunlight, stains may need to be reapplied every year or two; on the other parts, they usually need to be reapplied every three or four years. This isn't what most people have in mind when they decide to use stain instead of paint.

Despite what people think, exterior stains can also peel. I have a friend who wanted a white house but didn't want the problems he associated with paint, so he used a white exterior stain. To make a stain look white, you have to add a lot of pigment—that is, you have to make a thin watery paint that is almost as thick as a real paint. My friend's stain is now peeling on the outside of his garage, where he has a water-vapor problem. (Moisture rising from the garage floor pushes its way out through the unfinished walls.) Paint would have peeled there too, of course. The problem is the water vapor, not the coating.

HOW PAINT IS MADE

When it's time to make paint at Keeler & Long, the bags and drums of pigment are poured into openings in the floor. These openings lead to large machines, called pebble mills, in the factory below. The proper binder is then pumped into the mills from underground storage tanks. The mills are cylindrical vats lined with porcelain blocks and half-filled with round stones. The stones start out roughly the size of hens' eggs. When the mills are turned on, the binder and pigments are tumbled together with the stones. This breaks up lumps and disperses the pigments evenly through the liquid. It also wears down the stones, which, once they've been reduced to the size of large gumdrops, are sold to landscapers. (Of course, the parts that wear away are also sold, since they end up in the paint.) The mills are so noisy that they are usually run only at night, after everyone has gone home.

When the pigments and binder are thoroughly mixed, they are pumped into a thousand-gallon mixer, which uses enormous paddles to stir the paint. It is here that driers, tinting pigments, and other additives are introduced. Once the driers are in, the workers have to be on their toes. Long and I passed two guys who were cleaning a big machine whose pump had become clogged with "skins"—big sheets of dried paint that looked just like the horrible membrane that forms on the top of pudding and hot cocoa.

Working in a paint factory would be pretty much fun, I guess, except for the cleaning up. When I finish a painting project, I sometimes just throw away everything, including my clothes, because I hate coping with the mess. If you run a paint factory, though, you can't throw away all your million-dollar machines every time you make paint. All you can do is try to keep the cleaning to a minimum. For example, the people at Keeler & Long try to use only white ingredients in the pebble mills, so that the mills don't have to be cleaned every time they are used. That's why the tinting pigments aren't added until the glop from the pebble mills has been transferred to the mixers.

From the mixers, the paint is pumped into big tanks, where it's stored until it's needed. Long and I walked over to a man who was making some final adjustments in a batch of olive-drab paint for a pad-mounted electrical transformer. The man was adding teeny amounts of tinting colors, which he was taking from some big, spilly cans on a cart beside him. The initial tinting had been done in accordance with a recipe devised by Keeler & Long's color computer, which can analyze a sample and spit out a formula. It can also compare two samples and decide if they are the same. The man was tinkering slightly with the computer's recipe—partly, perhaps, to show the computer who was boss.

After its color had been adjusted, the olive-drab paint moved to the final station, where it was poured through a vibrating screen and then pumped into cans. The screen's mesh is so fine that water would stand on it if the screen weren't shaking. As paint passes through, it leaves sand, dirt, contact lenses, and other impurities dancing on its surface.

I stood beside this machine for a while and watched a man filling cans by hand with a hose. The cans are filled by weight, which is registered on a digital scale. The man had been doing this for so long that he was able to hit the proper weight, accurate to two decimal places, on the first or second try virtually every time. When a can was full, it rolled along on a conveyer belt to a machine that pushed down its lid. After a while the man ran out of cans and went to get some more.

Every paint order at Keeler & Long is a custom job. Most orders are for such small quantities that automation wouldn't be practical. Some orders are so small that *filling* them is scarcely practical. An example is wipe-on colors, a group of highly specialized paints that were invented, back in the 1930s, by Henry Long's father. Wipe-on colors are paints that are used on appliance knobs, automobile turn-signal indicators, plastic rulers, and other items containing tiny depressions or gradua- tions that need to be filled with paint. The paint is wiped across the surface of the item, allowed to dry for five or ten minutes, and then wiped off. The paint is formulated in such a way that the dried paint wipes cleanly from the surface of the item but remains stuck in the depressions. The paint in the depressions is then allowed to cure. One of the biggest customers for wipe-on paint is Masterlock, which uses it on combination-lock dials. Keeler & Long is pretty much the world's only source for this kind of paint. The monopoly isn't all that lucrative, though, because a single gallon of wipe-on color is enough for many thousands of items.

Long and I moved on and passed a small, tidy pile of old- looking paint cans, including one whose label indicated that it had been manufactured in 1954. These cans had been sent back to Keeler & Long by various customers. "Some of our customers send old paint back to us because that seems easier than getting rid of it properly themselves," Long said. Paint companies are really chemical companies, and paint is a hazardous waste. In recent years the government has issued strict regulations gov- erning its disposal. (Most such regulations don't apply to home- owners or other low-volume users.) Like all paint companies, Keeler & Long has a big still that it uses to reclaim solvents used in making paints and cleaning equipment. Gunk that can't be reclaimed is shipped, at great expense, to a licensed disposal facility.

MAKING PAINT STICK

When paint fails prematurely, most people blame the paint. These people are almost always wrong. The main causes of trouble are things like inadequate preparation, failure to follow instructions, and moisture. If the paint you put on your house last year is now peeling off in sheets, it isn't because Benjamin Moore forgot to add binder to the six gallons you bought at your hardware store.

Almost any paint works best if the surface to be painted is solid, clean, and dry. Simply remembering this would be enough to keep most people out of trouble. Problems arise when water, dirt, or other foreign substances come between the paint and the material to which it was designed to stick. House paints are designed to stick to houses, not to dirt. (Last summer I watched some teenagers paint the exposed deck of a boat house without even bothering to sweep it first. Most of that paint will be gone by next summer.)

Painters sometimes recommend letting new exterior wood "weather in" for as long as a year before painting. The theory is that lengthy exposure to the elements will clean and roughen the surface of the wood, making it more receptive to paint. In fact, very nearly the opposite is true. Leaving wood unprotected outdoors for even a couple of weeks can damage the wood's surface and reduce its ability to hold a coat of paint. The main culprit is sunlight, which is as bad for wood fibers as it is for skin. Unpainted wood also picks up dirt and other contaminants from the ground and from the air. This can create a layer of grime that prevents paint from adhering properly.

When bare wood is dirty or weathered, the best way to prepare it for painting is often to sand it. Sanding removes the damaged wood cells and leaves the surface clean and smooth. Contrary to what many people believe, the point of sanding is not to roughen the wood. Relatively smooth wood holds paint better than very rough wood does, even though rough wood soaks up more paint. When paint is applied to rough wood, the film is thin in some places and thick in others. As the weather changes, the thin parts expand and contract more readily than the thick parts. This creates unequal stresses that eventually turn into cracks, which let water and dirt work their way behind the film, which eventually peels off.

Previously painted surfaces need to be cleaned, too. Loose or peeling paint must be removed, either with a scraper specifically designed for that purpose or with a putty knife or similar tool.

If the existing paint is in uniformly terrible condition, it may need to be removed entirely. This is a dreadful job, but on an old house it is sometimes unavoidable. Unfortunately, paint that cries out for total removal is usually paint that, because of its age, is highly likely to contain lead.

Existing exterior paint almost always needs to be washed before it is repainted. In fact, if people would always wash their houses before repainting them, most of their problems with paint would disappear. Probably the best detergent for this purpose is trisodium phosphate, also called TSP, which is a potent and caustic cleaner. If mildew is a problem, chlorine bleach can be added to the TSP. TSP alone will also kill mildew, but mixing it with bleach makes it more effective.

One way to wash a house is simply to get out there with a ladder, a sponge, and a bucket. (Don't hold your arms up over your head if you do this. The soapy water will run down your arm and into your armpit if you do.) Another is to use a pressure washer, which is a device that sprays liquids under great pressure. Pressure washers are very fast and very effective, and they have become extremely popular with house painters in the last few years. Some professional models are so powerful that they remove not only dirt but also deteriorated paint. But pressure washers need to be handled with caution. If they are used improperly, they can damage siding. They can also force water up behind the siding, creating a reservoir of moisture on the wrong side of a new paint job. As this moisture later works its way out through the wood, it can take the new paint with it.

Whatever method is used, a freshly washed house needs to be rinsed thoroughly and allowed to dry before it can be painted. Some people think that leaving a film of bleach or TSP on their siding would be a pretty sharp idea, since that way the residue could continue killing mildew after the paint had been applied. But TSP and bleach can harm paint. Applying too strong a solution of either can even cause existing paint to peel.

Surface preparation is usually less critical indoors than it is outdoors. Except in kitchens and bathrooms, most people don't wash their walls before repainting them. This is fine. In fact, repainting is usually the easiest way to make a dirty wall look

43

clean again. There's no way to scrub children's fingerprints out of a flat wall paint; the dark streaks left by the sponge look worse than the fingerprints. It's easier to roll on a new coat of paint every once in a while. (Of course, it's even easier to leave the fingerprints alone and say the heck with it. Besides, having a good clear set of prints could be useful if the children are ever kidnapped.)

Previously painted interior woodwork and walls with a glossy finish usually do need to be cleaned before repainting. This is especially true in kitchens and bathrooms, whose walls tend to accumulate paint-antagonistic layers of grease and crud. Ideally these surfaces should also be sanded. Scrubbing with a mildly abrasive cleanser like Comet or Ajax can do the work of both cleaning and sanding. All surfaces should then be rinsed thoroughly and allowed to dry.

Before painting, nail holes, cracks, and gaps need to be filled with putty, spackling compound, wood filler, caulk, or some other patching material. Many painters do all this after the primer has been applied, because the primer makes the holes and gaps easier to see, and because most patching materials adhere better to primed or painted wood than to bare wood. A better though fussier method is to use a small brush to spot-prime all the areas to be patched, then to apply the patching materials, then to sand the patched areas, then to prime the entire surface, then to paint.

Painters used to make their own patching putties by mixing linseed oil with lots and lots of lead or some other pigment and perhaps some sawdust. You still run into painters who insist that the old ways are better, or who say that nail holes should be filled only with carefully hand-rolled balls and worms of glazing compound. But these guys are just old and out of it. There are a number of modern patching materials that are both more durable and easier to use.

Among the most interesting of these patching materials are a number of lightweight products based on technology invented by 3M. These products all contain what 3M calls Scotchlite Glass Bubbles. These are teensy-weensy glass beads that are bound together by a synthetic resin that is like the ones used in latex paints. Unlike latex paints, ultralight patching materials contain

44

very little water. This means that they dry almost immediately and that they don't shrink when they do. It also means that they weigh next to nothing. When you pick up a container from the shelf at the hardware store, you may wonder if it's empty. Inside is smooth white stuff that looks like cake frosting. It even smells a little like cake frosting—or at least like the kind of cake frosting you might be able to buy in a can at a hardware store.

Many painters don't bother to fill nail holes in exterior siding. This is not a good idea. Water and dirt collect in nail holes, as they do in all holes, cracks, and surface irregularities. The dirt holds the water and keeps the holes wet for long periods of time—as though the wood were in contact with the ground. This can cause the wood around the nails to rot. It can also cause even galvanized nails to rust. In time the nails can lose their grip on the siding. This can happen with almost unbelievable rapidity in parts of the country where the weather is warm and humid much of the time.

Larger gaps, such as those between the butt ends of siding boards and the trim around doors and windows, usually need to be caulked. Caulk is sold in long tubes and applied with a device called a caulk gun. A loaded caulk gun looks like a comically huge syringe, or like the kind of machine gun that terrorists use. Using a caulk gun engenders vague sensations of potency in the user. My success with my caulk gun increased substantially once I realized that pressing the small release button on the butt of the barrel disengaged the plunger and caused the caulk to cease oozing from the tip.

The easiest way to use a caulk gun is to pull it along whatever gap is being filled. Professionals sometimes recommend pushing the gun instead, on the theory that this will force the caulk deeper into the gap. But forcing caulk deep into a gap is not a good idea. A thick bead of caulk is much less elastic than a thin one. When shrinkage causes two boards to pull apart from each other, a thin bead of caulk between them will stretch while a thick one will merely stay stuck to one side or the other, creating a new gap. (Which is easier to stretch, a rubber band or a bicycle tire?) The idea is to bridge the opening with a layer of caulk that is thin enough to expand and contract readily, as the wood does.

45

David Owen

TIME TO PAINT

At the end of my tour of the Keeler & Long factory, Henry Long took me back to his office, where we chatted for a little while (about paint). I asked him how I should shop for paint, now that I understood why his company's products weren't what I was looking for. He said that it was possible to be guided to a certain extent by price. If a paint is cheap, he said, one can be nearly certain that it doesn't contain enough of the relatively expensive ingredients that distinguish good paints from poor ones. Because solvent costs very little—especially if the solvent is water—inferior paints tend to have a higher proportion of it. (To disguise this, they usually also contain chemical ingredients that make them seem thicker than they really are.) In the long run, he said, cheap paints are much more expensive than premium paints. Since they go on thinner, they deteriorate faster and need to be recoated sooner. Paying a few dollars less for a gallon of inferior paint is a false economy if you have to use twice as much and repaint twice as often. Besides, Long said, the major cost of a paint job isn't paint. It's labor.

This doesn't mean that there aren't real differences among top-quality paints. Different manufacturers make different compromises when they juggle the ingredients in their cans. Painters sometimes find that they simply don't like the feel of a particular paint. It may seem too thick or too thin, or it may surface-dry too quickly or too slowly, or it may have other characteristics that annoy some painters and appeal to others.

Whichever premium brand one settles on, one should stick with it. Top paint manufacturers design their paints not as individual products but as elements in coating systems. The best primer to use with a particular house paint is the primer made for that purpose by the same manufacturer. The two will have been formulated to stick to each other and to expand and contract at the same rate. Using someone else's premium primer probably wouldn't lead to trouble, but it might slightly reduce the life and performance of the coating. Why take chances?

46

The Walls Around Us

At last it was time for me to go. Long fished around in his desk and a closet to find some souvenirs for me. He came up with a Keeler & Long hat, a Keeler & Long memo pad, some Keeler & Long brochures, a Keeler & Long calendar, a Keeler & Long key ring, and a Keeler & Long ballpoint pen that doubles as a device for picking lottery numbers. The pen has a lot of tiny beads inside it. When you shake the pen, the beads roll into a column and show you which numbers you should pick to win millions of dollars.

I was a little sorry to have learned that the secret, miraculous paint of my dreams did not exist. Then again, why should our homes age more gracefully than we do? A peeling house is a reminder to its occupants that the scale of human striving is trivial in comparison with mighty forces like God and evaporated water. Besides, I would have my lottery winnings to console me. I thanked Long for his time and for my gifts. Then I went home to paint my house.

Chapter 3

Fear of Lumber

The night before I bought my first two-by-four, I lay awake for a long time. I watched the moonlight on the curtains. I listened to the ticking of a clock. I thought about getting up and figuring out a really great system for organizing all my tax-related receipts. In the morning I dressed slowly and drove by a circuitous route to the hardware store, where I spent ten or fifteen minutes looking at the various kinds of glue. Then I went out back to the lumberyard. When a lumberyard guy appeared, I managed to stammer what I wanted. The lumberyard guy nodded and asked, "Doug fir or KD?"

This was not, on the face of it, a malicious question. But I had not been thinking in terms of there being more than one kind of two-by-four. Most of my worrying had concerned the length of two-by-four I needed (ten feet) and whether in fact lumber could be purchased in this length without embarrassment.

Many substantially normal men feel a paralyzing fear when they have to buy something at a lumberyard or hardware store.

Women are afraid to shop at these places too, but for complex cultural reasons their fear doesn't matter. For men, these public exhibitions of ignorance are agonizing and, in fact, seemingly life-threatening. Someone could probably make a lot of money by setting up a company to sell building materials through the mail, anonymously—lumber without shame.

The first time I bought condoms I asked for seven, a number that, after virtually endless reflection, had struck me as being the sort of nonchalant-sounding quantity that a seasoned purchaser might request. The pharmacist replied that they were sold in either packages of three or boxes of a dozen. ("Doug fir or KD?") I said that in that case I would take nine. He said that in that case I might as well take a dozen, since the cost was about the same. I said oh, all right, sure, why not, hell, let's make it a dozen. At approximately that moment I pretty much decided to go back to just being a kid.

WHERE LUMBER COMES FROM

Although in many ways life in colonial times was more difficult than modern life, it was also in some ways simpler, in the sense there were no lumberyards. People who needed lumber were able to acquire it in unembarrassing ways, usually by making it themselves. Seventeenth- and eighteenth-century builders typically used mallets (called beetles) and wedges (called gluts) to split tree trunks into planks. Doing this was actually faster and less strenuous than sawing, because a tree's internal structure makes wood split readily in the direction of its grain. (This is why people use axes rather than saws to turn logs into firewood, but use saws rather than axes to turn trees into logs.) Wall studs and other smallish pieces of lumber were also split. The builder would find a straight limb of the proper size, split it in half, and then square three more sides with a froe, which was a tool that looked something like a long meat cleaver, but with the handle perpendicular to the slightly wedge-shaped blade. The builder would align the froe on the end of the limb and then whack it with a wooden maul. The rough surfaces of split lumber were smoothed with a plane.

Beams and other large timbers were made by hewing, which was really just a specialized form of splitting. A builder would prop up a tree trunk on blocks and mark a straight line down its length. The line was made by rubbing a piece of string with chalk or berry juice, stretching the string tightly from one end of the trunk to the other, and snapping it against the wood, like a bowstring (or, for that matter, like a modern carpenter's chalk line). The woodsman would then stand on the log and, using a long-handled ax, chop closely spaced vertical cuts into its side, the head of the ax miraculously stopping just short of both the snapped line and his toes. Then he would climb off the trunk and walk backward beside it, using a short-handled broadax to chip away the wood between the vertical cuts. Doing this was known as "hewing to the line." When one side had been squared in this manner, the builder would turn the log, snap a new line, and hew to it.

Not all lumber was split or hewn. Many larger boards and planks were sawn. In the very early days this was usually done manually, with enormous two-handled saws that were operated by two men, one of whom stood on top of the timber being sawn and the other of whom stood underneath it, in a deep trench called a saw pit. The man in the pit, who was known as the box

Froe

man, did most of the work. He also inhaled great volumes of sawdust and suffered disproportionately from respiratory ailments. The man on the top, who was known as the tiller man, kept the saw properly aligned, pulled it back up at the end of each stroke, and, undoubtedly, made humorous comments at which the box man did not laugh. (The cutting was done on the downstroke.)

The first American sawmill was probably one built at Jamestown in 1625 or so. Its saw had a straight blade that moved up and down, like a pit saw. The first circular saw blade was made in 1814 by a blacksmith named Benjamin Cummings. His shop was in Bentonville, New York. Circular blades were faster and more efficient than straight blades, and they dominated the lumber industry until the invention, half a century later, of the band saw. The blade of a band saw is a thin metal loop, or band, that runs continuously in one direction between two wheels, like a bicycle chain. Band saws could handle larger logs than circular saws could, and, because their blades were thinner, their kerfs consumed less wood.*

Modern lumber mills are paradigms of speed, efficiency, and noise. Raw logs are first stripped of their bark in gruesome machines called rotating ring debarkers. They then move one at a time into the mill's principal cutting contraption, which is called the head rig. A typical head rig is equipped with numerous grippers, levers, braces, and rollers and one or more laser-guided band-saw blades. The rig's moving carriage propels each log repeatedly past these blades, which slice off rough slabs called cants. The cants fall onto a conveyor belt that carries them to lesser saws, planes, kilns, and other finishing machines for final processing. The resulting lumber is shipped off to lumberyards and into the nightmares of men.

---

*A kerf is the groove or cut made by a saw. Too many lumber-industry publications have regular columns called "Off the Kerf."

David Owen

HARD AND SOFT

There are two broad categories of wood: hardwoods and softwoods. Hardwoods come from deciduous trees (the ones that lose their leaves): oak, maple, poplar, hickory, walnut, and others. Softwoods come from evergreen trees (the ones with needles): pine, fir, hemlock, spruce, cedar, and others. The most obvious difference between hardwoods and softwoods is that most hardwoods are—there is no other way to say it—harder than most softwoods. Driving a nail through a hardwood board without first drilling a pilot hole for it will often cause the board to split. Hardwoods also grow more slowly than softwoods, which is one of the reasons they're more expensive. One way to get pretty rich would be to go back in time, buy a lot of land, and plant a forest of black walnut trees on it.

But hardwoods also have a lot going for them. Their colors and grain patterns tend to be more interesting than those of softwoods. This means that they often look better than soft-woods do in natural or stained finishes. High-quality wood flooring is usually hardwood, both because it looks good and because it stands up to abuse. (High heels don't leave dents on oak floors, as they do on the pine floors in my house.) Hard-woods are also favored by woodworkers and furniture-makers.

Softwoods are, uh, softer than hardwoods. They're easier to cut, easier to nail, easier to tool. They're also easier to grow. As a result they are the species most commonly used in construc-tion. Virtually all of the wood in the frame of a modern house is softwood. So is virtually all of the lumber in a lumberyard. When you ask for a two-by-four at the lumberyard, softwood is what you get. (The kind of softwood you get depends largely on the part of the country in which you ask for it.)

The first thing to know about lumber is that the measure-ments used to describe its width and thickness almost never mean what they say. A two-by-four does not measure two inches by four inches; it measures about one and a half inches by about three and a half inches. Two inches and four inches are known as the nominal dimensions of a two-by-four. That is, they are its dimensions in name only. There are several explanations for why lumber is described in this way. Some of them have to do with the way lumber is manufactured, some have to do with tradition, and some have to do with economics (three and a half inches costs less to produce than four inches). There was a time in American history, long before Watergate and Vietnam, when a two-by-four really did measure two inches by four inches. If you want lumber like that today (as you may if you are remodeling a house that was built before everything became so terrible) you will probably have to order it from a sawmill that does custom runs.

Softwood lumber is divided into three main categories based on its nominal dimensions. The first category is timbers, which is wood with a nominal thickness of five inches or more (or a real thickness of roughly four and a half inches or more). A six-by-six is a timber. Timbers are used mainly as posts or beams for holding up very heavy loads.

The second category is dimension lumber, which is lumber with a nominal thickness of at least two inches but less than five inches. A two-by-eight (actually one and a half inches by seven and a half inches, of course) is a piece of dimension lumber. So is a two-by-four. Unless it's specially cut, the nominal dimensions of dimension lumber are always even numbers (two-by-two, two-by-four, four-by-six, two-by-ten). Dimension lumber is used mainly to frame houses. It's also used to build tree houses, sandboxes, and the wobbly, unlevel workbench in your basement.

The third category of softwood lumber is boards. This is just about the only instance I can think of where a term used by the lumber industry is the same as that used by regular, frightened men. A board is lumber with a nominal thickness of less than two inches. The most common nominal thickness for boards is one inch, which in actuality measures about three-quarters of an inch. Boards are usually sold in nominal widths of two, four, six, eight, ten, and twelve inches, although wider boards are sometimes available. (Sometimes wide boards for indoor use are made by gluing together narrower boards along their edges. My lumberyard sells these in sixteen-inch widths.) Confusingly, carpenters commonly refer to nominal one-inch boards both as "one-by" and as "three-quarter."

Boards are also sold in several other nominal thicknesses, not all of which are carried at all times by all retail outlets. I have often had reason to use boards with a nominal thickness of one and a quarter inches, a size usually referred to as five-quarter. (Very confusingly, a carpenter will sometimes speak of "three-quarter" and "five-quarter" in the same breath, referring in the first instance to an actual thickness and in the second to a nominal one.) Five-quarter is usually an inch thick, or a little more than an inch thick. I also often use half-inch-thick boards, which are usually referred to as half-by.

In figuring the price of lumber, the standard unit of measurement is the board foot, which is the volume of wood contained in a board that is one foot long, one foot wide, and one inch thick (nominally speaking, that is). In other words, a board foot is a piece of wood with a nominal volume of 144 cubic inches. A sixteen-foot-long two-by-four contains ten and two-thirds board feet of wood. So does an eight-foot-long two-by-eight. At a lumberyard where pricing is based on board feet, these two pieces of lumber would cost the same.

In addition to coming in different sizes, softwood lumber comes in different grades. Each piece is classified, by one of several regional lumber associations, according to a number of criteria having to do with appearance, water content, and method of manufacture. All this information appears in a label called a grading stamp that is printed on each piece. Decoding a grading stamp can be tricky, because different species are graded in different ways, and different grading associations use different terms and abbreviations. In addition, the people who work in lumberyards frequently use terms that are different from the ones used by the grading associations, or misuse those or other terms, or use terms they have made up all by themselves. Fortunately, the average person seldom has to be concerned with more than a small fraction of this complicated, boring information. Most lumberyards don't carry a dozen different grades or classifications of two-by-four. Instead, they carry one or two or three. This means that a smattering of general information is usually enough.

The Walls Around Us

Probably the single most important factor considered in the grading of lumber is the presence of knots. Knots, which are the remnants of small branches that were engulfed by subsequent tree growth, are generally a bad thing. A knotty board is usually weaker than a knot-free board. Knots also make extra work for the painter, because they contain resins that ooze out through paint. (The best way to seal these knots is with two or three coats of shellac applied to the knots before priming. In the olden days, painters sometimes sealed them with gold leaf.)

In my part of the country, softwood boards are almost always made of pine and are generally divided into two broad categories—usually called common and select—based primarily on the number of knots they contain. Common boards contain lots of knots; select boards contain few or none. Select boards also tend to be straighter and generally in better condition than common boards. Naturally, select boards are also more expensive than common boards—usually a great deal more expensive. A home center not far from where I live sells its pricey select pine boards individually "shrink-wrapped for your protection," according to its advertising supplement in the local paper.

The select and common categories are further divided into several subcategories. The names of these subcategories (along with the terms *select* and *common*) are mostly different from the terms used to describe comparable grades in other regions. Even within my own region, the terms are seldom used with precision. Select grades whose formal names are "C & Better" (abbreviated "C & Btr" on a grade stamp) and "D" are both referred to simply as "select" by the guys at my lumberyard. (Other retailers in my area refer to select boards as "clear," meaning that they are clear of knots.) Likewise, they refer to all the common pine boards they sell as "No. 2." This is the real name of a common pine grade in my region, but the No. 2 boards at my lumberyard aren't always strictly No. 2. This lack of absolute precision actually makes shopping for boards easier, since there are only two terms to remember.

If you don't live in my town, the boards at your lumberyard may well be described by different terms, and they may well be sawn from species other than pine. The grade known as "No. 1 Common" in my area is called "Select Merchantable" in certain others. To learn the local lingo, you may need to ask questions. There is relatively little shame in this, however, since only three or four people in the entire world understand all the finer points of lumber grading. (The best way to ask for lumber when you aren't familiar with the grading terminology is probably to ask for boards of a certain size—"I need some one-by-sixes"—and then see what sort of choice is offered.)

The best place to buy lumber is at a lumberyard—preferably one patronized by a substantial number of local carpenters. Home centers and big discount stores are usually cheaper, but the lumber they stock tends to be lower in quality. The select boards sold at a home center may be a couple of grade notches lower than the select boards sold at a reputable lumberyard. One way the big chains keep their lumber prices low is by buying inferior stock.

Defects other than knots affect the quality of lumber. Pieces are often warped, bowed, cupped, or otherwise bent out of shape. These defects can often be traced back to abnormalities (such as a bent trunk) in the tree from which the lumber was cut. The easiest way to check a piece of lumber for these problems is to lift one end of it to eye level and sight down one side. If the lumber is warped, the warp will be clearly visible. (Sometimes these defects don't become apparent until later, after the lumber has dried out a bit or after it has been cut.)

The system used for grading dimension lumber is different from the one used for grading boards, but it is standardized. That is, the grade names are the same in all regions and for all species. Building codes stipulate which grades may be used for which purposes. (A grade that is suitable for studs may not be suitable for joists.) If you're building something governed by code, you should follow the specifications. If you're just fooling around (say, building a big awkward thing in which to store old newspapers) you can ignore the grading terms and be guided by appearance and price.

Hardwood lumber is graded by yet another system, with still other terms and specifications. Some of these terms are misleadingly the same as those used to describe softwood. Yikes! But most people don't buy hardwood lumber, and most lumberyards don't carry much of it. The only solid hardwood I've ever bought (except for firewood) was yellow poplar, an extremely useful species that is very nearly as easy to cut, nail, and tool as softwood is. But the place where I bought it didn't have very much, and it was all of the same grade.

WATER AND WOOD

A living tree may contain twice as much water, by weight, as it does wood. After the tree is felled and sawn into lumber, this moisture level falls until it reaches equilibrium with the moisture level of the atmosphere. Contrary to popular opinion, wood never dries out once and for all. Its moisture content at equilibrium rises and falls in response to changes in humidity. Seasoned lumber may have a water content of 5 percent or less during dry winter months and 25 percent or more during a wet spring. When the weather changes, so does the wood.

As a piece of lumber releases moisture, it shrinks; as it takes on water, it expands. That's why doors sometimes stick in damp seasons and swing freely in dry ones. It's also why paint often cracks at the seams between boards. (Paint and other finishes may slow wood movement somewhat, but they won't stop it entirely.) All wood responds to moisture in this way, even if it is centuries old. The only way to avoid this problem altogether is to live in an arid region where the humidity is constant year-round. For everyone else, there is essentially nothing to do about changing moisture levels, except to take them into account when building or painting.

Most of the moisture-related dimensional change in wood takes place across the grain. That is, when a piece of lumber releases moisture, it usually shrinks much more in thickness and in width than it does in length. The reason for this has to do with the internal structure of wood. A piece of lumber is really a bundle of tiny tubelike vessels running parallel to the lumber's length. In a tree, these vessels carry sap through the trunk and limbs. After the tree is sawn into lumber, the vessels can still slurp up water like tiny wicks. The end grain of a piece of lumber—where the open ends of the vessels are exposed—is particularly vulnerable. If you stand a dry two-by-four on end in a bucket of water, it will draw a fair amount of the water into itself, becoming fatter (and considerably heavier) as it does. The same thing happens, though more slowly, if the two-by-four is merely exposed to humid air. This is why it's a bad idea to leave lumber lying around on the wet ground. Houses that are framed with excessively wet lumber often have problems—such as sticky windows and wallboard defects—later on.

When logs enter a sawmill, they are first sawn into rough lumber. Then the rough lumber is usually surfaced, or planed smooth. The rough sawing is usually done while the logs are still filled with most of the water they contained when they were living trees. Surfacing is usually done somewhat later, after much of this original moisture has been removed. The drying can be done either by putting the wood in a special kiln for several days or by letting it sit for a longer period in the open air. (It is sometimes said that air drying is better for lumber than kiln drying, but this isn't so. And kiln drying kills bugs.)

The grade stamp on a piece of lumber contains information about the moisture content of the lumber at the time it was surfaced. The lumber may be stamped S-Grn, meaning that it was surfaced while it was still green (moisture content above 19 percent); S-Dry, meaning that it was surfaced when its moisture content was 19 percent or less; KD-19, meaning that it was kiln-dried to a moisture content of 19 percent or less; MC-15, meaning that its moisture content was 15 percent or less; or KD-15, meaning that it was kiln-dried to a moisture content of 15 percent or less.

The main thing to remember about a moisture rating is that it refers to the moisture content of the wood at the time of manufacture, not at the time of purchase. Two-by-fours graded KD-15 may have a moisture content of twice that if they have been stored outdoors in wet weather. And two-by-fours rated S-Grn will dry to a moisture content of well below 15 percent if the weather and circumstances are right.

When the guy at my lumberyard asked me whether I wanted "Doug fir or KD," he was asking a question that did not, on the face of it, make sense; it was like offering a choice of "whole wheat or toast." The telling differences between the two kinds of two-by-four lay in what he didn't tell me. The two-by-four he called Doug fir was made of Douglas fir and had been stamped S-Grn and Std & Btr—that is, it had been surfaced while green and was of a dimension-lumber grade called Standard and Better. The other two-by-four, as it turned out, was also fir, but it had been kiln-dried to a moisture content of 19 percent before surfacing and was of a grade called No. 3. The lumberyard guy didn't tell me any of this (and probably didn't know it), and I wouldn't have known what he was talking about if he had told me. I just chose the two-by-four that was more expensive, because I didn't want him to think I was cheap.

PLYWOOD

The same busy people who invented just about everything else we now use—the ancient Egyptians, the ancient Chinese, and the ancient Greeks—also invented plywood. They did this by cutting or shaving thin layers of wood and gluing them together in a sandwich. The same thing was done by the eighteenth-century French and the nineteenth-century Russians. It was also done by a nineteenth-century New Yorker named John Belter, who made intricately carved furniture out of laminated wood that he had fabricated from as many as sixteen layers of veneer. It was also done by John K. Mayo, a New Yorker who, on the day after Christmas in 1865, received the first plywood-related patent issued by the United States.

But none of these people, as important as they may have been to the history of plywood, can be said to have invented plywood *as we know it.* This achievement belongs to Gustav A. Carlson. Carlson was a part owner of the Portland Manufacturing Company, a small producer of fruit containers, clothes hampers, and coffee barrels. In 1905 he was asked by the organizers of that year's World's Fair—which was to be held in Portland, Oregon, and which would coincide with the centennial of the Lewis and Clark expedition—to come up with something "new and unusual" for the fair's forestry pavilion. Carlson responded by cutting some thin sheets of softwood veneer and sticking them together with animal glue. According to Robert M. Cour, the author of a now rare text called *The Plywood Age,* "The animal glue smelled so bad that the men frequently had to seek the comfort of outdoors."

The new product—which the company originally referred to as "3-ply veneer work"—generated mild enthusiasm at the fair. A number of orders were taken. Over the next two and a half decades, Carlson's creation was used in gradually increasing quantities to make door panels, drawer bottoms, and a limited number of other products, including automobile running boards.

Two of plywood's main selling points were its strength and its stability. Then as now, the plies were arranged so that the grain of each one ran perpendicular to the grain of any adjacent one. (Plywood is always made with an odd number of layers, so that the grain on the two exposed faces runs in the same direction.) This crisscrossing makes plywood very strong. It also makes it highly resistant to moisture-related wood movement. Unlike a door panel made of solid wood, a door panel made of plywood expands and contracts very little (except in thickness) with the changing seasons. This eliminates cracking and minimizes many painting problems. Plywood is also easy to produce in widths that are impossible to achieve in sawn lumber.

The 1920s were very good to the infant industry. Sales rose steadily, and new factories were built. Annual production hit 358 million square feet in 1929. Then a double disaster struck: the Great Depression decimated demand for both doors and drawers, and automobile manufacturers began to make their running boards out of metal, which didn't delaminate when it got wet. (Early plywood glues were not only smelly but also water-soluble.) Plywood production fell rapidly, to 200 million square feet per year.

Those were dark times for plywood. But the industry soon rebounded, and, well, you know the rest of the story—how Norman Nevills, the famous daredevil, traveled six hundred miles down the Colorado River in a boat made of plywood; how the 1939 President's Cup race, held on the Potomac River, was won by a hydroplane made of plywood; how some of the pavilions on Treasure Island at the 1939 San Francisco World's Fair were covered with plywood; how Admiral Byrd's expedition to the South Pole used sleds and huts made partly of plywood. These triumphs had been made possible by the development, in 1934, of a reliable waterproof plywood glue. The new glue, which was based on phenolic resins, transformed the construction industry. Almost immediately, eager builders began turning to plywood for decking, sheathing, subflooring, siding, and paneling.

Then, as is well known, the Japanese attacked Pearl Harbor. Luckily for the plywood industry, "The friendly tough building material of peacetime proved a rugged foe in war," according to *The Plywood Age*. PT boats were made of plywood. So were army barracks and the seats of Flying Fortresses. When our GIs returned home in 1945, they brought with them positive feelings about cross-laminated wood veneer. By 1990, annual American production had soared to more than 22 billion square feet.

BUYING PLYWOOD

Since roughly the time of the Second World War, most softwood plywood has been graded. The original grading system was devised by a trade group that was known at the time as the Douglas Fir Plywood Association. (Douglas fir trees were named for a Scottish botanist named David Douglas, who came to Oregon in 1825 to collect tree specimens.) Today this group is known as the American Plywood Association. Every sheet of plywood manufactured by an APA member mill bears a grading stamp that conveys a great deal of information about it. These grading stamps can be more than a little intimidating to someone who is merely looking for half a panel to ruin with some new woodworking equipment. But with practice, grading stamps can be deciphered.

Plywood panels are graded first according to the quality of

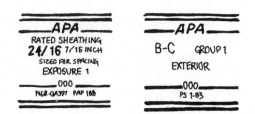

Plywood grading stamps

their face and back veneers—that is, their top and bottom plies. The standard grades are A, B, C Plugged, C, and D. A-rated veneers are smoothly sanded and are billed as being paintable, although discriminating painters may not agree. (A-rated veneers are allowed to have as many as eighteen football-shaped repairs—which are made to fill holes left by the removal of knots or other defects—and these repairs are difficult to conceal with paint.) D-rated veneers are rough, knotty, and full of splits, and they are generally not intended to be left on public view. B and C grades fall in between. C Plugged is a C veneer whose major defects have been rather crudely patched. There is also a premium grade, called N (for "natural"), which is often available only on special order. (My lumberyard refers to N-grade plywood as "clear.") Every plywood panel has two veneer grades, one for the face and one for the back. Plywood graded A-D, for example, has a smooth side and a rough side. You might use a panel like this to make the back of a bookcase or the bottom of a box, since in these applications only the face would be exposed.

Plywood panels are also graded according to the amount of weather they can tolerate, whether in service or just lying around the construction site before installation. There are four of these grades: Exterior, Exposure 1, Exposure 2, and Interior. Exterior panels are made with waterproof glues and can be left permanently exposed. This is what plywood siding is made of. Exposure 1 panels are made with the same waterproof glues used in Exterior panels but have surface characteristics (such as splits) that make them somewhat vulnerable to water and thus unsuitable for permanent exposure to the weather. Exposure 2 panels can be left unprotected for a brief time but need to be covered up as soon as possible. Interior panels are made with nonwaterproof glues and can't be used or stored outside. (Plywood intended for use indoors doesn't have to have an Interior rating. Exterior-rated plywood works just as well and looks the same in the same veneer grades. My lumberyard usually doesn't even stock much Interior plywood. Like most lumberyards, it also doesn't stock Exposure 2.)

Softwood plywood can theoretically be manufactured from more than seventy different species of wood, including apitong, keruing, mersawa, and quaking aspen. As a practical matter, most of these species have little to fear from plywood manufacturers. Most plywood is made mostly of Douglas fir. The standard sheet measures four feet by eight feet; standard thicknesses range between one-quarter and three-quarters of an inch and include such comical-sounding sizes as nine thirty-seconds and twenty-three thirty-seconds. As is true of no other lumber, the dimensions used to describe plywood are actual dimensions rather than nominal ones. That is, a sheet of three-quarter-inch plywood really will be just about three-quarters of an inch thick.

For fine furniture, cabinetry, paneling, and other serious applications, most woodworkers who use plywood prefer to use hardwood plywood. (So do the people who make golf-club heads, surfboards, shoe heels, gunstocks, banjos, and suitcases.) Hardwood plywood almost always looks better in natural or stained finishes than softwood plywood does. Hardwood plywood also usually makes a better substrate for paint.

Hardwood plywood is less plentiful, less standardized, and more expensive than softwood plywood, but it is extremely versatile. I've used it to build bookcases, boxes, and tabletops. My lumberyard carries only a few kinds—usually a limited selection of birch, mahogany, and oak—but others can be specially ordered. For users with special needs, custom mills can make panels in almost any configuration and in an almost inconceivable assortment of face veneers. (There's a mill in Vermont that will make panels measuring up to ten feet by twenty feet.) Mills that make hardwood plywood will also sometimes make top-quality softwood plywood.

Most softwood plywood today consists of veneers produced by a method known as rotary cutting. A big log (known in the industry as a peeler) is debarked and rotated on its long axis against a sharp blade, which peels away the wood in a thin, continuous sheet, like toilet paper being unwound by the cat. This big sheet, which can be more than a hundred feet long, is then cut into smaller sheets, which are shuffled, stacked, and glued.

Unfortunately for woodworkers, rotary cutting gives plywood a wildly wavy grain configuration that looks like something you might have seen on a black-light poster in 1968. This is because the blade follows a course through the log that runs roughly parallel to the growth rings. As a result, rotary-cut veneers seldom look very much like sawn lumber. In fact, they seldom look very much like anything but rotary-cut veneers.

Not all plywood veneers are rotary-cut. Some are produced by a method known as slicing, in which each log is shaved repeatedly in one direction across the grain. This produces a natural-looking grain pattern. There are several different methods of slicing, and several different methods of combining individual slices to make a complete face veneer. Sliced veneers are much less common in softwood plywood than in hardwood plywood, although they can usually be ordered from custom mills.

All plywood, whether rotary-cut or sliced, is subject to a manufacturing defect known as lathe checking, or knife checking. This is a pattern of small, closely spaced cracks that run parallel to the grain and often cover the entire face of the panel. It is the result of powerful stresses produced by cutting veneer and bending it as it comes away from the blade. Lathe checking may not become apparent until months after plywood is installed and painted or stained. This is a big concern with plywood house siding, since lathe checking can lead to rapid paint failure. It's also a concern with plywood used indoors. In the bathroom on the second floor of my house is a plywood vanity whose doors clearly show the effects of lathe checking. They are crazed with tiny lines that look almost like wrinkles.

OTHER KINDS OF ENGINEERED WOOD

The early twentieth century was a fertile period for the development of construction products based on wood that had been taken apart, fiddled with, and put back together, often in a dramatically different form. Plywood was the most broadly useful of these new products, but it was not the only one.

Much of plywood's competition as a building material comes from a class of reconstituted-wood products known generally (and in some cases specifically) as fiberboard. Fiberboard is made of pieces of wood that have been broken down into individual fibers and then mixed up and mashed back together under pressure, often with the help of glue. Except for the glue and a few other details, the manufacturing of fiberboard is in many ways similar to the manufacturing of paper, or of felt. The random interweaving of the fibers makes these products dimensionally stable and relatively strong, though not as strong as real wood. One of the great advantages of fiberboard is that it can be made from wood that is unsuitable for other uses.

The original fiberboard, and the kind with which most people are most familiar, is Masonite, which is known generically as hardboard or as high-density fiberboard. Masonite was invented in 1924 by a Mississippi engineer named W. H. Mason. One day, Mason was fiddling around with wood scraps, water, and a pressure cooker, trying to see if he could come up with something interesting. All of a sudden, the pressure cooker exploded, spattering fluff all over the walls. Eureka! By using heat to build up enormous pressure and then releasing the pressure, Mason had caused his wood chips to self-destruct, blasting themselves into their constituent strands of cellulose. (This is pretty much the same thing that happens to puffed rice, "the cereal that's shot from guns.") Mason then figured out a way to squeeze the fibers into a flat, hard mat, and Masonite was born. From there, it was but a few short steps to pegboard.

Hardboard is still an important product. It is used to make a variety of utilitarian objects, including the bottoms of drawers, the shelves in children's pretend refrigerators, and the clipboards carried by high school football coaches. The wafflelike texture on the back of many panels is a remnant of the manufacturing process, in which the mat of wood fibers is pressed against a fine-mesh screen to remove water.

An important modern descendant of Masonite is medium-density fiberboard, known to the trade as MDF. MDF is made of compressed wood fibers bonded together with glue. It is a wonderful material. It looks a great deal like particleboard (about which more in a moment), but it's denser and is made of finer particles. MDF is too expensive to use in rough construction, but it has many other uses, primarily in making furniture and cabinets.

My friend Ken used MDF to make a round marbleized top for a coffee table for his living room. The MDF was easier to tool than other materials would have been, and it holds paint better than plywood. The tabletop looks so much like real marble that people are invariably astonished when Ken tells them that it's not, as he invariably has to in order to receive any credit for his achievement. Like a number of other engineered-wood products, MDF is also an ideal substrate for veneers and laminates, because it doesn't shrink and expand the way real wood does. This means that laminates and veneers don't eventually loosen and pop off as a result of cross-grain stresses, as they often do when their substrates are made of solid wood.

Substantially less dense than MDF are the aptly named low-density fiberboards, including Homasote and beaverboard. These are the rough and somewhat cheap-looking panels that are often used in place of plaster or gypsum wallboard on walls and ceilings in beach houses, basement rec rooms, and summer cottages. Low-density fiberboard was once widely used as an insulating sheathing, since there's a fair amount of air trapped inside it. Now there are other products that do the same thing more effectively.

Particleboard, which was invented in Germany, is similar to fiberboard, except that it is made of small bits of wood rather than of even smaller wood fibers. These bits of wood are sprayed with glue and squished together under pressure. A similar product is waferboard, which is just like particleboard except that it's made from (somewhat) waferlike flakes of wood rather than smallish particles. Because flakes are larger than particles, less glue is required. Particleboard and waferboard are both used primarily in construction and in furniture-making.

Particleboard and waferboard are both being displaced by new products with better characteristics. One of the most important of the new products is oriented strand board (OSB), which is a little bit like a cross between waferboard and plywood. Like waferboard, OSB is made of small flakes of wood glued together under pressure. Like plywood, OSB consists of separate layers, each of which has its own grain direction. In the top and bottom layers, the wood bits are aligned so that their fibers run parallel to the length of the panel. In the middle layer, the fibers run perpendicular. This crisscrossing has the same strengthening and stabilizing effect that it has in plywood. OSB is less expensive than plywood but offers comparable performance in many applications.

Another interesting new product is laminated-veneer lumber (LVL), which is a close relative of plywood. Like plywood, LVL is made of laminated wood veneers. Unlike plywood, LVL is made of veneers whose grain all runs in the same direction. This makes LVL shrink and expand across its grain, just like ordinary lumber, but makes it less vulnerable to water damage, because the thirsty end grain is confined to the ends. (Because of the way it is made, plywood has at least one layer of end grain in every edge.) LVL and similar products are being used increasingly to replace solid-wood girders, headers, and other big members used in construction, because LVL is stronger and is much less prone to warping, twisting, and other common lumber defects. I-beams made of plywood and LVL, or of plywood and solid lumber, not only are stronger than solid wood but also weigh much less, and they can be produced in lengths of sixty feet or more.

The growing interest in engineered wood products arises in large measure from the fact that these products make extremely efficient use of timber resources. A traditional sawmill generates a huge amount of waste, not only in the form of sawdust and scraps but also in the form of finished lumber that is too knotty, warped, or blemished to use. Wood engineering makes it possible to fabricate superior building products from these waste materials and from trees that are too small or too defective to be cut into lumber. Many products can be made from sawmill floor sweepings. Plywood requires decent-sized trees, but making it generates very little waste, since the plies are peeled or sliced rather than sawn. Any waste that is produced can be turned into fiberboard. This efficiency has become increasingly important as old-growth forests have dwindled all over the world. The use of engineered wood greatly eases the pressure on the limited resources that remain.*

THE ENEMIES OF LUMBER

For every human being on earth, there are fifteen hundred pounds of termites. That works out to three tons for my house alone. Yikes! And that's just the termites. There are also powder-post beetles, old house borers, carpenter ants, carpenter *bees*, wood-destroying fungi, and several other troublesome enemies of lumber.

One spring day a couple of years ago I was out doing something in my yard when I noticed a sort of squirming mass on the ground. I crouched to get a better look. There were dozens of small winged insects crawling in the grass. No, wait, there were hundreds. Were they flying ants? Were they—termites? Still squatting, I took a little frightened hop backward and looked

---

*The only big drawback to engineered-wood products is that many of them are held together with glues that are hazardous. Most of these glues contain formaldehyde, a volatile and probably carcinogenic chemical that evaporates, or "outgasses," in significant amounts for as long as several years after manufacture. Some people are quite sensitive to formaldehyde vapors (which are also present in some new furniture, cabinetry, and carpeting). In addition, carpenters face a risk from working in close contact with these materials and from inhaling glue-laden sawdust. Formaldehyde outgassing from wood products has been reduced substantially in recent years, but it's still a problem, especially in tight, superinsulated houses that aren't well ventilated.

around again. The winged insects were everywhere. There were thousands of them. The grass around my feet was seething.

I picked up one of the bugs by the wings and took it inside for a closer examination. After holding it next to some drawings in a home-inspection guide, I became certain that what I had in my hand was a termite. Its antennae were not elbowed (an ant's would have been). Its two pairs of wings were the same size (on an ant, the back pair would have been smaller). Its body was of a roughly uniform thickness (an ant's would have had a pinched neck and waist). I went back out into the yard to wander around in small circles with a worried look on my face, stepping on as many insects as I could. My only experience with termites up to that point had been with the ones in the Saturday-morning cartoons on which I had wasted my youth. Those termites, you may recall, sound like buzz saws and are able to turn an entire tree into a single toothpick in a matter of seconds.

The next morning, all the termites were gone. At first I worried that they had moved into the house, but I couldn't find a trace of them anywhere. So I went to the library and learned that termite colonies often send out large swarms of "winged reproductives" a couple of times each year. (Some kinds of ants, including carpenter ants, do this too.) They swarm in order to start new colonies. Fortunately, they seldom succeed. Virtually all of the swarmers are eaten by birds, attacked by ants, or stepped on by me before they have a chance to make mischief.

This made me feel a lot better for a pretty long time. But then I realized that all those swarmers had had to come from somewhere. Swarmers are dispatched by existing termite colonies. That meant there had to be an existing termite colony located

Termite, ant

somewhere near my house. I got the chills all over again. Where was the colony? Was there more than one? Would the swarmers be back? Would their eggs all suddenly hatch? How worried was I supposed to be?

Well, I still don't know the answers to all of those questions. But upon reflection (and after still closer inspection of my house) I have decided not to remain in a state of constant agitation. There are woods across the road from my house, and the woods are filled with fallen trees, rotting stumps, decomposing branches, and all sorts of other things that look like dinner to a termite. There are undoubtedly many large colonies within striking distance of my house. My only hope is that in comparison with all the free food lying on the ground across the road, my house will always look relatively unappetizing. After all, the woods aren't covered with paint.

Still, my introduction to termites persuaded me of the importance of remaining eternally vigilant. My house has enemies everywhere! To keep them at bay, I have to make certain that I don't let things slide to the point where my dwelling begins to look like an easier meal than the stuff across the road. This is easier to do in my part of the country than it is in, for example, the South, where insect pests are both more numerous and more voracious. But I still have to be careful.

Termites are the pests that most people worry about most. There are in the neighborhood of two thousand species worldwide. Some of these species are quite exotic. The so-called compass termite, which lives in a part of northern Australia, builds enormous wedge-shaped mounds that can be ten feet long, twelve feet high, and three feet wide at the base. These mounds are always aligned on a precise north-south axis, an orientation that reduces exposure to the hot sun at midday and increases it in the cooler early morning and late afternoon, thus helping to maintain a constant temperature within the nest. Members of several African species build huge nests with elaborate underground fungus gardens, which they tend meticulously and from which they harvest food. At some airfields in Australia, bulldozers have to be dispatched each morning to level ten-foot-tall termite nests constructed on runways during the night.

The Walls Around Us

Termite colonies can consist of anywhere from a few dozen to several million individuals, depending on the species and the age of the colony. In all species, colonies are organized according to an elaborate caste system centered around a queen and king. The royal pair, as they are known to entomologists, do nothing but produce new termites at the rate of anywhere from several hundred to several million per year. The queen grows larger and more helpless as she settles deeper into egg production. In some species her abdomen may reach the size of a small potato. Her head remains tiny, her legs become vestigial, and she rapidly becomes incapable of feeding herself or venturing out of her egg-laying chamber—a prisoner in her own castle.

Fascinating creatures, certainly. Under any other circumstances, we would welcome them into our homes. But termites unfortunately eat wood and other materials containing cellulose, such as cardboard boxes, newspapers, and books. Cellulose is a carbohydrate that is indigestible to virtually all creatures, including termites. To extract nourishment from it, termites need the help of cellulose-consuming protozoa or bacteria that live in their digestive tracts and excrete substances that termites can digest. Termites don't have these parasites in their bellies when they are born. They acquire them from the saliva and feces of adult termites shortly after birth. (Termites are assiduous recyclers; they continually consume and reconsume not only their own bodily wastes but also the bodies of dead—and, occasionally, living—termites.)

Some species of termites have truly hellish appetites. In some parts of the world there are termites that would be capable of destroying an average-sized American house in a matter of weeks or even days. During the Second World War, wooden crates left on the ground on an island in the Pacific were rapidly (and invisibly) consumed to the point where they fell apart when soldiers attempted to lift them. In the 1950s, an entire village in India had to be abandoned because termites had pretty much eaten it up.

Termites are often referred to as white ants, although they are seldom white and are never ants. In fact, despite striking similarities in their appearance and social organization, ter-

71

mites and ants are essentially unrelated. The closest living relatives of termites are cockroaches, with whom they shared an
ancestor some 220 million years ago. (Nice family!) There is a
modern American cockroach, called the brown-hooded cockroach, that eats wood, has intestinal protozoa, and in many
astonishing ways (including the pattern in which it lays its eggs)
closely resembles the so-called Darwin termite, which lives only
in Australia. Taken together, these two widely separated insect
species are thought by entomologists to provide a glimpse of the
common ancestor from which both cockroaches and termites
evolved.

Fortunately for us, all the truly scary kinds of termites live in
other parts of the world, primarily the tropics. But Americans
still have forty species to contend with. These forty species are
usually divided into four major types: subterranean, Formosan,
dry-wood, and damp-wood.

In my area (and in most of the rest of the United States),
subterranean termites are the most common. These are what I
found swarming in my yard. They live in extensive underground colonies from which they stage their assaults on wood.
Like many termites, they must maintain continual contact with
a source of moisture. This means that they are most likely to
enter a house through some part of it that touches the soil, or
through some cellulose-rich material (including leaves, com-
post, firewood, and piles of old newspapers) that touches both
the soil and the house. One of the most common entry points is
through the dirt fill inside masonry porches, terraces, and steps.
This dirt is often heaped against wooden framing members,
providing easy, damp, protected access. Except during swarming, subterranean termites venture outside only under the cover
of slender tubes that they make out of mud, feces, vomit, and
saliva. These tubes, which can sometimes be found running over
the exposed parts of the foundations of infested houses, are one
sign of infestation that termite inspectors look for.

Like nearly all termite species, subterranean termites spend
virtually their entire lives out of sight. Unlike carpenter ants and
wood-boring beetles, they don't leave piles of sawdust on the
floor, and except when they're swarming they don't wander
around in plain view. This penchant for secrecy is defensive.

Most termite species go to great lengths to maintain an unbroken barrier between themselves and their predators, the most important of which are (surprisingly) ants. In addition, termites have soft bodies that aren't good at holding moisture. By remaining undercover, they cut water loss to a minimum.

The most aggressive termites in America are so-called Formosan termites, which are really a species of subterranean termite. They were accidentally introduced to this country from Asia at around the time of the Second World War. Unlike indigenous subterranean species, Formosan termites will sometimes travel short distances through the open air without constructing tubes. They will also chew through asphalt, rubber, lead, and other seemingly impregnable materials in order to get at a house or some other expensive wooden thing. Formosan termites live in vast colonies that can contain millions of individuals. These intruders, unfortunately, are spreading steadily throughout the southern United States and may gradually work their way somewhat to the north. (The range of all termites was extended northward early in this century by the spread of central heating.)

Dry-wood termites, unlike either subterranean or Formosan termites, don't require contact with the ground or with moisture. They can enter houses through almost any opening, including attic vents and gaps in siding. While subterranean termites usually infest (at least initially) the parts of houses on or near the ground, dry-wood termites are more often found in attics and in the wood around doors and windows. One telling sign of a dry-wood termite infestation is piles of tiny, seedlike feces pellets, which the termites sometimes push out of their galleries through small openings made for that purpose. Dry-wood termites are most common in southern California, Florida, and other southern states.

Damp-wood termites also venture into the open air, and they also leave piles of seedlike feces. They usually attack wood that is wet or rotting, although not necessarily wood that is touching the ground. Once they have gained access through a soggy spot, they may spread well beyond it, although they must always maintain contact with moisture. Damp-wood termites are most common in the Pacific Northwest.

In addition to termites, homeowners face a host of other

six-legged wood destroyers. The most common of these are carpenter ants. Unlike termites, carpenter ants don't actually eat wood; they tunnel through it in order to build nests. They are most likely to be found in wood that is decayed, or at least damp. In recent years builders have discovered that carpenter ants also love to burrow into rigid-foam insulation materials, such as the extruded-polystyrene panels used to insulate walls, ceilings, and foundations in many houses.

Carpenter ants can't survive without a steady source of moisture. If you find a nest in your house, maintain your composure long enough to determine where the moisture is coming from. Very often its source will turn out to be more worrisome than the ants themselves—perhaps a leak in the roof or some deteriorated flashing. If no moisture source is apparent, keep in mind that established colonies are sometimes able to maintain adequate humidity levels with nothing more than their own exhalations and excretions. This is especially likely to happen with nests built in rigid foam, which tends to block the escape of water vapor.

Carpenter ants are both messy and loud. They often leave visible piles of sawdust or chewed-up foam insulation near their excavations, and they can sometimes—usually at night—be heard munching and moving around inside a wall. (The stethoscope from your child's Fisher-Price medical bag is a useful instrument for detecting this activity.) They also stroll about boldly in broad daylight, looking like teenagers in leather jackets hanging around the shopping mall, waiting for opportunities to shoplift. Seeing carpenter ants in your yard is not in itself a cause for alarm. In fact, most of the ants in your yard probably *are* carpenter ants. But seeing more than an occasional intruder indoors should arouse your protective instincts. So should seeing a large group milling around purposefully in a corner of a garage or underneath a porch.

As a concept, carpenter ants are far less horrifying than carpenter bees, which sound like something that got away from the research laboratories at Genentech. Carpenter bees can be up to an inch in length and are similar to bumblebees in appearance. They bore round holes roughly half an inch in diameter, primarily in unpainted softwood. Carpenter bees use some of these holes as homes for themselves, and others as incubators for their offspring. On the positive side, carpenter bees make no great effort to hide what they are up to, and the damage they do is fairly limited, since their burrows usually extend just a few inches into the wood. Also, they don't travel in groups, and they almost never sting. (The males lack stingers; the females have them but seldom resort to them.)

Far more worrisome than carpenter bees are powder-post beetles, old house borers, and other wood-boring beetles. All such beetles, which can be as devastating to a structure as termites, lay their eggs on wood surfaces. When the eggs hatch, the minuscule larvae burrow into the wood, then tunnel around aimlessly for anywhere from several months to ten years, depending on the species. As they tunnel around, they grow. Finally, mature beetles bore out through the surface of the wood, leaving round exit holes and, usually, small piles of sawdust. Exit holes range in diameter from roughly a thirty-second of an inch for some kinds of powder-post beetles to roughly a quarter inch for some kinds of old house borers, which can be an inch long when fully mature. When woodworkers talk about "wormy" wood, they are talking about wood that has been bored by beetles and their larvae. (The larvae of wood-boring beetles are often called wood worms; their exit holes are often referred to as wormholes.) Unscrupulous antiques dealers sometimes try to make non-antiques look older by poking them with awls or even blasting them with shotguns.

Quite a few of the old beams and joists visible from my basement contain substantial numbers of holes made by wood-boring beetles. This is true of many old houses. As far as I can tell, though, none of the infestations in my house is active. I never see fresh sawdust, I never hear a gnawing or ticking sound (characteristic of old house borers), and I never see any beetles. This is also true of many old houses. The holes in my beams probably date from many years ago, when my house had a wetter and thus more inviting basement than it does today.

Still, wood-boring beetles are quite common and can be found in structures of any age. (Old house borers are actually more likely to be found in relatively new houses than in old ones.) Very often they migrate into houses from an old tree stump, a wooded area, or the house next door. They can also enter in a load of firewood or a piece of furniture. I once found beetle holes in a couple of boards that had come from my lumberyard. The boards had been kiln-dried, however, and kiln-drying kills beetles. Beetles can reinfest boards later, of course, but I decided that this was highly unlikely to have happened. So I touched up the boards with putty and used them.

Fungi, which are actually tiny plants, can also ruin lumber. When people talk about wood that has rotted or decayed, what they are really talking about is wood that has been consumed by certain kinds of fungi. Unlike green plants, these wood-destroying fungi can't synthesize their own food. Instead, they live off nutrients stored in the cells of the wood on which they grow. In doing so they give off enzymes that destroy the cell structure of the wood, causing it to fall apart.

Some wood-destroying fungi are commonly referred to as dry rot, because decayed wood is often dry and crumbly. But this nickname is misleading. No destructive fungi grow in dry environments. They require a significant amount of moisture to stay alive. The wood that is most likely to be affected is wood that remains wet much of the time, such as wood that comes into direct contact with the ground or wood in areas around sinks, showers, toilets, and cold surfaces (such as water pipes and toilet tanks) on which water condenses in times of high humidity.

Wood-destroying fungi pose a double threat to the structural integrity of a house. First, they destroy wood all by themselves. Second, they make wood more vulnerable to attack by insects. Termites and carpenter ants will often make their initial attacks in wood that has been softened by an infestation of fungus. Many species of termites are strongly attracted to wood-destroying fungi, which they can smell from far away.

ELIMINATING THE ENEMIES OF LUMBER

It is possible to thwart wood-destroying fungi simply by eliminating the source (or sources) of their moisture. Fungi can live on wood only if the wood has a moisture content of at least 20 percent or so. When the moisture falls below that level, the fungi die or become dormant and their damage is halted (though not reversed). The same is true of many wood-destroying bugs. In the case of damp-wood termites, eliminating an infestation can sometimes be as simple as repairing a leaking pipe.

Sometimes the steps that people take to eliminate moisture problems actually exacerbate them. For example, people with damp basements often ventilate them (by opening windows) in the hope of drying them out. This sounds sensible, but it's often not. The reason has to do with the nature of humidity. Warm air can hold more water vapor than cool air can. Opening windows on a humid summer day permits the warm, moist air from outside to mingle with the cooler air inside. As the humid air cools, it sheds moisture, some of which may appear as condensation on cold-water pipes. Opening the windows in this situation can have the unintended effect of making the basement wetter than it was before. A better solution would be to deal directly with the sources of the basement's dampness—for example, by upgrading an inadequate gutter system—or to close all the windows and turn on a dehumidifier.

Unfortunately, determining the source of a moisture problem is seldom simple. A small, hidden roof leak can create a hospitable environment for carpenter ants, yet remain unknown to the house's human occupants for years. In some humid southern states the air itself is so wet that controlling moisture may simply not be possible. And in areas where dry-wood termites are a problem, moisture is largely beside the point.

Most insect infestations of any size require the attentions of a professional. Even detecting the existence of an infestation can be difficult for amateurs. Unless it has been disturbed from the outside, wood that has been gutted by termites can look as sound as it did at the lumberyard. To find the problem, if there is one, it's useful to have the help of someone who knows how to poke around.

Until the government banned it in 1988, the insecticide most commonly used on termites and some other insects was a powerful chemical called chlordane. Chlordane was usually injected into the soil around and under foundations, ideally at the time of construction. Unfortunately, chlordane turned out to be toxic not only to termites but also to humans. It accumulates in the body and is believed to cause cancer and a number of other gruesome ailments. This can be a continuing concern for people whose houses were treated with chlordane in the past, because the chemical remains active for many years.

The principal replacement for chlordane has been a Dow Chemical product called Dursban. Dursban is also a highly toxic material, but it is believed to be substantially safer than chlordane. Unfortunately, it's not as good at killing termites, and it doesn't last as long. Still, it's the most popular chemical treatment not only for most kinds of termites but also for carpenter ants and carpenter bees.

Dry-wood termites and wood-boring beetles are usually attacked not with Dursban but with fumigants such as methyl bromide or sulfuryl fluoride (trade name: Vikane). Fumigants are often applied to an entire house, which is sealed off inside a plastic tent. There are parts of California where it is not unusual to see two or three tented houses in a single neighborhood. Fumigation is very effective at wiping out existing colonies, but it provides no continuing protection. Houses are vulnerable again as soon as the tent is removed.

In the past few years, similar results have been achieved with heat instead of chemicals. A tent is erected around the house, then high-powered heaters are used to raise the air temperature inside to around 140 degrees for several hours. This kills termites, carpenter ants, and other pests, but doesn't harm the house or its furnishings (except for candles and a few other vulnerable items).

The best way to prevent damage by insects and fungi is to build or maintain houses in ways that make infestations less likely to occur. Gutters and careful grading can divert rainwater away from foundations and keep houses too dry to be of interest to most pests. Cutting back trees and bushes can reduce moisture and eliminate access for carpenter ants and other insects. Storing firewood somewhere other than in the basement, beside the fireplace, or against the side of the house can make it harder for wood-boring beetles to find their way inside.

It is also possible to make the most vulnerable parts of a house unappetizing or deadly to the living things that want to consume it. The most common way to do this is by using so-called pressure-treated lumber. This is the faintly green stuff that decks, fences, and playground equipment are almost always made of nowadays. Pressure-treated lumber is wood that has been impregnated, at a pressure of about 150 pounds per square inch, with a solution containing a powerful preservative, usually chromated copper arsenate (CCA). Such lumber is highly resistant to wood-destroying insects and fungi. Some kinds are even used in place of concrete in house foundations.

Pressure-treated lumber is graded according to the amount of preservative it contains. This in turn determines the sort of uses to which it can be put. For use in decks, outdoor steps, sand-boxes, and the like, the lumber used should be rated for ground contact or have a CCA "retention level" of at least .40 pound per cubic foot. For a dock at the lake, the lumber used should be rated for contact with fresh water. Other grades are available as well. It is also possible to buy pressure-treated plywood.

Pressure-treated lumber is often extremely wet when sold. There are two reasons for this. First, pressure treatment itself raises the moisture content of lumber as high as 75 percent immediately after manufacture. (This high level then begins to drop.) Second, lumberyards often store pressure-treated lumber outside, uncovered, on bare ground. They do this because they figure the lumber can take it, which it mostly can, but as a result the wood is often sopping wet by the time it's sold. This is true even if the lumber is labeled KDAT (kiln-dried after treatment), as it occasionally is. The best idea is to let it dry for a while before attempting to build anything with it.

Most people who build decks from pressure-treated lumber

do so in part because they figure they'll never have to maintain them. This is a misconception. CCA scares away fungus and termites, but it doesn't protect the wood from a host of other dangers, including ultraviolet light. For maximum service, pressure-treated lumber needs to be cared for in pretty much the same ways that untreated wood is cared for. Decks should be protected with a surface-applied preservative or a water-repellent stain, both of which are available in formulations designed specifically for pressure-treated wood. And any preservative or stain should be reapplied every few years.

Manufacturers used to recommend letting pressure-treated lumber weather for as long as a year after installation before treating with a stain or a preservative, but most now say that such treatment should be done almost immediately. (Check the can for specific recommendations.) Prompt treatment can help to prevent checking, splitting, warping, discoloration, mildew, and other defects. The best time to apply a preservative or stain is before construction begins. This makes it possible to treat even the parts that won't show. Pressure-treated lumber can also be painted.

The use of pressure-treated lumber is controversial. The preservative used in making it is a powerful poison—in fact, a compound of arsenic. The lumber industry says that this preservative is permanently bound inside the wood and can't leach out. Various consumer groups dispute this and say that the lumber poses grave dangers, both to the people who live with it and to the builders who handle it. Builders are especially at risk. Few carpenters wear respirators when they saw, sand, or tool pressure-treated lumber, even though all three of these activities expose them to huge quantities of toxic, airborne sawdust. (Inhaling even nontoxic sawdust can cause serious respiratory problems, as people who work with wood sometimes discover in late middle age.) A carpenter who worked on my house told me that he is afraid that CCA-treated wood will someday be discovered to be "the next asbestos." Even so, he doesn't wear a respirator when he works with it.

Although CCA does bond powerfully into individual wood cells, these bonds are destroyed when treated wood burns. Ash produced by such fires contains a heavy concentration of arsenic and is extremely hazardous. For this reason, pressure-treated lumber scraps should never be disposed of by burning.

The danger involved in burning CCA-treated wood raises the disturbing question of what happens when all the pressure-treated lumber now in service ends up (as it inevitably will) in incinerators, landfills, and junk piles. CCA-treated wood may resist decay for a long time, but it doesn't last forever. In addition, there may come a time when our children or their children decide that they don't like greenish, aircraft-carrier-sized decks jutting out from the backs of their houses. What will happen when billions of tons of CCA-impregnated scrap wood ends up at the dump?

BORATE-BASED WOOD TREATMENTS

The most promising potential replacements for CCA and other toxic preservatives are borates, which are compounds of boron and, as such, close relatives both of the 20 Mule Team Borax that Ronald Reagan used to hawk on *Death Valley Days* and of the boric acid you use to kill cockroaches in your cramped, overpriced Manhattan apartment. Borate wood treatments, which have just begun to be commercially available in the last few years, kill cockroaches, too. They also kill termites, carpenter ants, powder-post beetles, and wood-destroying fungi. Lumber that has been treated with borate is as resistant to bugs and fungus as CCA-treated wood is, yet is nontoxic to humans. In addition, borate compounds don't cost much, are easy to apply, impart fire resistance, and don't change the color of wood.

In an experiment several years ago, wood scientists at the U.S. Forest Service placed a termite-infested log in each of two covered trash barrels. In one of the barrels they also placed several boards that had been treated with a borate solution. In the other barrel they placed untreated boards. After six months they checked the barrels. In the barrel in which untreated lumber

81

had been placed, the termites were still thriving and the un-treated lumber was infested. In the other barrel, all the termites were dead. Termites will nibble briefly at borate-treated wood, but the borate compounds kill the cellulose-digesting protozoa and bacteria in their guts. This also kills the termites, although not before they have returned to the colony and poisoned the rest of the nest.

One of borate's big advantages as a preservative is that it is water-soluble. This means that it often doesn't have to be ap-plied under pressure, the way CCA does. Some formulations can simply be sprayed or brushed on. Given enough solution and the proper conditions, some kinds of borate solutions will thor-oughly penetrate virtually any species of wood. The same is not true of CCA pressure treatment, which usually doesn't penetrate more than an inch below the surface and whose use is largely limited to a couple of species of pine (southern yellow and lodgepole) that have accommodating cell structures. Some man-ufacturers of log homes now soak all their logs in borate solu-tions before selling them.

Unfortunately, borate's solubility is also its main disadvan-tage. Extended contact with water can cause borate to leach out of wood to which it has been applied. This limits its usefulness outdoors, especially in applications where the lumber remains in permanent contact with the ground. Manufacturers of borate-based treatments say they are confident that the leaching problems can be solved, perhaps through the addition of poly-mers that will lock the compounds in place. In the meantime, leaching can be prevented or slowed by applying a standard wood preservative or water repellent to the surface of the borate-treated wood. This preservative should be applied within a day or two of treatment, and additional preservative should be applied every few years.

Borate-based wood treatments have been widely used for many years in Australia and New Zealand. They're just begin-ning to be used in this country, but within a few years they will be widely used here, too. Unlike CCA (as opposed to CCA-treated wood), borate preservatives can be sold directly to consumers. One of the first commercially available products is Bora-Care, an EPA-registered product that is made by Perma-Chink Systems, Inc., a manufacturer of products for log homes. Bora-Care's active ingredient is disodium octaborate tetrahydrate. It is sold as a concentrate that is meant to be diluted with an equal volume of water.

When I get around to it, I'm going to apply Bora-Care to the exposed beams and joists in my basement. This should kill any powder-post beetles that happen to be living in them at the time. It should also make the timbers permanently resistant to new infestations. I'm also going to apply Bora-Care to the underside of my porch and into a small space just above my foundation where part of the bottom of my house's frame is exposed to the outside. If I were building a house right now, I would be inclined to apply Bora-Care to much of the lumber in it, including the frame, the roof deck, the subfloors, the flooring, and the kitchen cabinets. I would be even more inclined to do this if I were building a house in an area where dry-wood termites are a problem.

Once I had done all this, I would sit back and open a beer and laugh at the termites across the road, secure in the knowledge that lumber didn't scare me anymore.

Chapter 4

Bones and Skin

During the first week my wife and I spent in our new house, Hurricane Gloria struck New England. There is a stand of tall white pine and blue spruce on a hill just behind us. When the storm hit I stood transfixed at the back door, watching the trees whip back and forth. Through the roar of the wind I could hear the big trunks groaning. Even the smallest of the trees, had it fallen in our direction, would have karate-chopped our roof and the back of our house and sent my wife, my daughter, and me to spend the night on cots in the gym of the elementary school. There we would have stumbled around in our underpants, sipping tepid cocoa with all the other unfortunates, our new neighbors. Had the previous owner known this storm was coming? What suckers we had been!

When I could no longer stand to watch the swaying trees, I went up to the third floor and climbed through a hatchway in the low ceiling and into the small attic above. I was looking for storm damage. Trembling slightly, I shined my flashlight among the perilously old-seeming rafters. I could hear the rain lashing against the shingles outside. In my mind I could see water pouring onto the scant insulation, streaming down through the walls, and squirting out through the electrical outlets in a house about to be split in two by falling pine trees.

But there were no leaks. The underside of the roof was dry. Braced by this reassuring discovery, I ventured farther into the attic, edging carefully along an old plank that had been laid across the joists of the ceiling below. Generations of mice had used this board as a latrine. Between the joists was a thin layer of gray insulation, and beneath the insulation was a layer of brick fragments and broken bits of plaster. The brick fragments dated from the demolition of the old twin chimneys. Over my head I could see patches in the decking where the chimneys had once passed through the ridge of the roof.

While I was shining my flashlight above my head, I suddenly noticed what looked very much like a large Roman numeral six carved near the end of one of the rafters. I looked closer. It *was* a large Roman numeral six. I shined my light at other rafters and found other Roman numerals carved into them. Not by Romans, of course, but by people from long ago.

At the time I didn't know what those numbers meant, but seeing them, and imagining the human hands that had put them there perhaps two hundred years before, filled me with strangely exhilarating feelings. The guy who had carved the numbers was dead, and his children were dead, and their children were dead, and their children were dead, and so on, and here I was, fit as a fiddle, two centuries later, shining my flashlight on his handiwork and having strangely exhilarating feelings. How could I worry about a mere hurricane when this house had stood intact, in all its Roman-numeraled glory, for six and a half times as long as I had been alive?

And then the storm suddenly got about 15 percent more intense, and I dropped my flashlight and practically jumped down through the hatchway and into the relatively unscary lower portions of my house.

David Owen

THE SKELETON OF A HOUSE

The first buildings built by white people in America were very crude. Early settlers in Virginia and elsewhere used a construction method that historians today call post-in-ground. A builder would clear a few trees, pace off his floor plan (usually a depressingly small rectangle), and dig a hole at each of the four corners and perhaps at a few points in between. Then, with the help of several shivering neighbors, he would tip a big wooden post into each hole, fiddle with it until it was plumb, and pack stones and dirt around it to hold it steady. Sometimes these posts were plain old tree trunks; sometimes they were tree trunks that had been squared up with short-handled broadaxes. When the posts were secure, beams were run between them to create a boxlike framework, and rafters (for holding up the roof) were notched into the tops of the beams.

When researchers today find evidence of post-in-ground houses, the evidence tends to be (to the layman) fairly unexciting, such as a surprisingly regular pattern of different-colored

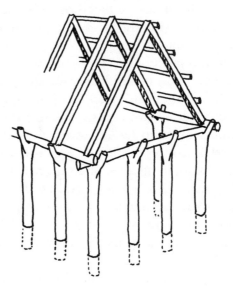

Detail of a simple post-in-ground frame

dirt. The reason there isn't more to look at is that the posts all rotted long ago. Early settlers were somewhat vague about the effect of wet soil on the longevity of wood. They were also in a hurry, and their first buildings weren't necessarily meant to last. The few old post-in-ground houses that do still exist are ones that were moved onto brick or stone foundations before their frames had been consumed by fungi, termites, beetles, ants, and rodents.

Outside of New England, the most common dwelling in many parts of early America was another termite-intensive structure: the log cabin. Like many deeply cherished American inventions, this one was invented in another country. The first examples in North America were built in 1638 by Swedes who were following an old Scandinavian design. The method of construction should be familiar to anyone who has played with Lincoln Logs (which were invented in 1916 by John Lloyd Wright, a son of the famous architect, and were inspired by a Japanese technique for building earthquake-proof buildings). Trees were felled, notches were cut, and the logs were stacked. The woodsmen who did this presumably didn't wander off to find something more interesting to do after stacking half a dozen trees, the way I used to do with Lincoln Logs. Instead they labored mightily, rapidly covering the American landscape with what would eventually become a potent, hokey symbol of our past.

Post-in-ground framing is really a crude subcategory of a medieval building method called post-and-girt. This method is characterized by its use of a small number of massive hand-hewn timbers to provide a sturdy skeleton from which the rest of a structure is hung. Post-and-girt framing remained far and away the most widely used building method until well into the nineteenth century, and it's still in use in house construction in a limited way today. (In its modern version, post-and-girt framing is usually known as timber framing.) It's also pretty much the same method as that used to erect office buildings and skyscrapers.

In erecting a typical post-and-girt house, an early builder would first build a stone or brick foundation and then lay four large timbers on top of it. The timbers formed a rectangular base called the sill. At each corner of the sill, the timbers were joined using a fancy, hand-carved joint, usually a mortise-and-

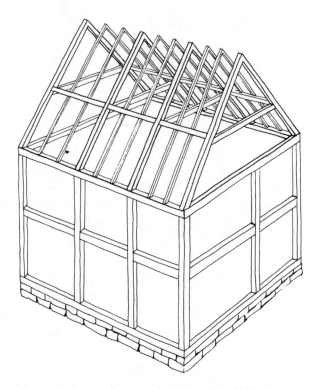

Post-and-girt house frame, simplified view

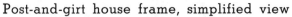
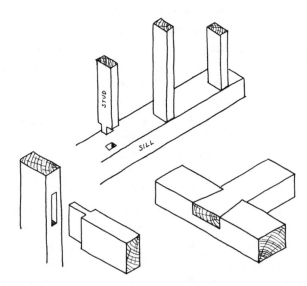

Some joints commonly used in post-and-girt construction

tenon. In a mortise-and-tenon joint, a tongue (or tenon) in the end of one member is fitted snugly into a slot (or mortise) in the side of another. You probably have some furniture that is held together partly with joints like this.

To secure tenons in mortises in a house frame, a hole was often drilled horizontally through each joint and a wooden peg pounded into it. The movie *Witness* has a nice barn-raising scene in which Harrison Ford wins the hearts of his grave Amish hosts in part by knowing how to do this. These pegs were called treenails, or trunnels. Occasionally, pencil-sized mini-trunnels were used to hold larger trunnels in place.

When the sill was in place, horizontal members called girts and joists were laid across it and notched into its sides. In my house the first-floor girts, which are visible from the basement, are hewn beams measuring, in cross section, eight inches by eleven inches. The joists are tree trunks or tree limbs whose top sides were hewn flat with a broadax so that floorboards could be laid level on top of them. Some of the joists still have most of their bark on the other sides.

Vertical members called posts were tenoned into the sill at the four corners and at several intermediate points. These posts

Trunnel

were typically a full two stories tall, and they often measured more than a foot thick. They were linked together at the level of the first- and second-floor ceilings by more girts, which were spanned by more joists. Between the posts, smaller vertical members called studs were notched into the girts, like bars in a cage. The function of the studs was not to hold up the structure but to provide ribs to which the inner and outer coverings could be attached. At the top of the box, rafters were notched into the front and rear girts, which were called plates. Where the rafters met at the ridge of the roof, they were notched and pinned together. (The ridgepole or roof beam is a fairly modern invention. Like most houses built before 1800, mine doesn't have one.)

A single person might hew the timbers for a post-and-girt house all by himself, perhaps over the course of several months. To keep things from getting out of hand, the builder would use a sharp tool to label each new member with a Roman numeral or some other symbol to indicate where it would ultimately fit into the finished frame. This was the purpose of the numbers I had seen on the rafters in my attic.

When all the timbers were ready, the homeowner-to-be would round up as many strong backs as possible to help assemble the frame. As we now picture them, these framing parties consisted primarily of fiddling, pie-eating, and good-natured merrymaking, with children in baggy shirts chasing dogs among the gingham-covered tables. But in the very early days, raising a house frame was probably just another grim chore, and a few weeks later the food ran out and everyone was killed by Indians or the flu.

BALLOONS AND STICKS

House-building technique didn't really begin to emerge from the Middle Ages until 1832, when a man named George Snow set out to build a warehouse in Chicago but was unable to obtain big timbers for a traditional post-and-girt frame. Like most of the rest of the Midwest, Chicago was short on big trees. So Snow framed his warehouse with the lumber at hand, which was the early-nineteenth-century equivalent of two-by-fours. To make up for their meager dimensions, he used lots of them. To hold them together, he used nails, which had recently begun to be mass-produced. Rather than concentrating the load of the structure on a few colossal timbers, Snow's method spread it over the entire frame. Studs became structural members, with each one playing a small part in holding up the building.

Like the posts in a post-and-girt house, the slender studs in Snow's warehouse ran unbroken from the sill to the roof plate, enclosing the interior space in a thin, balloonlike shell. As a result, Snow's innovation became known as balloon framing. At any rate, I think that's why it became known as balloon framing. It also became known as stick framing, because two-by-fours and other sawn lumber seemed dinky and sticklike in comparison with mighty chestnut beams.

The transition from post-and-girt framing to stick framing would not have been possible without the invention, around 1800, of a method for mass-producing nails. Before that time, nails had been made by hand, using a method that hadn't changed since the Roman era. A blacksmith would heat a slender iron bar known as a nail rod and hammer the end of it to form a sharp point. Then he would break off a nail-sized piece from the sharpened end, whack it half a dozen times to create a head, and dunk it in water to cool it. When he had done all this, he had a pile before him that consisted of one nail. There's a church in a town near mine that was built in the mid-eighteenth century at a cost of two hundred dollars. Of the total, one hundred dollars was for nails. Old houses and barns were often burned so that the nails could be salvaged and reused.

The new nail-making machines, which used sharp blades to stamp-cut nails from sheets of metal, changed all that. The nails they made, called cut nails, were cheap and readily available. If a carpenter dropped one while he was working, he didn't necessarily bend down to pick it up.

Cut nails and hand-wrought nails are both referred to nowadays as "square nails," but they aren't the same thing. Wrought nails are truly square in cross section, and they have four distinct sides that taper to a point; cut nails are rectangular in cross section, and just two of their sides taper. Wrought nails also usually look cruder and have lumpier heads. Because the change from wrought to cut nails was so rapid and so complete, and because it conveniently took place near the turn of a century, nail type is often used by architectural historians to date old houses. The presence of cut nails almost always indicates post-1800 construction. The people who built my house used wrought nails, although the only ones remaining are in some old walls downstairs and in the floors upstairs. Just about everything was remodeled later, after cut nails were introduced.

Most modern nails are made by a method that is reminiscent in some ways of the old method of making nails by hand. The process is mechanized, of course, and the raw material is huge coils of metal wire rather than short lengths of nail rod, but the idea is similar. The wire is fed into a machine that flattens one end (a process known as cold-heading) and pinches off the other at the proper length, to give it a point. Because they are made of wire, such nails are known generally as wire nails.

The only truly old-fashioned thing about modern nails is the confusing system used to indicate their sizes. This system dates back to the fifteenth-century English practice of referring to nails in terms of their cost per hundred. In the 1400s, a ten-penny nail was a nail that cost ten English pennies per hundred, or a tenth of a penny apiece. Today the designation refers only to size. The bigger the number, the bigger the nail. An eight-

Wrought nail, cut nail

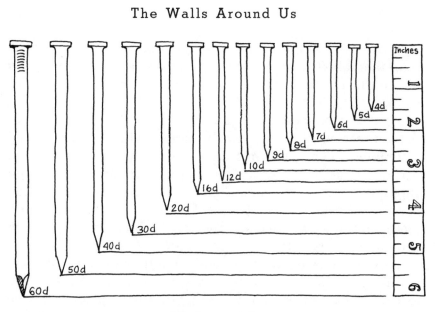

Modern nails

penny nail (about three inches long) is a good bit larger than a two-penny nail (about an inch long) and a good bit smaller than a sixteen-penny nail (about three and half inches long). To make this system still more confusing, the abbreviation for *ten-penny* is *10d,* because *d*—which stands for *denarius,* the name of an old Roman silver coin—was the English abbreviation for *penny.*

Nails today are sold by the pound. The proper pronunciation of "10d" is "ten-penny," although a 10d nail is often referred to simply as a ten or, less frequently, as a number ten. Swaggering into the hardware store and asking for a hundred twelve-dee nails is likely to attract the sort of amused attention that may make one reluctant to swagger into a hardware store ever again. The best way to buy nails, I've found, is to figure out what kinds and sizes are needed ahead of time and then pick them out in silence.

Fueled by the ready availability of cheap nails, stick framing supplanted post-and-girt framing fairly rapidly. As our ax-wielding forebears decimated America's old-growth forests, big timbers became harder and harder to find. So did the skills required to hew and join them. Nailing together a frame made of two-by-fours was easier and faster than carving a lot of mortises and tenons. Stick framing also liberated builders from the boxy designs that followed naturally from post-and-girt engineering. By the end of the century, almost no one was building with tree trunks.

Nowadays balloon framing itself is seldom used. For most of this century, most houses have been built with a closely related technique called platform framing or with one of its several variants. Like balloon framing, platform framing is based on sticks, but it uses them in a slightly different way. Rather than running all the way from the sill to the plate, the studs in a platform-framed house rise to the height of one story only. Each succeeding story is framed from scratch on the "platform" created by the story below it. (In a balloon-framed house, the second-floor joists are hung from the sides of the studs in the exterior walls, which is harder to do.) Building a platform frame is easier and safer (there isn't as far to fall) than building a balloon frame is. It also permits the use of shorter sticks. This is a big advantage, since the quality of a piece of modern lumber is often inversely proportional to its length.

Modern stick framing is so easy, relatively speaking, that it's possible for one person to frame an entire house all by himself or herself. Off and on over the course of several months, I watched (from my slowly passing car) a single carpenter frame a new house not far from mine. First he bolted two-by-six sills to the top of the poured-concrete foundation. Then, on top of the sills, he installed the first-floor joists—which were two-by-twelves laid edgewise—and covered them with plywood decking. Then he built the frame in sections. He built each section by laying out his sticks on the first-floor platform and nailing them together. Then he raised it, plumbed it, and nailed it down, and moved on to the next wall.

The sticks with which this carpenter framed his walls were two-by-sixes. Until not long ago, walls were almost always framed with two-by-fours, but in recent years many builders have switched to wider studs. The reason has to do with the price of energy. A wall framed with two-by-sixes can hold two more inches of insulation than a wall framed with two-by-fours. Some builders in cold parts of the country even use two-byeights as studs in exterior walls. Others frame walls with two parallel but slightly separated rows of two-by-fours. This is expensive, but it has a lot of advantages. The gap between the two rows of studs eliminates thermal bridging, which is the transmission of heat through framing members. (Wood is a reasonably good insulator, but it conducts more heat than insulation does.) The gap also gives the electrician a convenient, ready-made channel through which to run wires.

The carpenter I watched placed his two-by-six studs twenty-four inches apart, measured from the center of one stud to the center of its neighbor. This spacing is referred to in the trade as "twenty-four inches on center" or "24 in. o.c." Traditional stud spacing in a stick-framed house is sixteen inches on center (which is why most tape measures have special marks at sixteen-inch intervals), but the wider spacing is often used nowadays. One reason is that a frame made of two-by-sixes on twenty-four-inch centers is as sturdy as a frame made of two-by-fours on sixteen-inch centers. Another is that twenty-four-inch spacing requires less labor and lumber and is therefore cheaper.

The spacing of studs affects many aspects of construction, including the configuration of some building materials. Standard sheets of plywood and gypsum wallboard, for example, measure four feet by eight feet, dimensions that are evenly divisible by both sixteen and twenty-four. This means that if one edge of a panel is aligned on the center of a stud, the opposite edge will be aligned on a center as well, ensuring solid surfaces for nailing. Knowing about stud spacing is useful in performing numerous handyman activities, including hanging pictures, installing medicine cabinets, and putting up moldings and other trim.

After I had watched the lone carpenter work for a while, I went home and, with the help of my younger brother, used what I had learned about platform framing to build a tree house for my daughter. A tree house is something my brother and I had always wanted but never had. Still smarting from this privation, we ran a band of two-by-fours about six feet off the ground around the trunks of four closely spaced medium-sized trees. This gave us the equivalent of a sill. We then laid two-by-four joists on edge sixteen inches apart on top of this sill and secured them with L-shaped metal braces called framing angles. Then we nailed down a plywood deck on top of the joists. Then we built a two-and-a-half-foot-high stud wall—in sections, on the ground—and nailed it in place around the perimeter of the deck. Then we covered the studs with some old weathered barn siding that we had found by the side of the road. Then we added a ladder made from two-by-fours and a trap door that could be locked from above. Then we stood in our tree house for a long time and drank beers and looked at what we had done (while my daughter pounded futilely on the door from below).

A SKIN FOR THE SKELETON

In the earliest post-in-ground houses, the spaces between the posts were filled with a medieval building material called wattle and daub. A mat of woven sticks (the wattle) was erected between the posts and covered on both sides with several applications of a plasterlike mixture of clay and sand (the daub). Wattle and daub had been used in Europe for centuries, but it didn't hold up well in the harsher weather of North America. When the early settlers grew tired of watching their houses rinse away in driving rains, they switched to wood.

The first wood siding consisted of overlapping horizontal boards that had been hand-split, or riven, from short oak logs. These boards were called clapboards, for reasons that experts still argue about. The least-likely-sounding explanation is that clapboards are called clapboards because when two of them are struck together they make a clapping sound. (Wouldn't any pair of boards do this?) Another explanation is that *clapboard* is derived from *cloveboard*—that is, boards that had been cloven. At any rate, the *p* is silent, as in *cupboard*.

To make clapboards, a log was stood on end and split radially with a froe, the same wedgelike tool used in splitting boards (see Chapter Three). This technique, which was borrowed from barrel-making, was also used in making shingles. Riving later gave way to sawing, which made it possible to produce longer and more uniform boards.

Unlike the log cabin, the clapboard really was an American invention. It provided a local solution (wood) to a local problem (unbelievably ugly weather—much uglier than the weather that, for better or worse, we have now). Today wood clapboards remain a popular siding choice in new construction. They also provide the model for the design of many other forms of siding, including those made of aluminum and vinyl. After more than three hundred years, the clapboard style is still what most Americans think of when they think of a house.

In the early days, clapboards were nailed directly to the framing. This made for some pretty drafty houses, since the horizontal seams between clapboards are not uniformly tight enough to keep out icy winter winds. My house was built this way. When I venture up into my attic, I can see daylight between some of the clapboards. I can also feel a fairly invigorating breeze. By the end of the eighteenth century, though, most builders had begun to enclose their house frames with wide boards before nailing up the clapboards or other siding. These wide boards, which were known as sheathing, were nailed horizontally across the studs. Then the clapboards were installed on top of them. Sheathing made houses a bit more weathertight. It also made them stronger. The sheathing boards acted as braces to

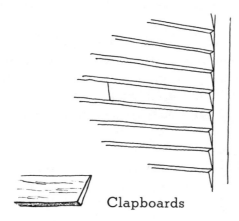

Clapboards

keep the frame from racking under various stresses. To increase this bracing effect, later builders installed their sheathing boards diagonally. Doing this anchored the vertical members not only to each other but also to the sill, the outer girts, and the plates.

Nowadays houses are usually sheathed in plywood, OSB, foam insulation board, or some other manufactured product. Sheathing a house in one of these materials is faster than sheathing it in sawn lumber, because plywood and similar products come in bigger pieces. Panel sheathing also makes for tighter houses, because there are fewer seams for the wind to sneak through. (To make houses even more windproof, builders often cover the sheathing with a fabriclike covering known as a house wrap, the most common brand of which is Tyvek.) Most important of all, modern sheathing products are very strong and very stable. They strengthen frames and keep houses from twisting slowly in the wind.

At some point early in our history, builders discovered that it was possible to go beyond sheathing in protecting a house from chilly weather. They began to fill wall cavities with bricks (called nogging), corncobs, hay, pine cones, or other mildly insulating materials. These helped to slow the flow of air through the walls and improved somewhat the ability of early houses to retain the heat given off by their smoky and wildly inefficient fireplaces. (Most of the warmth these fireplaces produced went straight up their chimneys, a problem that wasn't really addressed until Benjamin Franklin invented his famous stove, in 1742.)

Quite a few other old houses had, and continue to have, no insulation in their walls. My house is one of these. Virtually all of its wall cavities are empty, save for a mysterious double course of crudely mortared bricks laid on top of the sill. These bricks are puzzling. Could they have been intended to deter bugs or gnawing animals? I don't know, and I've never heard or read of such a practice.

The only walls in my house that are insulated are ones that have been stripped down to the studs in the course of some remodeling project or other. When a wall is fully opened, it's easy to fit the insulation snugly and to install a proper vapor retarder (see Chapter Two). Properly fitted insulation is more efficient than insulation that leaves gaps. In new construction, insulation is often installed poorly, even haphazardly, by people who either don't know or don't care what they are doing. These people's mistakes are impossible to see and expensive to correct once the interior walls have been installed.

In old houses, inadequate wall insulation is often less of a problem than actual gaps in the walls. Loosely fitting window sashes can negate the benefit of even the thickest insulation. Even electrical outlets (which often have no insulation behind them) can be sources of icy drafts. The easiest way to make quick reductions in heating costs is often to plug these leaks. Loose doors and windows, which are usually the worst offenders, can be replaced, weather-stripped, or fitted with storms. Actual holes in the walls, both inside and out, can be patched or caulked. Electrical outlets can be fitted with foam inserts or with special cover plates designed to block the flow of air. Each of these alterations is relatively minor, but all of them taken together can make a house not only less expensive to operate but also more comfortable to live in.

So far, most of my weatherproofing efforts in my own house have focused on plugging holes. I intend to insulate all the walls eventually, but I'm taking my time, because all methods for injecting insulation into existing walls—various foams, chopped cellulose, several others—leave something to be desired. In retrofit jobs, these materials are typically pumped through small holes drilled into the exterior walls. Gaps and missed areas are inevitable. Some materials shrink substantially, reducing their performance. In addition, all such products (as well as other types of insulation) can alter the sometimes fragile ecology of an old house, by blocking the flow of air and water vapor or simply by filling cavities that have been empty for centuries. Injecting insulation into old walls is certainly possible, but it isn't a handyman job. It should be done carefully and with the help of an experienced and reputable specialist.

David Owen

MODERN SIDING

Anyone building a house today has a somewhat baffling array of siding products to choose from. Making such a choice can leave the homeowner fraught with anxiety, since the siding is the part of a house that most people spend most of their time looking at and, therefore, judging its occupants by. Is my siding whispering to strangers that I am cheap? Pretentious? A swell guy? The answer depends largely on the prevailing taste of the neighborhood, which varies greatly from one part of the country to another.

The most popular siding material in my part of the country is wood. The first wood siding in America was oak, a wood that wasn't all that well suited to the task. Oak is very hard, and it tends to split. After a relatively brief heyday it was largely replaced by other woods, including cedar, redwood, and pine. Cedar and redwood—which are naturally resistant to bugs and rot—remain the best choices, although they are also the most expensive. In the premium grades, cedar and redwood are uniformly grained, free of knots, and easy (and aromatic) to work with. With proper care, they can last essentially forever. The cedar clapboards on my house are more than a hundred years old, and they probably have at least another century left in them.

Clapboards are also known as bevel siding, because the way they're sawn gives them a beveled or triangular profile. The most commonly used boards have a nominal width of six inches, which means that they are really about five and a half inches wide. These are typically overlapped by anywhere from two inches to a little less than an inch. The boards have one rough side and one smooth side, either of which can be exposed. The smooth side is better for painting. The rough side, which has a slightly furry appearance that some people like a lot, is usually exposed when the house will be stained rather than painted.

The term *clapboard* covers a lot of territory. It is used not only for traditional bevel siding, like the stuff I just described, but also (loosely) for just about any kind of horizontal lap siding. Other terms are used, too: weatherboard, shiplap, drop siding, novelty, Dolly Varden. There are many names, many styles, and many variations, some of them peculiar to certain parts of the country. But all these subspecies bear a distinct family resemblance to the original: they all consist of overlapping horizontal boards, a siding innovation that has endured because it works. Because clapboards overlap, the protection provided by them is unaffected by the cyclical cross-grain expansion and contraction of wood. Clapboards also shed water readily while providing an easy escape path for water vapor.

Some builders recommend priming clapboards front and back before installing them. Priming the backs (which is called backpriming) can sometimes reduce cupping in situations where large amounts of moisture accumulate inside the walls. Prepriming the fronts (which is never called frontpriming, so far as I am aware) makes it possible to get some paint on what will ultimately be the covered portion of the face of each clapboard. Prepriming is a good job for a homeowner who wants to pitch in and possibly save some money. Doing this requires good weather (so that waterlogged clapboards from the middles of the bundles can be given time to dry out before they're painted) and a lot of room in which to spread out. It also helps to have access to a herd of sawhorses.

In some parts of the country, the preferred form of solid-wood siding is cedar shingles. Shingles are extremely labor-intensive (and thus expensive) to install, and they also cost a lot themselves, particularly in the premium grades. But they look great, they require virtually no maintenance, and they can last for a very long time. Cedar-shingle siding typically lasts much longer than cedar-shingle roofing does, because siding receives much less abuse from the sun and the weather. This is true even if, as is often the case, subpremium shingles are used on the sides. I've seen houses sided with hundred-year-old unpainted, untreated shingles that still had plenty of years left in them. Even shingles whose exposed surfaces have weathered to the thinness of shirt cardboard aren't necessarily done for. A wood technologist once told me that he had squeezed half a dozen more years out of his own exhausted shingles by putting a coat of paint on them.

One minor drawback to cedar shingles (and, less frequently,

other forms of wood siding) is that woodpeckers sometimes find them irresistible. This doesn't necessarily indicate a bug problem. Woodpeckers just like to peck wood, and they can become attached to certain parts of certain houses. One way to get rid of them is to cover the preferred pecking area with window screen or aluminum foil. This usually sends the bird back to the woods, or at least down the street to a neighbor's house. When the bird is gone, the damaged shingles can be replaced. Indeed, one of the advantages of cedar shingles is that small areas and even individual shingles can be replaced without much trouble.

The most popular siding choice in America by far is plywood. Roughly 1.5 billion square feet of plywood siding products are installed each year. Much of it doesn't look very much like plywood, at least from a distance. Some is grooved, so that it resembles (sort of) narrow boards laid side by side. Some has vertical battens applied to its surface. Some is cut into clapboardlike planks that are lapped horizontally. All of these treatments are available in a variety of textures and surface veneers. Any kind of wood that can be peeled or sliced into thin sheets can be used for the exposed ply.

Plywood siding's main selling point is that it's inexpensive. The material itself doesn't cost very much, and it's easy (and therefore cheap) to install. A pair of carpenters can cover an entire house with plywood panels in less time than it would take to cut and fit cedar clapboards for a garage. Because of its strength, plywood siding can usually be attached directly to the studs, without an intermediate layer of sheathing. This also saves money.

Plywood siding's main disadvantage (aside from any aesthetic objections) is that it's susceptible to water damage. If water penetrates a panel, the glue that binds the plies can weaken, causing the veneers to delaminate. Plywood siding with decorative grooves is most prone to this kind of damage, since the grooves provide numerous entry points for water, but all plywood is vulnerable along its edges. As a result, the edges of all panels (and of all cutouts for doors and windows) need to be sealed carefully with a wood preservative or primer, or with wood preservative *and* primer, and joints between panels need to be protected as much as possible. The homeowner also has to be scrupulous about maintaining the paint or stain. This can be difficult to do, because plywood doesn't hold paint as well as solid wood does (because of lathe-checking—see Chapter Three), especially outdoors.

One of plywood siding's closest direct competitors is hardboard siding, which is a member of the class of engineered wood products known as fiberboard. As such it is a close relative of Masonite, although it is less dense. Like all fiberboard products intended for exterior use, it's treated in various ways to make it water-resistant. Even so, it is highly susceptible to moisture, which can make it swell and warp. Because of this vulnerability, the paint on hardboard siding needs to be maintained with even more care than does the paint on plywood siding. Damage can follow quickly once the barrier is broken. Hardwood siding should be inspected regularly, and paint problems should be dealt with immediately.

Most hardboard siding is sold preprimed; some is sold fully painted. Preprimed hardboard, like any primed exterior surface, needs to be painted as soon as possible to keep the primer from breaking down in sunlight. Failing to paint promptly will also usually void any warranty. Lazy people sometimes decide that the factory prime coat looks just fine to them, a decision they usually begin to regret six months or a year later.

Most hardboard siding is made to look like clapboard or some other form of horizontal lap siding, although it is available in other styles, too. It is usually embossed on the exposed surface with a wood-grain pattern that is intended to make it resemble solid wood—despite the fact that high-quality solid-wood siding usually has no visible grain pattern. In fact, the presence of richly textured knots and wavy grain lines is almost always a dead giveaway that a particular siding is fake. The genuine-cedar clapboards on my house are perfectly smooth.

One of the fastest-growing siding products is vinyl. It still accounts for a fairly small percentage of the total market, but it is relatively new. It has even begun to find acceptance among former wood purists. The reason for this is that high-quality vinyl siding can look very much like real wood siding while being nearly maintenance-free (except for a good washing every once in a while). There's a nice old house on the village green in my town that I've always admired. I didn't realize until I leaned up against it one day that it is sided with vinyl.

Vinyl siding is made from polyvinyl chloride, or PVC. You may have drain pipes, plumbing, or lawn chairs made from essentially the same stuff. Vinyl siding comes in several grades and thicknesses. The thicker, more expensive grades usually look better and last longer than the economy grades. They also hold their color better. (Vinyl siding can't peel, because the color is blended into the material, but it can fade.)

Vinyl siding becomes soft in hot weather and brittle in cold weather, two conditions in which it is particularly vulnerable to damage, but it doesn't dent or scratch the way aluminum siding does. If damage does occur, individual courses, which usually consist of two or three "clapboards," can be removed and re-placed. (Both installation and repair should probably be left to qualified professionals, since there are genuine tricks to the trade.) Vinyl siding is harmed by exposure to ultraviolet light, but the harm takes place very slowly. Some brands are guaranteed for as long as fifty years, with the usual host of limitations and exclusions.

Like hardboard siding, most vinyl siding is embossed with "realistic" phony wood grain, although several manufacturers do offer a limited number of smooth or nearly smooth versions. (A vinyl salesman once told me that a genuinely woodlike smooth finish would be viewed as a "nonfeature" by his customers, who wanted to be able to feel and see that rich, rich grain.) The most successful vinyl sidings, in my opinion, are the ones that attempt the most straightforward knock-offs of classic wood styles. These often look quite good, at least from a distance of several feet, and certainly from the street.

One aesthetic difficulty with vinyl siding is the metal channels used to anchor it around doors and windows and at inside and outside corners. These pieces are often the most obvious clue that vinyl has been used. The channels almost always look tacked-on and out-of-place, especially in retrofit installations on old houses. The corner pieces stand out because they're usually much narrower than the pleasingly wide wood pieces they are meant to imitate.

The obtrusiveness of these details can be minimized by a sensitive architect or carpenter, however. Trim can be designed in such a way that the channels blend into it, or the channels can be applied so that they don't overwhelm existing details. Another way to disguise a vinyl siding job is to use real wood shutters, if shutters are called for, rather than the now ubiquitous plastic ones. A wood-sided house with phony shutters looks much phonier than a vinyl-sided house with wood shutters. A front door that's made of wood instead of steel can also help.

People often turn to vinyl (or aluminum) as a solution to paint problems. Most of the time these paint problems are not paint problems at all, but rather water problems. If a house's paint is peeling off in sheets because its roof is leaking or because too much water vapor is pushing its way out through the walls, vinyl siding won't help. It may hide the symptoms for a while, but it won't cure the disease, and it may even make it worse, by permitting it to progress unnoticed. All such problems should be investigated and dealt with before burying them out of sight behind new siding of any kind.

Vinyl siding hasn't been around long enough for anyone to be entirely certain what happens to it in the very long run. Recent versions are a big improvement over the earliest ones, but no vinyl siding stays pristine forever. Even if you had to replace it in thirty years, though, vinyl siding would still end up costing substantially less than wood and paint. If I were building a house today, I'd be tempted. Vinyl siding is a better imitation of wood clapboards than asphalt shingles are of wood shingles. If putting vinyl on the sides would make it possible for me to put wood on the roof, I might do it.* My main hesitation would be my fear that friends would shake their heads and decide that I was just a vinyl-siding kind of guy.

*Even on a house with solid-wood siding, it might make sense to use vinyl on any dormers or other isolated, hard-to-get-at details. No one would ever suspect, and the painter would be spared some climbing. It's also possible to buy vinyl or vinyl-covered trim pieces, vents, soffits, lattice (great for under porches), and other items.

The rise of vinyl siding has decimated the market for aluminum siding. There was a time when this stuff seemed modern and even futuristic. Now it is on its way to becoming the leisure suit of residential construction. There is still a market for it, but that market is declining.

Aluminum siding has a number of serious disadvantages in comparison with vinyl, not the least of which is that it costs more. Another is that it is fairly easy to dent. Ladders, baseballs, hailstones, and blown branches can leave it looking battleworn (and kick up quite a clatter in doing so). In addition, the color on aluminum siding is a coating, not an integral part of the material as in vinyl siding. This coating can be scratched off. It also erodes over time. In recent years, aluminum siding (whose main selling point has always been the claim that it doesn't need paint) has provided a profitable new growth market for the paint industry. Many manufacturers offer primers and paints specifically designed for it. Regular latex primers and house paints work fine, too. Fortunately, aluminum siding is an excellent substrate for paint, as long as it is cleaned thoroughly—to remove dirt and chalk—before the paint is applied. (Vinyl siding can also be painted, though with some difficulty. Consult a paint manufacturer beforehand.)

The siding material that most Americans associate with luxury is not wood or any of its imitators but brick. There are some parts of the country where virtually all new housing has at least a small amount of it in the exterior, usually in some highly visible place, such as the area around the front door or a gable end that faces the street. This bit-of-brick look arises from a pair of powerful but conflicting human emotions: a yearning to live in magnificent opulence and a horror of spending money. The conflict between these feelings leads to some pretty peculiar house designs, in my opinion. I recently saw a wholly unappealing new house whose exterior siding included not only brick but also vinyl clapboard, battened plywood, and imitation stucco.

In virtually all brick houses, the brick has essentially no structural function. That is, it doesn't hold up the building. It's just siding, called brick veneer. The house is framed and sheathed in the regular way—with wood—and then a shell of brick is erected over the sheathing. A small air space is left between the bricks and the sheathing to help prevent moisture damage and to leave "finger room" for the mason. The brick shell is attached to the frame with metal ties spaced a couple of feet apart. Regularly spaced weep holes are placed (or should be placed) in the mortar at the bottom of every wall and at various other points in order to provide escape routes for water that makes its way behind the shell. When properly installed, the bottom edge of the shell is kept well above grade, both to maintain the effectiveness of the weep holes and to prevent subterranean termites from gaining easy access to the wood framing underneath.

People think of brick as being extraordinarily strong, but this isn't necessarily true. A house made of sticks might actually be harder for a Big Bad Wolf to blow down than a house made only of bricks. In fact, it's the sticks that provide most of the strength in a brick-veneer house. Among the buildings hit hardest by San Francisco's 1989 earthquake were ones made entirely of brick—that is, houses without structural wood or steel frames. When the earth shook, these buildings collapsed into a heap of rubble.

The main advantage of brick, aside from the fact that it makes some people feel rich, is that it requires very little maintenance, assuming that it is properly installed. Brick doesn't rot and you don't have to paint it. Just about the only thing you have to do is keep an eye out for cracks (which can indicate expensive

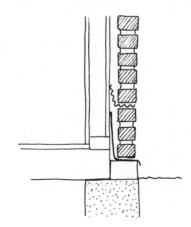

Construction details, brick veneer

107

structural problems) and for deteriorated mortar and flashings (which can let water behind the shell). One thing you definitely should *not* do is treat bricks with any sort of waterproofing material. Doing this can cause moisture to build up inside the wall, with predictable results.

When the surface of the mortar between bricks erodes or becomes crumbly, it needs to be repaired. This repair process is often referred to popularly as tuck-pointing, although the proper term is pointing or repointing. (Tuck-pointing is a special, decorative method of applying mortar.) In pointing, deteriorated mortar is removed from brick joints with a chisel or a grinder, and then new mortar is smoothed in place with a skinny tool known as a pointing trowel. Except for small projects, pointing is a job probably best left to professionals.

Sometimes houses (and interior walls) are covered with thin slices of brick or bricklike material that are bonded to plywood sheathing or some other substrate. Many people confusingly refer to this material also as brick veneer. But it's not the same thing. There would be less confusion if people would simply refer to the slices as fake brick. Several years ago my friends Kurt and Anne bought a house that had an expanse of fake brick over the fireplace. At some point during their negotiations with the previous owner, they indicated that this fake brick was one of the few things they didn't like about the house. The previous owner seemed puzzled by this aesthetic judgment, but did his best to reassure my friends. "There's *real* brick underneath," he said.

There are a lot of other siding choices, including stone, tile, synthetic stucco, fiberglass-reinforced cement, and, well, a lot of others. They add up to a small segment of the total market, but there are a lot of them and new products are introduced regularly. Using some of the very newest products can require a certain spirit of adventure, since they may not have been around long enough to have a track record. Before straying too far from the beaten path, you should do some careful research and be insistent about long-term, ironclad written guarantees.

MAINTENANCE

A house's siding is usually fairly well protected from the elements. Rain rolls off it. The sun doesn't burn down on it the way it does on a roof. Even relatively crummy siding will protect a house for quite a while. But all siding performs better and lasts longer if it is properly maintained.

One of the main enemies of almost any siding, as of almost any other building material, is water. Water ruins paint, nourishes mildew, promotes rot, destroys mortar, and encourages infestations of insects. Maintaining the skin of a house consists primarily of ensuring that water is kept away from places where it isn't supposed to go. The most obvious way to do this is to keep the paint or preservative in good condition, but other measures are usually necessary as well.

The most devastating forms of water damage are usually caused by contact with the ground. Wood siding that touches the dirt seldom lasts very long. Prolonged ground contact promotes rot not only in the siding but also in the framing, leading eventually to the weakening of the entire structure. To keep this from happening, sills (and the trim or siding that covers them) should be at least six inches above grade.

It's not uncommon for old houses to require the installation of new sills, an expensive process that involves jacking the house off of its foundation and fitting new timbers underneath. There's a beautiful old barn in my town that is actually a couple of feet shorter than it was when it was built; at some point someone dealt with its rotten sills simply by trimming away the bottom part of the structure, a repair that left the first-floor windows eerily close to the ground. Ground contact also provides an easy and continuous entryway for termites, carpenter ants, and other insects.

Old houses on inadequate foundations will sometimes simply sink into the ground, bringing their sills and siding into contact with the dirt as they do. Or, if the house is built on a slope, the ground above the house may slowly slump toward it, like a sluggish amoeba attempting to engulf its teeny prey. If it's caught early, a problem like this can be dealt with by regrading the ground around the perimeter of the house, improving drainage, and replacing a few boards. But people tend to ignore problems like this until the time for simple solutions has passed.

I once saw a nice-looking raised flower bed that had been constructed along one side of a house. The gardener had made a frame from two-by-tens laid edgewise and then filled the frame with rich topsoil. The stratum of dirt overlapped the house's siding by several inches, creating a fertile zone of decay that the gardener watered daily. A garden like this can eventually do hundreds or even thousands of dollars' worth of damage to a house.

The flowers themselves were probably causing problems too. Vegetation of any kind that grows too close to the sides of a house can shorten the life of the siding and its paint. Dense shrubs and bushes give off large amounts of water vapor and greatly reduce the flow of air around a house, promoting infestations of mildew and making it harder for wet siding to dry out. Trees that grow too close to a house do the same thing. They can also damage siding directly, as their branches scrape against the house in the wind.

Older houses often have foundation plantings that, through years of inattention, have become wildly overgrown. The people who live in such houses often don't notice that they're being overwhelmed, because the growth takes place gradually. All such vegetation should be trimmed back fearlessly, to leave the siding plenty of breathing room. Doing this can often make a big improvement not only in the health of the siding but also in the appearance of the house, which was almost certainly never intended to bob in a sea of shapeless bushes. People who drastically cut back old foundation plantings often discover that their houses look taller and more majestic than they had imagined.

Water that is shed by the roof of a house can also damage siding. A roof collects rainwater from a large area and concentrates it in a very small area along its bottom edges. Unless this water is conducted away from the house by a properly designed gutter system, it can do great damage to the siding. Often the damage is done on the rebound. When the cascading water strikes the ground, it splashes back up against (and often under-neath) the lower portions of siding, usually bringing with it a film of dirt. The water encourages rot and makes paint peel. The dirt keeps the siding from drying out promptly and fosters the growth of all sorts of undesirable life-forms. The damage can occur especially rapidly on houses with vertical siding, whose end-grain is exposed and close to the ground.

Builders often save money by installing gutters only over doorways, if they install them at all. But a good set of gutters can add a lot of life to a house's siding. (They can also go a long way toward keeping a basement dry.) My garage has a gable roof that slopes to the front and back. There is no gutter in the front. In a rainstorm, water pours off the front of the roof in a sheet and splatters back against the garage doors and the wood trim around them. Much of the paint has peeled from the wood nearest the ground. The bottoms of the doors and the lower portion of the trim have begun to rot. The asphalt nearest the doors has begun to erode. A hundred dollars' worth of gutters and leaders would have prevented this from happening. (It would also keep me from being drenched every time I open or close the garage door in the rain.) I haven't gotten around to tackling this problem yet, but someday I intend to.

Gutters alone don't solve runoff problems. The water that they collect has to be conveyed as far from the house as possible. It is not at all unusual to see gutter systems whose downspouts empty straight down onto the ground beside the foundation. This creates more problems than it solves. It takes water col-lected over a large area and pours it on an area about one foot square right next to the house. In a heavy rain, the basement will leak.

My house is on the side of a hill, so I didn't have any trouble getting rid of the water from my roof. I hired a college student to dig trenches leading from my downspouts to various points farther down the hill. He and I then installed polyvinyl chloride (PVC) drainpipes in these trenches. The pipes we used were four inches in diameter and came in ten-foot lengths that fit together without fasteners or adhesives. My hardware store sells them five to a bundle at a cost of a little more than fifty cents a foot.

It also sells angled connectors that permitted us to turn corners and follow the contour of the ground. When it rains, the water from my roof flows into the gutters, down the downspouts, into the drainage pipes, and at least fifty feet from the foundation before being dumped onto the ground.

If a buried drainage system is out of the question (either because of the slope of the lot or because such systems are prohibited by local ordinances), it should at least be possible to use a horizontal leader to carry the water ten feet or so out into the yard. This will keep the earth near the foundation from becoming saturated, and it should significantly reduce the severity of water problems in the basement. The little concrete splash blocks sold at gardening centers aren't adequate in most situations.

My new drainpipes have gone a long way toward eliminating my anxieties about big storms. When rain lashes against my house now, I cheer myself with thoughts of my underground drainage system. And if another rogue hurricane comes my way, I won't stand fretting by the back door or creep around up in my attic. I'll put on my raincoat and grab a flashlight and go out to the edge of my yard to watch the water from my roof—which used to end up in my basement—sluicing harmlessly down the hill.

Chapter 5

The Walls Around Us

W hat to do with the interior walls of one's dwelling is a problem of antique standing. For a surprisingly large stretch of human history a frequent response to this problem has been plaster. The pharaohs' toilers crumbled gypsum, heated it, mixed it with water, and spread the resulting paste over rough walls made of stone, brick, mud, or reeds. A wide variety of ancient peoples did essentially the same thing, using gypsum, lime, clay, and other materials. In doing so they anticipated with their usual uncanniness the way we do things today (except that, for the most part, we don't do this thing today, the plasterer's art having gone the way of the other arts—but I'm getting ahead of myself).

From the time of the Egyptians onward, plaster has been viewed as a remarkable substance, and indeed it is one: as richly smooth and pliant as the material Freud called the child's first gift, yet clean, white, pristine—primordial slop bleached of unpleasant associations. When properly maintained, it is sturdy enough to mock the eons, yet its supple plasticity endears it to the artist, who, with a delight presumably not unlike that of the Shaper of the original clay, et cetera, et cetera.

Plaster, like almost everything else, reached its aesthetic zenith during the Renaissance. Exacting craftsmen filled magnificent rooms with moldings, reliefs, and other ornaments, achieving a degree of interior decoration seldom aspired to nowadays beyond the city limits of Las Vegas. When Michelangelo sprawled on his back for four years beneath the ceiling of the Sistine Chapel, it was onto wet plaster (*fresco* means "fresh," the condition in which the surface to be frescoed must be) that he painted his astonishing vision.

Plaster has utilitarian virtues as well. It deters rodents and is of no interest to termites. Plaster made with lime is antiseptic and helps in a small way to control the spread of disease. Plaster is poor at transmitting sound, which means that a house with plaster walls is quieter than one whose walls are made of wood. All plaster is fire-resistant. A modern wall made with gypsum wallboard—basically, two pieces of heavy paper with a layer of plaster in between—can hold its own against flames for about an hour. Plaster walls were viewed, correctly, as one solution to the fires that regularly blackened London for so many centuries. "Bild up an hous of fyne lyme playster to keep away the flames" was the wording, perhaps, of some medieval edict.

In the earliest days of the American colonies, the inner walls of houses were made of wooden boards. These were nailed directly to the studs. Soon, though, plaster became the covering of choice for most walls. At first it was used just in the public rooms, and often only on the upper portions of the walls, where it was less likely to be thumped by boots and chair backs. Much of the wonderful woodwork in old houses—chair rails, wainscoting, baseboards—was installed to protect what was viewed at the time as even more wonderful plaster.

Until the late nineteenth century or so, plaster in American houses was typically made of lime, sand, and the hair of animals. Sand and animal hair are familiar to all; lime is calcium oxide. It is produced by crushing and then calcining (by heating to more than seventeen hundred degrees Fahrenheit) limestone, seashells, Tums, or some other rich source of calcium carbonate. Freshly calcined lime is called quicklime; pouring water into it causes a hot, nasty chemical reaction. After this nasty reaction has taken place, quicklime is known as slaked, or hydrated, lime. It is from this that lime plaster is usually made.

A very similar substance is calcium sulfate, or gypsum, whose use as a building material is reputed to have been introduced to America by Benjamin Franklin. Franklin had learned about gypsum in France. When he returned home, in 1785, he adopted the French practice of grinding gypsum to a powder and sprinkling it on his fields. This powdered gypsum was known as land plaster. It improved the quality of the soil and made crops grow better. Thanks in part to the interest of Franklin, gypsum eventually found its way into a host of useful products, including concrete, chalkboard chalk (which is made of soft gypsum plaster), toilet bowls, beer, tofu, and toothpaste. The average American, it has been estimated, ingests a bit less than half a pound of gypsum per year.

"THE ROCK NOBODY KNOWS"

If you habitually worry that we may one day run out of gypsum, you should read "The Rock Nobody Knows," a pamphlet published by the National Gypsum Company, which makes plaster, wallboard, and other gypsum-based products. There are two main gypsum belts in the United States, it turns out. One extends from southwestern Texas all the way to the banks of the Niagara River in New York State. The other begins in California and spreads into Utah. The amount of gypsum in these two belts, according to the pamphlet, is unlimited.

Gypsum occurs naturally in many forms, including satin spar and alabaster. As a lad, I had a piece of satin spar in one of those boxed rock collections sold at souvenir stands in national parks. As hard as it is to believe, I think my mother later threw it out. Wherever it is today, that little chunk of satin spar, like all gypsum, contains a great deal of water: roughly 50 percent by

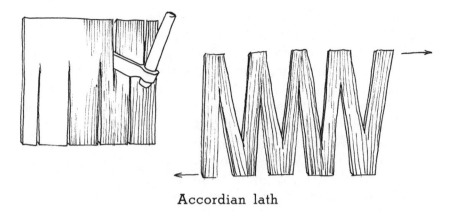

Accordian lath

volume, not including the dab of amber glue that held it in the box and belied my claim, made to various friends, that I had found this handsome treasure while digging in my yard.

Crushing and calcining drives off most of the water in gypsum, yielding the remarkably useful material known as plaster of paris. Gypsum wall plaster is usually made of plaster of paris and additives that keep it from setting too quickly. When water is mixed back in, the gypsum's original crystalline structure re-forms. The water content of hardened gypsum plaster is about the same as that of gypsum rock. It is this internal water that accounts for gypsum plaster's resistance to fire. For roughly a hundred years now, most plaster has been made of gypsum.

Plaster, like cake frosting, needs to be spread on something. Not cake, of course. The supporting surface onto which it is spread is called lath (rhymes with *bath*). From colonial times until well into this century, lath was made of wood. One of the earliest versions was called accordion lath. It was made from thin oak slabs that were split, with a froe, on alternate sides and then pulled apart, like an accordion. The expanded slab was nailed to the studs and plaster was spread across it. The wet plaster oozed through the splits and sagged over the back of the lath. When the plaster dried, these sagging oozes—known as keys—held the plaster firmly in place.

Accordion lath was replaced by narrow wood strips nailed horizontally across the studs. Small spaces were left between the strips, so that the plaster could ooze through and form keys. My house contains two kinds of wood lath: hand-split oak strips from the late eighteenth century and sawn strips from the nineteenth. The hand-split laths are of uneven width and thickness and are held up with wrought nails. The sawn laths are uniform and are held up with machine-cut nails. I have a box in which I keep about a dozen laths that I have extracted from my walls at one time or another. These laths seemed extremely interesting to me at the time I put them into the box. They seem somewhat less so now.

In our century, wood lath was replaced by metal lath. Several of the most popular versions were made by punching short slits in sheet metal and then pulling the ends of the sheet, creating diamond-shaped holes. Metal lath is still used in some applications. Far more common is so-called gypsum lath or Rocklath, which consists of smallish wallboardlike gypsum panels. These panels are nailed or screwed to the studs and covered with two or three coats of plaster.

The durability of an old plaster job was determined in part by the skill of the lather, as a person who installs lath is known. Using lath that was dirty or too dry could cause the plaster to set improperly, weakening its bond. Leaving too little space between the laths (which was sometimes done to save plaster) could prevent the formation of good keys. Butting the ends closely could cause cracks when the house shifted or settled. Sometimes, at the end of a wall, a lather would find that his laths were a few inches too short to reach all the way into the corner. Rather than stopping to cut short strips, he would nail up one or two laths vertically. Where he did this, the plaster would eventually crack. The wood grain in the vertical pieces was perpendicular to the wood grain in the horizontal pieces. When the laths swelled and shrank in response to changes in humidity, the difference in grain direction created stresses and the stresses created cracks.

Of course, the quality of a plaster job was also greatly determined by the skill of the plasterer. Plastering was (and remains) an exacting trade requiring a good eye, a steady hand, and a long apprenticeship. Wet plaster hardens quickly and permanently,

David Owen

leaving the plasterer little time to fuss over mistakes. Anyone who has ever tried and failed to spread spackling compound evenly over a previously unnoticeable dent in a wall will have no difficulty appreciating the level of skill required to spread plaster evenly over, for example, the ceiling of Grand Central Station.

MODERN TIMES

Shortly before the dawn of the twentieth century a dreamer named Augustine Sackett had an idea that marked the beginning of the end of the plaster era. Sackett sandwiched three thin layers of plaster of paris with four layers of heavy paper, creating what he called Sackett Plaster Board. Each board was thirty-six inches long, thirty-two inches wide, and a quarter of an inch thick. The quality of the early product was such that it could be used for very little. It was ugly, heavy, rough, and weak. However, it was fast. Before Sackett's invention, walls had usually consisted of three coats of plaster on wood lath. After Sackett's invention, they still usually consisted of this, but sometimes a builder would save himself a good deal of trouble and money by nailing plaster boards directly to the studs, covering them with a thin layer of plaster, and letting it go at that.

In 1909, Sackett (whose business by then spanned the globe from Garbutt, New York, to Fort Dodge, Iowa) sold out to the United States Gypsum Company, a mining-and-manufacturing concern that had been founded seven years before. The company refined Sackett's invention—for example, by eliminating the two internal paper layers. In 1917 the company introduced the product that has been the mainstay of its business ever since, a much-improved gypsum panel called Sheetrock. Unlike Sackett Plaster Board, Sheetrock was a total substitute for lath and plaster. All that an installer had to do was cover up the joints and nailheads by troweling on a relatively small amount of plaster-like compound. Doing this was fairly easy, and it became ex-

118

tremely popular. If you're like a lot of people, you can touch some Sheetrock from where you're sitting right now.

Along with Kleenex, Kitty Litter, and Windbreaker, Sheetrock is, I think, one of the world's outstanding trade names. People tend to use it, improperly, as a generic term for gypsum wallboard, but in proper usage it applies only to various products of USG Corporation, as the company is now known. Wallboard is also often referred to as drywall and sometimes as gypsum board or even gypboard. If you would like to do this, too, you may. *Drywall, gypsum board,* and *gypboard* are not trade names.

USG is the biggest manufacturer of gypsum wallboard in the world. It ships about seven billion square feet of it in America in a year. Seven billion square feet works out to 160,700 acres, 65,000 hectares, or 26 million square rods. That's a lot. Still, two thirds of all the gypsum wallboard shipped in America is made by other companies. The second-biggest producer, with something more than five billion square feet, is National Gypsum Company, which makes Gold Bond brand wallboard.

Whatever the brand name, gypsum wallboard has a lowly reputation. When people complain about how much worse things are nowadays, wallboard is one of the things they often complain about. You never heard of people putting their fists through walls before Augustine Sackett came along, these people will say while poking you in the chest with their stubby fingers. Wallboard is usually less rugged than lath and plaster. It's also cheap, which makes it irresistibly attractive to the sort of people who are irresistibly attracted to cheap things. Since this describes almost everyone, almost everyone has some.

Because wallboard is relatively easy to install, it is often installed by people who don't know what they're doing. These ignorant people include not only recklessly ambitious do-it-yourselfers like me but also highly paid professionals. Once it occurs to you to look, you can spot bad wallboard jobs almost anywhere, including, quite possibly, in your own house. When I find myself waiting in someone's office, I pass the time by looking for evidence of sloppy wallboard jobs. It isn't hard to find.

Still, gypsum wallboard doesn't have to be crummy. Skillfully installed, it can be as handsome and enduring as three-coat-plaster. People who rhapsodize about old plaster walls tend to forget that old plaster walls weren't always so great. They cracked and crumbled and pulled away from their lath. Owners of old houses are susceptible to a silly form of reverse snobbery in which ancient plaster is cherished *because* of its imperfections.

The problem with modern walls is not the materials but the spirit in which they are used. In most new construction the walls aren't given much thought. Architects and their clients worry more about where walls will be placed than about what they'll be made of. But people who really care about well-made walls can still have them today.

WALLBOARD TO THE RESCUE

As I mentioned in Chapter One, when my wife and I bought our house it was filled with horrible wallpaper. This wallpaper—vast geometric schemes in clashing colors, floral fantasies, perching birds garlanded with fruit—had been put up with oceanic thoroughness by the previous owners, and much of our first year in residence was devoted to getting rid of it.

Getting rid of it turned out to be harder than we had anticipated. In the first place, our house's relationship with ugly wall coverings proved to have been not a passing fancy but rather a marriage of some two centuries' duration. In one room an exploratory core sample revealed (from the surface inward) ugly wallpaper, oldish gypsum wallboard, ugly wallpaper, a thin veneer of plaster, ugly wallpaper, and a proper plaster wall.

In the second place, the previous owners' devotion to wallpaper considerably outran their skill at putting it up. We found several walls that had been incorrectly prepared before being papered over and were thus unwilling to surrender the offending layer without surrendering much of themselves as well. In other places the wallpaper was serving less a decorative than a structural function—in fact, preventing the walls from tumbling down.

My wife and I, at times resembling one of those happy, industrious couples in cigarette advertisements, scraped wallpaper off as many walls as we could. Simply painting over the remaining wallpaper was considered but for the most part rejected; in most rooms there were too many bumps, lumps, tears, holes, gaps, cracks, and crevices. Demolishing the walls and starting from scratch was a possibility, but a messy and expensive one. It was at this point in our thinking that we called in a pro.

The pro we called in recommended that we deal with some of our remaining wallpaper by burying it beneath a layer of gypsum wallboard. The wallboard, he said, could be attached directly to the existing walls. This idea was attractive for several reasons. First, it would leave the old walls intact but out of sight. Second, putting new walls over old was clearly a tradition in our house. Third, it would leave the walls thicker, sturdier, and somewhat less drafty than they had been before. Fourth, it would be relatively inexpensive. We decided to start with the front hall and the living room.

The people who put up the wallboard in our house were the first people that my wife and I had ever hired to do any sort of work in a place where we lived. Once, when we were living in New York, we had had our apartment painted, but the painter had been hired and paid by the owner of the building. Also, it took him less than four hours to paint all four rooms, and the walls still looked terrible when he was finished.

When the workmen came to install wallboard in our house, I spent a lot of time watching them work. "I have conceived of a plan, and now skilled craftsmen are executing it in my behalf!" is approximately what I was thinking. When the workmen left for the day, I would walk slowly through the hall and living room, looking at the stuff they had left lying around. Before this, I had never thought very much, if at all, about wallboard. Now I began to think about it all the time.

Laminating wallboard over existing walls is made somewhat

difficult by things that stick out from the walls: moldings, base-boards, window trim, and the like. The cornice molding in our hall and living room, for example, was in the way. Fortunately, it had been put up by the previous owners, not by Thomas Jefferson. The workmen pulled it down and threw it in their dump truck. If the molding had been something special, they would have saved it and put it back up later, after trimming it to fit walls that would be slightly closer together than they had been before. Instead, when they were finished, they put up new molding that gratifyingly looked older than the old molding.

The windows in our living room and the principal doorways are old and nice. Taking them down was out of the question. Fortunately, the casings around them stuck out an inch and a half from the old plaster walls. Likewise with the top of some old raised-panel wainscoting along one wall. Reducing the pro-trusion by the thickness of the wallboard made no difference. The baseboards in the hall, which had been installed during the house's dormitory days, were ordinary modern pine boards three-quarters of an inch thick. Setting half-inch wallboard above them cut the protrusion to a quarter of an inch and actu-ally made them look more in keeping with the age of the house, because colonial builders used to nail baseboards and certain other trim pieces to the framing and then apply the wall plaster flush with them. They did this partly because they liked the way it looked and partly because it permitted them to use the trim pieces as guides in smoothing and leveling the surface of the plaster.

The transformation of the walls in our house was astonish-ing. The living room, which had previously seemed dark and mausoleumish, now looked almost cheerful. The walls were the color of naked wallboard—gray—but even so they looked much better than they had looked in the days when they had been smothered by large-patterned, sepia-toned, ugly-wrapping-paper-reminiscent wallpaper. For the first time since we had moved in, I fully noticed and appreciated the windows. My wife and I joked that we liked our new walls so much that we might just leave them unpainted. And the really great thing was, we were able to continue making this joke for a little over two years. But that's another story.

WALLBOARD BASICS

At a wallboard factory, a plasterlike gypsum slurry is sandwiched between layers of special paper on a moving line perhaps a quarter mile long. The sandwich, which is four feet wide, is squeezed to the desired thickness by heavy rollers. The edges are shaped and the paper is wrapped and sealed around them. The gypsum begins to harden. At the end of the line, the quarter-mile ribbon of new wallboard is chopped into marketable lengths and stacked in an enormous kiln for final drying.

Wallboard is much heavier than I would have guessed before I used it. The standard panel—which is eight feet long, four feet wide, and half an inch thick—weighs a bit under fifty-eight pounds, or about as much as a third-grader. When I built my office, which is on the third floor of my house, the only part of the construction process that I didn't like was carrying the wallboard from the garage, where the lumberyard guys had stacked it, across the yard and up two flights of stairs. When you lift a sheet of wallboard by yourself, all fifty-eight pounds of it bear down on a narrow band across the base of your fingers. This is particularly agonizing on stairs, because you have to hold the panel at exactly the right angle to prevent it from hitting the ceiling, then the steps, then the ceiling, then the steps.*

Although wallboard is heavy, it's easy to work with. You don't have to saw it (although you can). If you score the facing paper with a utility knife, you can break the panel cleanly with your bare hands, like Bruce Lee. Professional wallboard hangers (known in the trade as rockers, as in Sheetrockers) use four-

---

*Carrying third-graders would be a lot easier, because you could pick them up under their arms. On the other hand, they would probably begin to squawk and kick you in the shins by the time you got them about halfway up the stairs. So it's probably a toss-up.

foot-long T-squares, called wallboard squares, to guide their knives during full-width cuts. You can hang a wallboard square on the edge of a panel, hold the bottom of the square in place with your foot, run your knife down the side of the square, snap the panel back to break the gypsum core along the line of the cut, then run your knife down the back of the crease to free the two pieces. The pros do this at a blinding pace, with one rocker calling out measurements while another cuts and snaps.

For most of its history, gypsum wallboard has been put up with nails. There are several specialized kinds. Some are coated with a cement that bonds to wood. Others have little rings around their shafts that do the same thing. The ringed nails work better than the coated ones, but neither kind works as well as screws. Screws hold tighter than nails (which means you don't have to use as many), and they're faster to install. They're also easier on walls. Hammering nails into wallboard on one side of a wall will often loosen the nails holding up wallboard on the other side. And if there's plaster on the other side, all that hammering may crack it or cause the keys to break off.

Wallboard screws usually have a black coating that makes them somewhat rust-resistant. (Similar screws are available in galvanized or cadmium-coated versions for use in truly moist conditions, such as outdoors.) All wallboard screws are self-tapping, which means that they don't require pilot holes the way ordinary wood screws do. This makes them extremely useful for all sorts of fastening jobs. I keep a large supply in my basement, in about six different lengths (ranging from three-quarters of an inch to three and a half inches), and I use them constantly. In fact, the workbench on which I keep all my wallboard screws is put together with wallboard screws.

The most important part of a wallboard screw is its head, which is flat on top and concave on the sides. In

Wallboard screw

profile it looks a little like the bell of a trumpet or a bugle, and, in fact, wallboard screws are also known as bugle-head screws. When a wallboard screw is driven into wallboard, the shape of the head causes the face paper to wind tightly underneath it. This holds the wallboard snugly against the framing. Properly driven wallboard screws are much less likely than nails to tear the face paper. This is important, because virtually all of the strength of a wallboard panel is in the paper. A fastener that tears the paper is holding up nothing at all. (For attaching wood trim and doing other carpentry chores, I like to use so-called trim-head wallboard screws, which have small heads that are easy to countersink.)

Screws virtually eliminate one of the most common and annoying problems with wallboard: nail pops. A nail pop is, to use technical terms, a nail that has popped. As wet framing lumber dries out inside a wall, it shrinks away from the wallboard nailed to it. It also shrinks away from the shanks of the nails. Everything looks fine until someone leans against the wall. Pop! The round nailheads poke through the surface, looking like buttons you might push to open secret passageways. Screws, in contrast, follow the wood as it shrinks, taking the wallboard with them. Contractors who still use nails (and many of them do) are ignorant, stubborn, cheap, or all three. If I were looking to hire a wallboard contractor, I would eliminate from consideration anyone who didn't plan to use screws.

Trimhead wallboard
screw

Wallboard screws are installed not with a screwdriver but with a wallboard screwgun. Mine is a Makita variable-speed. It looks almost exactly like my Makita variable-speed electric drill, but it has a much more specialized function. The motor, which can be operated at speeds of up to four thousand revolutions per minute, has a clutch that doesn't engage until a few pounds of pressure have been applied to the tip.

I stick a screw on the tip (which is magnetized), pull the trigger, press the point against a sheet of wallboard or a piece of wood, and—zzzzip!—the screw is screwed in. An adjustable sleeve causes the clutch to disengage at the exact moment the screw has been driven to the depth I have selected. Big-volume contractors sometimes use magazine-fed screw guns, which reload themselves after each screw has been driven and look like automatic weapons. I tried one of these at an exhibition once, and then spent about an hour trying to make myself believe that I needed to buy one.

Wallboard screw gun

TAPING

The most time-consuming part of any wallboard installation is covering up the heads of the fasteners and the joints between the panels. Screws and nails are always driven slightly below the surface of the panels—not so far as to endanger the paper, but far enough to create a slight depression. (A sixteenth of an inch is said to be about right, but how on earth would one measure it?) This depression—called a dimple in the trade—is filled with two, three, or more applications of a spackling-compoundlike material called joint compound or mud. Repeated applications are necessary, because almost all joint compounds shrink as they dry. Dimples made by screws are smaller than those made by nails and thus easier to fill—another reason to prefer screws. Tossing around a little casual banter about "mudding the dimples" is a good way to make a wallboard installer think you're out of your mind. (I did once hear a professional taper speak of "spotting the nails.")

Joints between panels are harder to cover than dimples. First the joints are "buttered," or covered with a thin layer of compound. The compound is applied with a spatulalike knife (called a wallboard taping knife) four or five inches wide. While this compound is still wet, a strip of two-inch-wide paper tape is embedded in it, smoothed with the knife to remove all air bubbles from underneath, and covered with an extremely thin layer of compound. Joint tape reinforces joints. In the old days it was always perforated, to facilitate bonding; nowadays it usually isn't. Instead, its surface is mechanically roughened, giving it a slightly hairy texture.

In recent years an increasing number of wallboard installers have switched to fiberglass mesh tape for reinforcing wallboard joints. Most such tape is self-sticking, which means that the initial, embedding coat of compound can be eliminated. This makes the mesh tape seem easier to use. Most people also believe that mesh tape is stronger than paper tape—the mighty power of mesh.

Unfortunately, mesh tape is actually much weaker than paper tape, and it doesn't work nearly as well. In fact, studies done at USG's extensive testing facility have demonstrated that a joint reinforced with mesh tape has very little more strength than a joint that isn't reinforced at all. The reason is that mesh tape, unlike paper tape, tends to stretch when it comes under stress. When it stretches, the compound cracks. Hardware-store clerks (and some wallboard-supply manufacturers) push mesh tape

Taping knives

127

because it costs much more than paper tape and is thus more profitable to sell. But you should be firm. Using mesh tape can ruin a wallboard job and lead to expensive and inconvenient repairs once the cracks have appeared.

The long edges of wallboard panels are almost always tapered. Placing two of these tapered edges together creates a shallow depression. Repeated applications of joint compound fill this depression, concealing the reinforcing tape and creating a uniform surface across the panels. Harder to conceal are the joints between the butt ends of the panels, which are not tapered. Putting tape and compound on these joints creates a hump that has to be disguised by spreading the compound far out onto the panel. Even good tapers tend to have trouble with these joints. The only entirely satisfactory method of dealing with them is to eliminate them entirely by using longer panels (or shorter rooms).

Corners also require special treatment. For inside corners, paper tape is folded lengthwise along the factory-made crease that runs down its center. The corner joint is buttered on both sides, just as a flat joint would be. The folded tape is pressed into the compound so that the crease is aligned with the angle of the corner. The tape is embedded with a taping knife, covered with a very thin layer of compound, and allowed to dry. Successive coats of compound are applied to just one side of the corner at a time: left side one day, right side the next, left the next, right

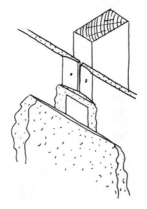

Taping details

the next. Doing the second side while the first is still wet is possible in theory but enormously frustrating in practice. Some people like to use an angled corner trowel, known in the trade as an angle plow, which smooths both sides of the corner at once, but getting good results is easier with a regular knife.

Outside corners are reinforced not with tape but with wallboard corner bead, which is a perforated metal strip that has been creased along its length into a V-shaped profile. Corner bead, which is sold in eight-foot lengths, is nailed, stapled, or crimped (but never screwed) onto outside corners. It is then covered with at least two coats of joint compound. Doing this is just about my favorite part of installing wallboard, because, for some reason that I do not understand, I really enjoy spreading joint compound over perforated metal.

When the embedding layer of compound is dry—usually a day or two later—a second layer of compound is spread over it with a somewhat wider taping knife. After it has dried, the second coat is followed by one or two additional coats, which are applied with successively wider knives. Each new layer of compound is "feathered," or squished flat, beyond the edges of the previous one. This is done by keeping the outside edge of the knife (the one farthest from the joint) pressed firmly against the wallboard as the knife is drawn over the joint. At the same time, the inside edge of the knife is allowed to ride slightly above the surface. The idea is to disguise the buildup of compound over the joint by making its edges fade smoothly into the surface of the wallboard. On butt joints, some tapers use knives whose blades are two or three feet wide, so that they can feather the compound over a broader area.

Professional tapers will sometimes finish a job by applying an extremely thin layer of joint compound over the entire surface of all the walls and ceilings. This thin layer is called a skim coat. It helps to eliminate a number of common wallboard defects by creating a uniform finish and eliminating texture differences. In applying a skim coat, a wide knife is used to spread a swath of compound, then the same knife is used to remove virtually all of the compound just applied. This is repeated until the entire surface has been covered with a uniform film. It's usually hard to keep the edges of the knife from occasionally (or frequently) leaving little ridges in the compound, but these can be scraped off later with a clean taping knife once the compound is dry.

When the final layer has dried, the joint compound is sanded to eliminate bumps, lumps, and trowel marks. Careful sanding can compensate, to some extent, for less-than-perfect taping, but it's always a mistake to rely too heavily on sandpaper. For one thing, sanding joint compound is extraordinarily messy. It creates a blizzard of abrasive white dust that takes several years to vacuum up. For another thing, sandpaper can scuff the wallboard's face paper, raising a fuzzy nap that is easy to see and troublesome to get rid of. (Applying a skim coat before sanding prevents this from happening.)

An excellent alternative to sandpaper is a wet sponge—preferably a tight-celled cellulose sponge. A sponge is slower than sandpaper, but it doesn't produce dust. It also doesn't scuff the face paper or leave scratches in the compound. In any taping job, though, the goal should be to produce work that requires as little sanding or sponging as possible. The most skillful tapers can get away with next to none.*

THE JOY OF JOINT COMPOUND

Before it turns into dust, joint compound is one of the most wonderful and thoroughly satisfying building materials there is. I have used it not only to finish wallboard joints but also to patch cracked plaster, to resurface ugly ceilings (by skimming), and to make little pretend animal cookies for my daughter. Once, when I was resurfacing the ceiling of my daughter's bedroom, I stepped down from the stool on which I had been standing and into an open bucket of joint compound. The smooth white material felt cool and luxurious against my foot,

*One thing that wallboard dust gets into is window screens. If you're working with the windows open, remove the screens before you sand. If you don't, you'll have to wash the screens.

which, as luck would have it, was bare. I extracted my foot, scraped it with my taping knife, hopped down the stairs and out the front door, and cleaned up with the garden hose.

There are several kinds of joint compound, including taping, topping, and all-purpose. Taping compound bonds powerfully both to paper tape and to wallboard but is difficult to sand; it is intended for embedding tape. Topping compound is weaker but shrinks less and is easy to sand; it is intended for the final coat. All-purpose is a compromise between the two. The best all-purpose compounds are the new lightweight versions. USG's, which is called Plus 3, weighs about a third less than other joint compounds. It also shrinks less, is noticeably easier to feather, and eliminates the need for separate taping and topping compounds, since it bonds as powerfully as taping yet is as easy to sand as topping.

A few specialized kinds of joint compound set rather than dry. They are, in effect, plaster. The main advantage of setting joint compounds is that, like plaster, they harden very quickly (in as little as fifteen or twenty minutes) and they don't shrink when they do. They are also extremely strong. Their main disadvantages are that they are tricky to work with and they can't be sanded (because they're too hard). As a result they are almost never used for topping. But they can be extremely useful for other purposes, such as embedding tape and applying an initial coat to corner beads. (They are also good for patching cracks in walls and ceilings.) If a setting compound is used as the initial coat in wallboard finishing, a second coat (of a regular, drying joint compound) can usually be applied the same day. This saves time and money. It also produces stronger joints. USG's setting joint compound is called Durabond. Gold Bond's is called Sta-Smooth. Both are known in the industry as "hot mud."

Nonsetting joint compound has a great deal in common with spackling compound (and can be used for the same purposes indoors), but the two are not the same thing. Joint compound is thinner and wetter and thus easier to spread evenly over large surfaces. It's also easier to feather. Until 1977, virtually all joint compounds contained substantial quantities of asbestos. Asbestos made joint compounds easier to spread and had other beneficial effects that did not, in the end, outweigh the fact that it sometimes killed the people who manufactured it and used it. Nowadays no joint compound contains asbestos, although old walls can pose a danger during remodeling.

One of best things about joint compound is the swell plastic bucket it comes in. (Setting joint compounds are sold in powder form rather than premixed in buckets, for a reason that should occur to you in a moment.) I now have about twenty of these buckets. They are made of heavy-gauge plastic, and they have sturdy metal handles and tight-fitting lids. I use one to hold my plumbing tools, one to hold my paint-stripping tools, one to hold birdseed, one to hold charcoal, and four or five to carry water from the dehumidifier in my basement, which has no floor drain, to my yard. The rest I hoard.

My hardware store sells a five-gallon bucket of joint compound for about twelve dollars; it sells an empty five-gallon plastic bucket for about six-fifty—and that's without a lid. Why would you buy an empty plastic bucket when you could get the same bucket plus more than sixty pounds of one of the world's most interesting substances for less than twice as much? If you somehow end up with more empty joint compound buckets than you want, you can always sell them in Haiti, where they can bring five dollars apiece on the black market.*

WATCHING PROS

Professional wallboard hangers—as opposed to professional builders or carpenters who hang a little wallboard every once in a while—work at a pace that can give an average

---

*Joint compound buckets, like any large buckets, pose a danger to very small children. A five-gallon bucket half filled with water weighs more than twenty pounds. If a toddler pulls himself up on the side of it and tumbles in headfirst, the bucket may very well not tip over and the toddler may be unable to free himself. According to the Consumer Product Safety Commission, sixty-seven children between the ages of eight months and a year drowned in buckets between 1985 and 1987.

do-it-yourself the vapors. I discovered this one very cold day while watching two deft rockers named Billy and Spanky put up walls and ceilings in a brand-new house not far from where I live.

When I arrived at the construction site, Billy and Spanky were standing in front of a big kerosene heater, smoking cigarettes and trying to get warm. The house was fully enclosed and insulated, but the furnace hadn't been hooked up. Finally Billy stubbed out his cigarette, went into the dining room, and cut about a foot off the end of a twelve-foot panel. (Using twelve-foot panels rather than eight-foot panels in this eleven-foot room made it possible to eliminate all butt joints, which would make life easier for the tapers later on.) With Spanky's help he hoisted the shortened panel into place on the ceiling. The two of them quickly banged in half a dozen nails to hold it in place. Then Spanky "screwed off" the panel with his screw gun, putting in a screw roughly every foot along each joist. While he did this, Billy measured and cut the next panel. The entire ceiling took about ten minutes to finish.

Billy and Spanky's ceiling technique was not entirely by the book. First, they used nails, although they didn't use many. Using screws alone would have been just as easy, and it would have eliminated the risk of nail pops. Second, in applying fasteners they worked from the ends of each panel towards the middle. Doing this can create stresses in the panel that can lead to surface defects later on. A far better technique is to secure the middle of the panel first and then work out toward the edges.

The walls went even faster than the ceiling. The front wall had a picture window in the middle of it. Billy and Spanky nailed and screwed a big panel over the top part of the entire wall, covering up half the window. Then Spanky used a small router with a special bit to cut an opening around the window. He did this by running the router around the outside of the window jamb, using the jamb itself as a guide. After removing his cutout, he could pop the panel snugly into place around the jamb. He did the same thing around electrical boxes for light fixtures, light switches, and outlets. This, too, was not exactly by the book. The recommended procedure is to measure and cut all openings before hanging panels. But Billy and Spanky got good results in less time doing it their way.*

While Spanky was making cutouts and screwing off, Billy was measuring and cutting panels for other parts of the room. As he did this, he was thinking several moves ahead, like a chess player: a window cutout from the dining-room wall might become the ceiling of the front-hall closet; the fourteen-foot panels stacked in the living room would work better in the kitchen, which was a little over thirteen feet wide.

Billy and Spanky quickly established a brisk rhythm, which they maintained between infrequent cigarette breaks. They didn't talk, except to call out measurements. I stayed out of the way by standing quietly in what would one day be a closet but at the moment looked like a tiny jail cell with two-by-fours for bars. Billy and Spanky were being paid not by the hour but by the panel, which meant that every question I asked cost them money. Their average production rate was eighty or ninety twelve-foot panels a day—roughly four tons of Sheetrock. On a really good day, when no one was pestering them, they sometimes installed more than a hundred panels.

The main enemy of a rocker is a sloppy framer. When studs and joists are improperly spaced, misaligned, or out of plumb, the rockers have to stop to make adjustments. Billy and Spanky didn't have many complaints with this job, because the framing was basically straight. (Where it wasn't, they whacked it into line with their wallboard hammers.) The worst jobs, Billy said, are in condominiums, where construction crews tend to be sloppy and the framing is almost always out of line. The second-worst jobs, he said, are rehabilitations in old houses like mine, where the framing is *always* out of line. On those jobs he charges by the hour, not the panel.

Rocking this new house took Billy and Spanky one and a half days and consumed close to ten thousand square feet of Sheetrock. Then they took off for another job. A few days later, a

*Another good way to mark locations for cutouts is to rub chalk, Vaseline, lipstick, or something similar on the edges of the electrical boxes and then carefully press the backs of the panels against them.

different crew arrived to begin taping, a distinctly separate trade. Billy and Spanky talked about tapers the way doctors talk about dentists. Tapers, meanwhile, view rockers as brawny louts with no sense of artistry. Of course, every crew that passes through a construction site blames the previous crew for all its problems. Painters, for their part, view tapers as unschooled thugs who conspire to make paint jobs look bad.

I didn't go back to watch Billy and Spanky's Sheetrock be taped, but I did spend some time with another taping crew, a husband-and-wife team working on a big two-story addition to the house of some friends. The tapers' names were Bill and Mary. They were from Arkansas, where they worked during the winter but where there weren't enough jobs to keep them busy all summer long. Bill had been taping for seventeen years. Mary worked with him during the summers and when he needed an extra pair of hands.

Good tapers establish a rhythm in their work, but it isn't the frenetic rhythm of rockers. Every motion Bill made was fluid and spare. He would start at one corner of a room and work his way around it, spreading joint compound the way a pastry chef spreads butter cream. He wore a belt that had a shallow container for mud (called a bread pan) on the front and a spool for tape at one side. When he spotted screws, he would cover three or four at once with a single downward swipe of his knife and then skim away the excess with a swipe in the other direction. Much of the work he did was done with his arms held over his head. Mary told me that after seventeen years of this, Bill sometimes felt uncomfortable when his arms were hanging at his sides.

Bill and Mary were in a good mood, because the rockers who had preceded them had done a good job. There were only one or two butt joints in the entire addition, which meant the taping would be easier. Also, the rockers had used screws and dimpled them properly, so that there were no screwheads sticking above the surface of the wallboard. When a screw isn't countersunk sufficiently, it clicks against a taping knife passing over it and makes a ripple in the compound. (Protruding fastener heads are known in the trade as tits.)

135

Despite the high quality of the rocking on this particular job, Bill said, taping walls and ceilings in Connecticut required a lot more labor than taping walls and ceilings in Arkansas. In new construction in Arkansas, he said, most walls and ceilings are covered with textured finishes. That is, the fasteners and joints are given just a single coat of compound and then the walls and ceilings are sprayed with a joint-compoundlike coating that can be given a number of different textures. The best-known texture is the one used on so-called acoustical or popcorn ceilings, which are ubiquitous in some parts of the country, even in high-end construction. If you've ever hung by your ankles above a big rectangular vat of cottage cheese, you have a pretty good idea of what it's like to look up at one. (Some ultra fancy textured ceilings are sprayed with glitter while they're still wet.) Popcorn ceilings and other textured finishes are popular with builders because they save time and money. The thick coatings cover up sloppy joints and rocking mistakes. Taping can be finished in a day instead of being spread over most of a week. And textured finishes are often left unpainted, or are tinted before application, which means that painting costs can be eliminated as well.

In the sort of high-volume work where textures are most common, preliminary taping is often done not with knifes and trowels but with specialized tools that dispense tape and mud at the same time. The most common of these tools is a long, tubular device known as a bazooka. (There's a similar, smaller device called a banjo.) Also available are automatic corner finishers, corner rollers, nail spotters, flat finishers, and other gizmos. These tools are very fast, but they don't always produce terrific results. Whatever the quality of the tools themselves, they're most often used in situations where speed is of much greater concern than quality.

DOING IT MYSELF

By the time I went to watch Billy, Spanky, Bill, and Mary, I had done a little rocking and taping of my own. One of the nice things about gypsum wallboard, as opposed to genuine plaster, is that an amateur can handle it. And no matter how lousy one's own work is, one can always be assured that somewhere out there is a professional whose results are worse.

My first wallboard project was repairing a badly deteriorated plaster wall in the upstairs hall of my house. Simply patching the cracks in this wall might have been possible, but the cracks were so big and the plaster was so loose that concealing all the flaws would have been extremely difficult. Instead, I decided to bury them. Measuring, trimming, and nailing up two eight-foot panels took me most of an afternoon, or about as long as it took Billy and Spanky to finish four entire rooms, including ceilings and cutouts. Taping was intimidating but not impossible. I got a little jaunty with the joint compound, but with careful sanding and judicious picture hanging, the wall ended up looking pretty good.

My second wallboard project was in the children's playroom. Once again, I laminated new wallboard on top of old walls. To make everything come out right, I had to install new cornice moldings and new baseboards, and I had to make new casings and stops for the windows. But the work I replaced had been ugly to begin with, and the buried wallpaper had been hopeless. All things considered, I did a pretty good job, and the end result was extremely satisfying. Indeed, I would be unashamed to display my playroom joints (except for one small one, now hidden behind a couch) beside the joints of almost anyone. The same goes double for my dimples.

The only real setback I encountered involved a wallboard screw that made a funny noise as I drove it in. I looked at it for a while and then unscrewed it. A thin column of water streamed horrifyingly through the hole. Like most plumbing disasters, this one occurred late on a Saturday night.* I had to shut off the water in the basement, drain the line, and rip a big hole in the wall I had just put up. I made a temporary patch in the pierced copper pipe by dipping the wallboard screw in epoxy glue and driving it back in. This, surprisingly, kept us dry until the plumber was able to come, on Tuesday.

My next wallboard project was in the dining room. While patching a crumbling plaster wall there one day, I noticed a small splash of color behind the lath and decided to find out what it was. Using a hammer, a crowbar, and a saw, I knocked a hole in the wall and stuck my head into it. Behind the dining-room wall, I discovered, was a six-inch air space filled with extremely old-smelling air and, beyond that, another lath-and-plaster wall, probably an original one. In keeping with the rest of the house, this wall was covered with ugly wallpaper (an off-white print with a brown border of flowers).

A few weeks later, burning with curiosity, I decided to get a better look behind the wall. I knocked down all the crumbling plaster on a six-foot-wide section between a window and a corner. The plaster was made of lime and sand. I could see wisps of animal hair along the broken edges when I held pieces up to the light. Then I pulled down all the lath, which was held up with small machine-cut nails. The studs were two-inch-thick oak or chestnut slabs, one of them more than eight inches wide. The studs had bark on their edges: they were thick slices of tree limbs.

And then there was the older wall. In places where the plaster had crumbled, I could see the old lath, which was hand-split oak. The nails were handmade and had huge, lumpy heads. The older studs, surprisingly, were evenly sawn on all four sides;

*When I have a plumbing disaster at night, I usually call the telephone-answering service that is used by most of the plumbers in my area and ask the receptionist to leave a message for all the plumbers on her list. This saves time and phone calls. When one of the plumbers calls me back and agrees to take care of my problem, I call the answering service again and ask the receptionist to cancel all my other messages. I learned about the answering service one night when I was frantically calling plumbers and realized, after about the sixth call, that all my calls were being answered by the same woman.

they were also notched into the sill below and the girt above. The plaster ended abruptly about two and a half feet above the floor. Had old wainscoting been removed at the time the newer wall was installed? Was it the same raised-panel wainscoting that now runs the length of the living room? I removed samples of everything, took a few pictures, and signed "George Washington" in pencil on the wallpaper. Then I closed the opening with Sheetrock.

My biggest and most satisfying wallboard job to date was in a new three-room guest suite that my friend Ken had built in a space that had once been part of his garage and workshop. Ken had designed and built his entire house, but he had never tried to install wallboard. Like many people, he was afraid of wallboard, and terrified of taping. Using various powerful arguments, I persuaded him that he and I should install the wallboard ourselves. If we screwed up, I reminded him, our mistakes would be seen only by houseguests, who would be in no position to complain.

In comparison with hanging wallboard in my house, hanging wallboard in Ken's house was a breeze. The framing was straight! The corners were square! The floors and ceilings were level! Rocking took just two afternoons, and we did the taping in small installments over the course of a little more than a week. A taping session always goes very rapidly, especially on a relatively small job like this one. Homeowners are sometimes annoyed when the tapers they have hired drop by for an hour or two and then disappear, but that's just the nature of taping. Once the compound is on the wall, there's nothing to do but let it dry. This makes taping a good do-it-yourself chore, since there is no need to set aside huge blocks of time in which to do it.

When we were finished, we primed the walls with USG's Sheetrock First Coat, a new primer that is especially formulated for gypsum wallboard. First Coat is a high-solids latex paint that is designed to mask minor wallboard-finishing flaws. Its primary pigment is calcium carbonate, which is also the main filler in wallboard joint compounds. I like to use two coats. I also like to use First Coat as a first coat when I repaint previously painted walls.

139

HIGH-END WALL SYSTEMS

The work that Ken and I did in his guest suite was very standard, as far as wallboard installations go. There are several things we could have done to fancy it up, had we felt like it. One way to do this would have been to use a special glue in addition to screws in attaching wallboard panels to studs. Using this glue—which is known as wallboard adhesive and is sold in the same sort of cartridges that caulk is sold in—holds the panels securely against the studs and makes it possible to use many fewer screws. This reduces the likelihood of fastener problems later on. Glue is especially useful for ceiling panels.

Another way to upgrade our work would have been to use five-eighths-inch panels instead of half-inch. The thicker panels feel sturdier, resist fire longer, and absorb more sound. (Five-eighths-inch panels are required by building codes for some applications in some parts of the country.) Using thicker panels would have been an easy and relatively inexpensive way to make Ken feel extravagant.

To make him feel really extravagant, we could have used a double layer of wallboard. In double-layer systems, the first layer, installed vertically, is glued and screwed. The second layer, installed horizontally, is bonded to the first with blobs or beads of joint compound. Screws are used only along the edges of the panels, which are later taped. Double-layer installation eliminates fastener problems and can produce walls that are anywhere from three-quarters of an inch to an inch and a quarter thick—the kind of walls you can really pound your fists on. When I patched the exploratory hole I cut in my dining-room wall, I used two layers of half-inch wallboard, because their combined thickness exactly equaled the thickness of the lath and plaster I had removed.

People who really want to show off can use plaster instead of wallboard. There are two ways of doing this. One is to use two or three coats of plaster on gypsum lath. This is seldom done in houses, though. It's expensive, and skilled plasterers are hard to find. Historical restorations and buildings that get a lot of wear and tear, such as hospitals, schools, and prisons, are among the few remaining outlets for this sort of plaster work.

A somewhat less daunting alternative is so-called veneer plaster, which is a very thin layer of plaster (an eighth of an inch thick or less) that is applied to special backing panels, which are just like regular wallboard panels except that they have a different facing paper. Veneer plaster can actually be more durable than a traditional three-coat plaster job, and it's less expensive. A USG spokesman told me that using veneer plaster in an average-sized house costs about four hundred dollars more than using standard wallboard. (He also told me that USG markets a special veneer-plaster system to prisons; its main selling point is its toughness.) Veneer plaster can also be used as a skim coat over existing plaster.

One of the side benefits of veneer plaster is that it is very fast: a house can be veneer-plastered in a single day and be ready for painting after two days—assuming that you can find someone who's good enough with a trowel to put it on for you. And you do have to find someone to put it on for you. Veneer plaster is not for do-it-yourselfers.

REVIVING CRUMMY OLD WALLS
AND CEILINGS

In major historical restorations, technicians sometimes go to (I think) absurd lengths in preserving old plaster. Small fragments are removed, numbered, cleaned, and glued back in place on the lath; tiny vacuum nozzles are inserted into tiny cracks to remove tiny pieces of grit from tiny sections of sagging plaster; siding is removed so that costly glues can be injected through holes drilled in the backs of the laths. This is the sort of work that would never be done if there weren't grants to pay for it.

For people who don't have the backing of a foundation or the federal government, the same tools and materials that are used to install and repair gypsum wallboard can also be used to repair old plaster. Doing this sort of work in my house has given me so much pleasure that I sometimes wonder whether I might have enjoyed being a dentist. Removing decay, scraping away various foreign accumulations, applying filling material—these dentistry-evocative activities are among my favorite home-improvement chores.* Whatever the reason, I find that I deeply enjoy repairing plaster, and when I do it I sometimes pretend that I am a famous specialist, called in only in the most desperate situations. (Working on my house and playing golf are pretty much the only times that I still pretend to be other people in roughly the same way that I once pretended to be, for example, the Man from U.N.C.L.E.)

Sometimes it is possible to restore old plaster simply by throwing some joint compound at it. The previous owners of my house painted all the ceilings with a popular textured paint containing sand. The ceilings look a little like what coarse sandpaper would look like if you painted it white. Many people like this texture and think that it looks old. I don't. (I think it looks like sandpaper.) I used to brood about it a lot. Scraping it off was impossible. Applying multiple coats of paint made it less noticeable but didn't hide it completely. Then I realized that I could get rid of it by covering it with a couple of coats of joint compound. I've skimmed five ceilings as of this writing, and I intend to finish the rest before I die. The skimmed ceilings look smooth, cool, and, I think, beautiful—in fact, they look pretty much exactly the way the ceilings looked before the previous owners painted them with sand.

Joint compound can also be used to repair surface problems on walls. In my daughter's room, the graffiti-covered paint beneath the wallpaper was solid, but it was etched with a web of tiny cracks. These cracks were in the paint, not in the plaster. Despite the cracks, the paint was firm, so I simply skimmed everything with joint compound. Now the walls look great— much better than they would have if I had simply tried to paint

---

*Equally satisfying, I suppose, are the ways in which repairing plaster does not resemble dentistry: the tools are large, the work is not done inside people's mouths, walls don't have breath.

directly on top of the old paint. (Skimming is a good do-it-yourself activity, but it's also easy to find a painter or wallboard taper to do it for you.)

When plaster has real cracks in it, skimming isn't enough. There were several cracks like this in my daughter's room. I repaired them by taping them with paper tape and joint compound—exactly as though they were wallboard joints—before skimming the entire wall. I also taped the room's corners, which had all cracked at the time the house was moved. Before taping the largest cracks, I prefilled them with Durabond. The Durabond set rapidly and created a continuous surface on which to apply tape and regular mud. It also helped to hold the cracks together.

When a crack is large and the plaster is old, it's usually a good idea to stabilize the plaster sections on either side before taping. This is especially important with ceiling cracks, or with any crack around which the plaster has begun to pull loose from the lath. To secure the plaster in these situations, I use plaster washers, which are perforated-metal disks applied with wallboard screws. Plaster washers greatly increase the holding power of the screws and can clamp sagging plaster firmly to its lath and to the framing. The washers are then covered with joint compound. Because the washers stand out slightly from the surface to which they are attached, they usually require at least a couple of coats of compound and careful feathering over as broad an area as possible.

The most extensive plaster repair I've ever done was in my son's room, whose ceiling had a large crack that ran from wall to wall. The lath and plaster on one side of the crack had sagged more than half an inch near the middle of the room, creating a vast, spooky fissure that would have been impossible to conceal with anything less than major surgery. I began by removing all the plaster for about six inches on either side of the crack. Then I resecured the loose laths with ring-shank wallboard nails. I also tightened the remaining lath and plaster by installing many wallboard screws with plaster washers in an area extending several feet on ether side of the gap. (I installed the screws and washers at eight-inch intervals along the ceilings

143

joists, which ran perpendicular to the crack.) I replaced the missing plaster with pieces of half-inch wallboard, which I cut to match the irregular outline of the gap. Then I used Durabond to embed paper tape over the seams between the wallboard and the plaster, and I skimmed the entire ceiling with Plus 3. You would never guess by looking at it now that the ceiling was once well on its way to falling down.

Joint compound can also be useful in dealing with the problem that I seem to spend much of my life dealing with: ugly old wallpaper. In one bedroom on the second floor of my house, I decided not to remove the existing wallpaper (which was in fairly solid shape) but to paint over it. Usually, painting over old wallpaper isn't a great idea. The paint can loosen the paper—not enough to make removal possible, but enough to make the new work look terrible. The most troublesome areas are the seams, which are often loose to begin with. Various stresses (including shrinkage caused by the drying of wallpaper paste) can cause the edges of wallpaper strips to pull away from the wall. Even if paint doesn't make this problem worse, it almost always makes it look worse. The seams tend to show throw the paint.

In the bedroom in question, I eliminated the seam problem by eliminating the seams. Using a taping knife and my fingernails, I peeled back a little of the wallpaper on either side of

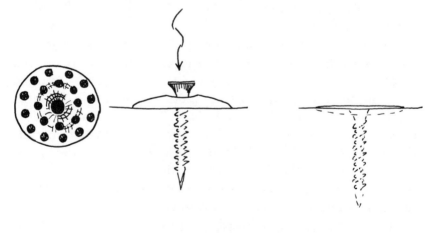

Plaster washers

every seam. This left me with a ragged gap an inch or two wide running the length of every seam. In some cases I was able to do little more than tear away some of the facing of the wallpaper—like trying to tear the price tag off a package. That was fine. In fact, it was good. I did the same thing with scattered loose spots in the middles of the strips.

When all the edges and loose spots had been peeled, I used a six-inch taping knife to fill all the ragged seams and bare spots with just enough joint compound to bring them flush with the surface of the remaining paper. Over the next couple of days, I skimmed the entire surface with two coats of joint compound. Then I sanded and painted. When I had finished, every wall was smooth and uniform and revealed no trace whatsoever of the ugly wallpaper entombed within it. And that, as far as I'm concerned, is the mark of a good wall.

Chapter 6

Electricity

One day when I was in the second grade, two friends of mine and I decided to get rid of a mean kid in our neighborhood by using my Lionel train set to electrocute him. We put several pieces of track on the seat of a chair in my room and attached them to the train set's control box. Our plan was to lure the mean kid into my house and, by various stratagems, cause him to sit on the chair. We would then turn the throttle on the train's control box to ninety miles an hour and reduce him to a pile of ash.

For a number of reasons, this plan came to nothing. In the first place, luring our tormentor into my house proved to be impossible. (We were afraid to speak to him.) In the second place, our invention did not work, as we discovered when we tested it on ourselves. One of my friends said he felt a tingling in his bottom, but my other friend and I felt nothing. We soon abandoned our research and returned to an earlier project: trying to turn a foot-long piece of copper tubing, which we

146

had found while trespassing at a construction site, into a hand-gun.

If I had been born with a different sort of mind, my childhood failure to build a practical electric chair might have spurred me to make many breathtaking discoveries in the field of electrical science. But it did not. Instead, I abandoned this seemingly impossible subject and devoted the bulk of my intellectual energy to writing poetry about how depressed and alienated I (wanted everyone to think I) felt. As I grew older, my ignorance of electricity grew with me until, by the time I graduated from college, it comprised virtually everything there was to know about the topic.

After I had lived in my house for a year or two, I decided that it was time for me to try to come to terms with electricity. I bought a couple of books and a few tools and started tackling simple projects. I replaced a few defective light switches and updated some old outlets. This went on for a while. My projects were interesting and easy, and I didn't electrocute myself. Gradually I became more ambitious. I extended an old circuit, then wired a new one. I installed some light fixtures. I put lights in my garage. Nothing terrible had happened to me up to this point, so I was feeling pretty good about myself and about electricity in general. And yet I still had essentially no understanding of why, for example, I was able to read a book in my house at night. Finally, not all that long ago, I decided to go for broke. I decided to see if I could figure out just exactly what on earth electricity actually is, and how it makes its way around a house.

THE HISTORY OF ELECTRICITY

Our word for electricity—*electricity*—comes from the Greek word *elektron,* meaning amber. At some point long ago, the ancient Greeks noticed that rubbing amber with wool caused the amber to attract dust, bits of grass, leaves, and other light materials. Numerous explanations for this phenomenon were advanced: the gods, invisible liquids, demons, tiny hooks, magic, etc. As is now well known, all of these explanations were wrong.

If the ancient Greeks had had access to a modern encyclopedia, they would have realized that the behavior they had observed in amber had less to do with amber than with rubbing. Stroking the amber with wool caused electrons from the wool to be transferred to the amber, leaving some atoms in the amber with more than their usual complement, and some atoms in the wool with fewer.

The transfer of electrons from the wool to the amber gave the amber what we now call a negative electric charge, and the wool what we now call a positive electric charge. (The practice of describing electrical charges in this way originated with Benjamin Franklin, who believed that electricity was a "fluid," and who really did fly a kite in a thunderstorm.) What is sometimes true of people is always true of electrically charged matter: opposites attract, and likes repel. When a negatively charged piece of amber is held close to, for example, a positively charged bit of leaf, the two are attracted to each other, and the leaf sticks.

Electricity in its amber-and-leaf form is called static electricity, because the electrical charges that constitute it are, for the most part, static, or at rest. Fortunately for people who own electrical appliances, there is also another form of electricity, known as current electricity. This consists of electrical charges moving continuously through materials that are capable of conducting them (such as the copper wire inside an extension cord, or the water in a bathtub).

The history of current electricity began in 1780, when an Italian professor of anatomy named Luigi Galvani stuck a brass wire into the spine of a dead frog and suspended the frog above an iron plate. Each time the dead frog's feet touched the iron plate, its legs jumped. Because Galvani had earlier produced this same reaction by zapping the frog with static electricity, he deduced that the dead frog must contain its own source of power. This was sort of right, although not in the way that Galvani thought it was. As was soon demonstrated by Alessandro Volta, another Italian professor, the jumping of the frog was caused not by what Galvani had called "animal electricity" but by an electrical current arising in a chemical reaction between the brass of the wire and the iron of the plate.

To prove his hypothesis, Volta constructed a stack of zinc and silver disks. Between each pair of disks he placed a piece of paper that he had wetted with salt water. As in Galvani's experiment, electricity was produced. It was in the form of a steady current running through a wire connecting the top and bottom of the stack. The salt water had brought about a chemical reaction between the two dissimilar metals, causing the silver to lose electrons and the zinc to gain them. A current-producing arrangement like this is now known as a voltaic pile. It is a rudimentary battery. If you have fillings in your teeth, you can create a miniature voltaic pile in your own mouth by biting down on a piece of aluminum foil.

Many terms used nowadays to describe electrical quantities or phenomena are derived from the names of people who made important electrical discoveries in the late eighteenth and early nineteenth centuries. The terms *volt* and *voltage,* for example, are derived from the name of Professor Volta. The flow of electricity through a wire is often likened to the flow of water through a pipe. In such a comparison, voltage is roughly analogous to water pressure, and volts are the units in which it is measured. Voltage—which is also referred to as potential difference, electromotive force, and electrical pressure, among other things—exists when a material that contains an excess of electrons is connected in a particular way to a particular kind of material that does not contain a surplus of electrons. (Voltage can also exist between a material that has a deficiency of electrons and a material that does not.) Because nature abhors this sort of inequality, electrons will flow between the two materials until the inequality no longer exists.

Another useful term is *ampere.* It is derived from the name of André-Marie Ampère, a French physicist. An ampere is a unit of measurement that is used to describe the quantity of electrons moving along a wire—referred to as amperage, or simply as current. In the water-pipe comparison mentioned above, amperage is analogous to the volume of water moving past a given point in the pipe in a given period of time. Amperes are usually called simply amps. A one-amp current is a current flowing at a rate of 6,280,000,000,000,000,000 electrons per second. Sheesh!*

A third important term is *ohm*, which is named for George Simon Ohm, a German physicist who died in 1856. An ohm is a unit of measurement that is used to describe a property known as resistance, which is the degree to which a given material hampers the flow of electricity through it. All materials resist the flow of electricity to some extent. Those that resist it most are called insulators. Those that resist it least are called conductors.

Resistance, amperage, and voltage are all related, as Ohm himself stated in a formulation now known as Ohm's Law. Loosely speaking, the law states (in one of its several forms) that if resistance is increased, voltage must also be increased in order to maintain a constant current. When my friends and I failed to be electrocuted when we sat on my Lionel train tracks, it was because the resistance of our pants and skin was more than enough to resist the extremely low voltage of the current that ran my train set.

When a conductor resists an electric current flowing through it, some of the energy in the current is converted to heat. The greater the amperage, the greater the loss. That's why wires get hot. The heat produced by resistance can lead to all sorts of problems, including fires. But resistance isn't always a bad thing. It can also be put to work. In an electric range, it is resistance that makes the burners get hot. In an electric heater, it is resistance that warms your feet. And in an electric light bulb, it is resistance that produces light.

---

*It is amperage, rather than voltage, that is the real muscle of an electric current. When I was in the sixth grade, I had a science teacher named Mr. Whitson, who liked us to see things for ourselves. When we studied electricity, Mr. Whitson had us hold hands in a big semicircle and then zapped us with fifty thousand volts. Fifty thousand volts sounds like enough to kill dozens of sixth-graders, but it didn't even make us feel sick. The reason was that the amperage was microscopic. If the ratio had been reversed—if the voltage had been low and the amperage had been high—my school would have had to replace its entire sixth grade.

EDISON

If Thomas Edison had set out to electrocute a mean kid, no doubt he would have succeeded. Edison was a born experimenter. At the age of six, he set fire to his family's barn, "just to see what it would do," he later explained. He also had the idea that bicarbonate of soda, if consumed in sufficient quantity, might fill a person with so much gas that the person would be light enough to fly. He tested this hypothesis on a young servant, who became ill. The ultimate outcome of both experiments (and of most of Edison's other early forays into science) was that Edison was whipped by his father.

At sixteen, Edison was hired as a nighttime operator in a telegraph office in Stratford Junction, Ontario. Nighttime operators were required to transmit the number six in Morse code (dash-dot-dot-dot-dot) to the train dispatcher every hour, to prove that they weren't sleeping on the job. Using a clock, a notched wheel, and some other items, Edison built a machine that automatically sent this signal for him, permitting him to sleep without interruption.

In 1869, at the age of twenty-two, Edison received his first patent. It was for an electric vote-recording device. Over the next few years he invented, among many other things, a stock ticker, a telegraph key with an alphabetical dial (which could be used by operators who didn't know Morse code), the mimeograph machine, and a system for sending four telegraphic messages simultaneously on a single wire. At the age of twenty-eight he came within a short distance of inventing the telephone. At thirty he invented the phonograph.

Let's see, when I was thirty—well, it isn't really a fair comparison. I had a lot on my mind that year. Besides, all the easy inventions were taken up. What was I supposed to do? Go to graduate school? Also, unlike Edison, I wasn't deaf. (Probably as the result of boyhood ear infections and other illnesses, Edison had lost most of his hearing by the time he was thirteen. He listened to his phonograph by resting his head against it. "But if there is some faint sound that I don't quite catch this way," he told an interviewer in 1913, "I bite into the wood, and then I get it good and strong.")

In 1878, at the age of thirty-one, Edison embarked on the project for which he is most widely celebrated today. Practical electric illumination had been the dream of many researchers for several decades. In 1801, the English chemist Humphry Davy (who was twenty-three at the time) had invented the so-called arc lamp, in which the source of illumination was an electric current arcing between a pair of narrowly separated carbon electrodes. In the late nineteenth century, arc lights came to be used in lighthouses, in a few big stores, in some offices, on city streets (hence Broadway's nickname, the Great White Way), and in a few other applications, but they were not well suited to domestic illumination. They were too big, too bright, too noisy, too smelly, and too dangerous, among other things.

When Edison took up the illumination problem, he focused not on arcing but on incandescence. If the current passing through a conductor is strong enough, resistance can cause the conductor to become heated to the point at which it glows, or incandesces. Other scientists had worked with this phenomenon for a number of years, but their results had been only vaguely promising. The lamps they had devised produced virtually no light and burned out almost immediately.

Edison's goal was to create an electric lamp that would reliably produce at least as much light as a gas lamp, and at a competitive cost. One of the keys lay in finding a suitable material to use as the incandescent filament. He focused on carbon, which is a relatively resistant conductor that has an extremely high melting point. Edison and his assistants used an oven to carbonize a wide variety of materials, including graphite, cardboard, the fuzz from a coconut shell, bits of the coconut shell itself, fishing line, wood scraps, cork, flax, boxwood, tissue paper, cedar shavings, twine, and whiskers from the beard of a houseguest named J. U. Mackenzie.

Edison achieved his first significant success with carbonized sewing thread, in a lamp that burned for forty hours between October 19 and October 21, 1879. He soon achieved still greater success with carbonized paper and bamboo. (Carbonized-bamboo filaments were still being used in electric lamps as late as 1908.) Tungsten filaments, which are used in light bulbs today, were developed in 1911 by a man named William D. Coolidge.

The light bulb itself was but a single element in the electrical system that Edison created. He also invented metering equipment, better generators, switches, fixtures, and a way to "subdivide" electric current so that lamps on the same circuit could be turned on and off independently of one another. What Edison ended up inventing was not just a practical electric lamp but an entire system for creating electrical power and putting it to work in homes and businesses. In 1880 alone, he applied for sixty patents. (Not all concerned electricity; one had to do with a new method of preserving fruit.) During that same year, he also sold his first lighting system, to a San Francisco–bound steamship called the *Columbia.*

Not long afterward, Edison bought two run-down buildings on Pearl Street, in Manhattan, and wired them for electricity. It was from these buildings that the electrification of the world began. By 1884, Edison had 508 customers.

DC, AC, AND TESLA

Edison's electrical system was based on so-called direct current, which is abbreviated DC. In a circuit carrying a direct current, the electrons move in one direction only, from the negative to the positive pole of the voltage source. This is the kind of current produced by a voltaic pile, a battery, or a generator designed to produce direct current. All of Edison's generators were of this type.

Direct current has advantages as a power source in certain situations, but it also has serious disadvantages. The most important of these is that it is very difficult to transmit over long distances. The reasons for this have to do with the relationship between amperage, voltage, and resistance described in Ohm's Law. A direct current transmitted at a high enough amperage and low enough voltage to be of use in a home dissipates fairly rapidly through the conversion of electrical energy to heat, caused by resistance, as it travels on a wire away from its generator. The amount of electrical energy lost in this way grows geometrically as the amperage is increased. Edison planned to work around this problem by constructing an electrical generating station every couple of blocks—and in every factory and on every farm—thus limiting the distance that the current would have to travel.

At around the time Edison was developing his electrical system, a few researchers were working with another kind of electric current, called alternating current. Alternating current, which is abbreviated AC, doesn't flow continuously in one direction. Instead, it reverses direction many times a second. It does this because the generators that produce it operate in such a way that their positive and negative poles constantly switch places. Instead of streaming in one direction, an alternating current shuffles back and forth. (*Shuffling* probably isn't the right word. Standard household AC reverses direction 120 times a second, making a complete cycle every sixtieth of a second. Since electrons move through wire at close to the speed of light, each half-cycle is long enough to send an electron zooming roughly fifteen hundred miles.)

For complicated reasons having to do with magnetic fields and the induction of electric currents, this back-and-forth shifting of electrons makes it possible to do things with an alternating current that cannot be done with a direct current. By using relatively simple devices called transformers, for example, one can easily raise or lower the voltage of an alternating current. A transformer can be used to "step up," or increase, voltage so that electricity can be transmitted over very long distances with little loss of current to resistance. Another transformer can then be used to "step down" the voltage so that the current can be used. DC had to be generated in each neighborhood, which meant that coal to fuel the generators had to be transported to each neighborhood; AC could be generated at the mouth of the mine and transported by wire.

The electricity in your house is alternating current. It was generated at anywhere from a few thousand to more than twenty thousand volts by your power company, stepped up to as much as 765,000 volts for long-distance transmission, and then stepped down substantially for local distribution. That big gray cylinder at the top of the utility pole in the corner of your yard is a transformer. It takes the multithousand-volt current carried by local distribution lines and turns it into the 120-volt current used by, among other things, your toaster oven.

That the electricity in your house *is* alternating current had nothing to do with Thomas Edison. In fact, Edison bitterly fought AC for many years, partly out of a sort of constitutional crankiness and partly because he had an enormous amount of time and money invested in his own electric system, which was based entirely on DC. The person responsible for introducing AC, and for creating the modern system of generating, distributing, and using electricity, was a young immigrant who, though not widely remembered today, was surely one of the most brilliant and fascinating figures in the history of science. His name was Nikola Tesla.

Tesla was born in 1856, in what is now Yugoslavia. Like Edison, he exhibited his scientific bent early in life. As a very young boy he theorized that hyperventilation would make his body light enough to float through the air. One day, he climbed to the roof of a barn, panted until he was dizzy, and jumped from the roof while holding an umbrella. He was injured severely. At the age of nine, he built a small windmill and glued sixteen live June bugs to its arms. When the June bugs beat their wings, the windmill spun rapidly, turning a drive belt (made of thread) that Tesla had strung between two tiny pulleys. Tesla had planned to follow this prototype with a hundred-bug engine, but a playmate ate his supply of insects, an act that nauseated Tesla and gave him an abhorrence of June bugs that lasted the rest of his life.

In his late teens, while studying physics, Tesla developed a fascination with electricity. He became interested, in particular, with the possibilities of alternating current, which had first been generated some years before but whose usefulness was severely limited by the fact that no one had succeeded in building a practical motor that could use it. In fact, the scientific consensus at the time was that an efficient AC motor was an impossibility. Tesla disagreed and vowed that he would one day build one.

Late one afternoon, in February of 1882, Tesla went walking in a park with a friend, whom he entertained by reciting from memory lengthy chunks of Goethe's *Faust*. Tesla was very tall and very thin, and he had dark, piercing eyes. Suddenly he stopped and fell into a deep trance. While staring into the setting sun, he later said, he had a vision of the entire cosmos pulsing with alternating current along a broad spectrum of frequencies. At the center of this vision, appearing as though it were standing directly in front of him, was a new kind of electric motor. "See how smoothly it is running?" he said to his friend. "Now I throw the switch. . . ." The motor in the vision ran on AC.

Since early childhood, Tesla had had both a photographic memory (he was able to recite entire books) and a remarkable ability to visualize objects about which he was thinking. These visions were so vivid that he was initially unable to distinguish them from real objects. As a child he had struggled to suppress his frightening ability, but in school he realized that it gave him a leg up in math classes, where he astonished his teachers by solving complex problems almost instantaneously. (He worked them on a sort of mental blackboard.) This same ability later enabled him to test engineering concepts without a laboratory. He would "build" an electric motor in his mind, leave it running for several weeks, then mentally take it apart to see how it had performed. When, several years later, he finally built a working model of the motor he had conceived in that fateful trance, he was able to specify and assemble the parts without making drawings or pencil-and-paper calculations. He took all the measurements directly from the images in his head.

In 1884, Tesla moved to New York in the hope of persuading Edison of the superiority of alternating current. Edison gave the young man a job but could not be swayed on the matter of direct current and later grouchily refused to pay for extensive improvements Tesla made in Edison's generators and distribution system. Tesla quit and batted around for two dreary years, one of them spent as a menial laborer. This period, he later said, was the low point of his life. Finally, though, he found financial backing and was able to establish a laboratory of his own.

With money and a laboratory, Tesla was at last able to build a number of different machines and devices that up until that point had existed only in his mind. He did so rapidly, in the space of a few months. (Like Edison, Tesla seldom slept more than a few hours a night.) In 1888, based on this work, he was awarded the first of a series of related patents that would eventually cover essentially every aspect of the generation, transmission, and utilization of alternating current. Later that same year he sold the rights to his system (for one million dollars) to George Westinghouse and his brand-new Westinghouse Electric Company. In all important particulars, the electrical system that Tesla invented is the one we use today. In the words of an electrical engineer who, thirty years later, presented Tesla with an award for his work, "He left nothing to be done by those who followed him."

Tesla and Edison were fiercely competitive. On at least a few occasions each man professed sincere admiration for the intelligence and ingenuity of the other, but for the most part they fought like kindergartners. When Tesla's ideas were first becoming known, Edison waged a bitter and small-minded battle against them. He claimed, among other things, that alternating current was more dangerous than direct current, a dishonest assertion that he "proved" by publicly using AC to electrocute some stray dogs. Edison got his comeuppance in 1895, when Westinghouse generators were installed at the world's first massive generating station, at Niagara Falls. Edison's DC system rapidly proved to be the evolutionary dead end that Tesla had always said it was, and Edison's company was forced to license Tesla's technology from Westinghouse.

During the next few years Tesla made a truly astonishing series of discoveries. It is now generally agreed among scientists that he invented radio at least two years before Marconi made his first feeble transmission, and that he discovered X-rays (and demonstrated their usefulness as a diagnostic tool) at least a year before Roentgen. He also invented or closely anticipated the loudspeaker, the vacuum tube amplifier, radar, the electric

clock, the bladeless turbine, the electron microscope, the cyclo-
tron, the neon sign, the robot, and the fluorescent light, which
he used to illuminate his laboratory. (Unlike the version introduced by others forty years later, most of the fluorescent lamps
in Tesla's lab were wireless.) He also discovered that an otherwise deadly electric current could be rendered harmless by dramatically raising its frequency. He demonstrated this at the
1893 Chicago World's Fair, where he passed a high-frequency
million-volt current through his own body, causing a flamelike
aura to flicker about his skin and enabling him to make light
bulbs glow and wires melt by touching them with his hands.

For a number of years around the turn of the century, Tesla
was an international celebrity whose fame burned at least as
brightly as Edison's. He wore stylish clothes and was pursued by
romantically ambitious women. He had famous friends (including Mark Twain) and wealthy backers (including J. Pierpont
Morgan), and his lectures were viewed in the scientific commu-
nity as epochal events. Yet long before his death, his renown had
dissipated. One reason for this was that Tesla had very little
commercial sense and virtually no patience for marketing his
discoveries. (Many of his ideas were so far ahead of their time
that even most scientists were unable to comprehend them.)
Another reason was that his New York laboratory, which was
just down the street from Edison's, was destroyed by fire in
1895, when he was near the peak of his inventive powers. Another was that he seldom wrote down anything, partly because
he didn't need to and partly because he had a secretive disposi-
tion. Unlike Edison, he had few assistants to spread the word
about his work. The only invention with which his name is
widely associated today is the Tesla coil, a kind of transformer.

In the final decades of his life, Tesla withdrew further and
further from public view and deeper and deeper into the eccen-
tricities that had marked most of his life. (He could not tolerate
the smell of camphor, the act of shaking hands, or close contact
with the hair of other people; he strongly preferred numbers
that were divisible by three; he was unable to eat or drink anything without first calculating its volume; he counted his steps;
he washed his hands compulsively; he hated pearls and other

objects with smooth, round surfaces; he never married, but he told a friend that he had once loved a particular pigeon "as a man loves a woman"; when he dined, alone, at Delmonico's or the Palm Room of the Waldorf-Astoria, he ordered ahead of time by telephone, arrived at exactly eight o'clock, used eighteen linen napkins to wipe germs from the silver and crystal, and left at exactly ten.) He died, impoverished and forgotten, in 1943.

KNOBS AND TUBES

In the earliest household electrical installations, inadequately insulated wires were run right along the surface of walls, where they must have occasionally appeared tempting to people looking for a place to hang a picture. The exposed wires were supported every few feet by cleats or knobs made of wood. Wood is more nearly an insulator than a conductor, but when it is damp it can carry a current quite readily. Every so often this happened. Soon supporting knobs were made of glass or porcelain instead.

Gradually it began to occur to people that this interesting new technology would be every bit as interesting if it were concealed inside walls. The result was a wiring system known as knob and tube. The knobs, which were made of porcelain, were quite similar to the supporting knobs used in exposed wiring. They were attached at close intervals to the sides of studs and joists, and the wires were strung between them. The mildly phallic-looking tubes, which were also made of porcelain, served as insulating sleeves or bushings at points where wires had to pass through the framing.

A couple of years ago, my friend Ken and I installed half a dozen new canister-type lighting fixtures in the ceiling of my kitchen. To install and wire the canisters we had to cut holes in the ceiling. Whenever I cut a hole in my house, I like to poke around inside it for a while with a flashlight. I did this and discovered a lot of old knob-and-tube wiring running along the joists. (The old wiring in my kitchen ceiling had long since been disconnected, although there are plenty of old houses in which knobs and tubes are still in use.) Before closing up the ceiling again, I extracted an old tube, which I now keep on my desk and occasionally use as a tiny spyglass for looking at my computer screen when I can't think of anything to write.

From the vantage point of the safety-conscious present, early electrical wiring practices seem astonishingly reckless. Early conductors were only minimally insulated, sometimes with hemp, paper, or shellac-impregnated cloth. Short circuits were common, and fires were frequent. In the early years, new wiring was sometimes simply strung on top of the lath and covered with plaster, a great-seeming idea that rapidly turned out to be not so great, since the lime in the plaster ate through the insulation, and no one could ever remember exactly where the wires had been laid. One day when I was patching an old wall in my house, I noticed what looked like the tip of a nail poking through the plaster. I gripped the end of it with a pair of pliers and pulled. The nail turned out to be not a nail at all but a foot-long piece of electrical wire. Was this the remnant of an old under-the-plaster wiring scheme? I don't know. You find a lot of strange things in an old house.

In the very early days, Edison sometimes mounted incandescent fixtures on existing gas lamps. The idea was that the gas could serve as backup if the newfangled power source should fail, as it often did. Later, when electric service was more reliable and people had given up gas lamps for good, wiring was often run through the same metal pipes that had once carried gas. (This gas, incidentally, was not the clean-burning natural gas that people today use for cooking and heating; it was a dirty, stinky, dangerous, nauseating, semi-incombustible gas made from coal.) Soon similar types of pipes, or conduits, were developed specifically for carrying insulated wires. These conduits protected the wires from stray nails and gnawing rodents. Their direct descendants are still used in several applications today, although most modern electrical cable is sheathed simply in vinyl.

When Edison began providing electrical service to his first customers in New York, he ran all his supply lines underground, in wood conduits. This didn't work very well at first. With no foolproof method of insulating wires, moisture was a persistent problem. But Edison thought overhead wiring was absurd. "You don't lift water pipes and gas pipes up on stilts," he said.

Today, New York's power lines still run underground, as do the lines in the hearts of most big cities. The same is not true in most of the rest of the country. In my town as in most communities, virtually all power and other utility lines are carried overhead, on tall poles. This practice is actually a holdover from the early days of the telegraph. Samuel Morse had originally wanted to run his telegraph lines underground, but the lack of dependable insulation had made this impractical. To get his system into operation in a hurry, he settled for poles. When electrical service spread beyond New York City, poles were used because poles were fast, cheap, and familiar. They have been with us ever since.

Overhead utility lines have been part of the landscape for longer than most of us have been alive, so we tend not to notice them. This is a good example of how familiarity can make even unspeakably ugly technology invisible. If you want to appal yourself sometime, go for a walk in your neighborhood and make a point of looking closely at the utility poles and wires. If you're like me, you'll be so astonished at how intrusive and ill-conceived the system appears that you'll never feel quite the same about your neighborhood again. The poles loom up everywhere, leaning at goofy angles. Sagging wires slice the view. Otherwise graceful houses seem weighted down by mantles of cables. Satellite-television antennas are so new that people are still capable of being horrified by the way they look, but ordinary utility poles, which are far uglier and vastly more numerous, raise little comment. We made ourselves blind to them long ago.

Nowadays, in new communities and developments, utility wires are often buried. Doing this makes both the houses and the landscape look better in a way that one notices without quite being able to put one's finger on. In addition, underground wires last longer than wires that are exposed to the weather, and they require less maintenance. (On the other hand, performing maintenance on buried lines is trickier and more expensive than performing maintenance on overhead lines.) My local electric company is spending millions of dollars this year to cut back tree branches that have grown too close to power lines and that, in a storm, could knock those lines down. This is work that wouldn't be necessary if the lines were underground.

LIVING WITH ELECTRICITY

On a rainy summer afternoon a couple of years ago, I decided to clean a clogged gutter on the front of my house. I had meant to clean this gutter for some time, but because the weather had been dry I hadn't gotten around to it. Now, though, water was spilling over the edge of the gutter and splashing next to the foundation. I got my extension ladder, which (because I had had the foresight not to put it away the last time I had used it) was conveniently lying in my yard. This ladder is tall enough to reach my roof only if it is fully extended, so I stood it up in my yard and began to hoist the extension, using the not entirely satisfactory rope-and-pulley arrangement that is standard equipment on an extension ladder.

All of a sudden the ladder became extremely difficult to extend. No matter how hard I pulled on the rope, I couldn't seem to make the extension rise more than a few feet. I adjusted my grip and pulled the rope harder. I felt almost as though the top of the ladder had encountered some sort of obstacle that was preventing it from rising to its full height. I dug in my feet and yanked the rope as hard as I could. No luck. I kind of glanced up at the top of the ladder to see if the rope had become entangled in the ladder itself, as sometimes happens. Through the raindrops spattering on my glasses I saw that the top of the ladder was being restrained by the telephone and electric power lines serving my house. It had lifted these lines two or three feet above the level at which they normally hang.

Residential service lines are almost always insulated (very

old lines sometimes are not), but the insulation takes a beating from sun, wind, rain, ice, scampering squirrels, tree limbs, and so on. Over the years this insulation can crumble or become cracked, exposing the conductor. I was barefoot, standing in wet grass, and clinging to a wet aluminum ladder. The wire against which I had jammed the extension was carrying enough current to kill me many times over. Even a pinhole-sized break in the insulation would have been enough to do me in. When I realized what I had done, I jumped backward from the ladder and let it crash to the ground. Trembling in my yard, I resolved to sell all my personal belongings and gratefully spend my remaining days in service to others.

On further reflection, after I had put on dry clothes, I decided to keep my personal belongings and not spend my remaining days in service to others, but I did resolve to be a lot more careful with ladders from then on.*

Electricity can travel continuously only along an unbroken conductive path, called a circuit. Turning on a flashlight completes a circuit that begins and ends at the battery. The current flows from the battery's negative pole, passes through the filament in the tiny lightbulb, and returns to the battery at the positive pole. The current continues to flow as long as the battery continues to produce voltage—that is, as long as the chemicals and other stuff inside the battery continue to create an imbalance of electrons between the negative and positive poles. Each time the battery pushes electrons out one door, electrons rush in the other. Both doors have to be open in order for an electric current to exist.

Electric service provided by a power company works essentially the same way, though on a different scale. The company's

---

*It wasn't even completely my ladder. My friend Rex and I had bought it together, figuring that neither of us would be able to keep an entire ladder busy all the time. When we bought it, the guy at our hardware store filled out two separate charge slips for us. He wrote "½ ladder" on each one. I'm pretty sure that, for sentimental reasons, my wife would have wanted to keep my half. But what about Rex? Would he have continued to use his half, which had meant so much to the two of us, knowing that I had come to such a gruesome end while attempting to use it to clean my gutters? You can never tell how people are going to react in this situation.

customers are all tied into a huge electric circuit that begins and ends at the company's generating station. Current generated at the station flows out over one set of wires, is put to work in homes and businesses, and returns to the station over another set of wires.

In certain situations, the returning current can follow a different path back to the generating station. If a falling tree breaks a power line, for example, a broken end of the line may fall to the ground (or into a pond, or onto a branch of another tree) and complete a circuit whose return path to the generating station lies not through a wire but through the earth itself, which acts as a giant conductor. If my aluminum ladder had come into contact with a break in the insulation on the power lines serving my house, the ladder and my body would have completed just such an electric circuit. Current from the generating station would have flowed along my house's service wires, down the ladder, through my body, through the earth, and back to the generating station. The current would have continued to flow along this deadly path for as long as the ladder and I continued to accommodate it. The danger to me lay in the fact that I was "grounded"—that is, I was part of a conductive return path.

If both myself and my aluminum ladder had somehow not been in contact with the earth or with any even slightly conductive material in contact with the earth—that is, if I had not been grounded—the circuit would have been incomplete and no current would have flowed. This is why birds can sit on trolley wires and other uninsulated lines without being fried. A sparrow may feel a tingle when it lands on a wire, as its body becomes an electrically charged extension of the hot conductor, but it isn't vaporized. Similarly, a squirrel running along a power line is in no danger of being electrocuted, unless it simultaneously comes into contact with a wet tree limb or some other grounded conductor. In some parts of the country, utility workers make repairs on live high-voltage wires while suspended from helicopters. Since the workers aren't grounded, they are (sort of) safe.

The power lines against which I had been pushing the ladder are known in the trade as service wires. At my house as in most houses, there are three of these wires. Two of them are "hot," carrying current at 120 volts or thereabouts. (For lots of different reasons, the voltage on these wires isn't perfectly uniform and can range from around 115 to around 125 volts.) The third wire is "neutral." Its job is to complete the electrical circuit serving my house by carrying current after it has finished running my dishwasher. Unlike the hot wires, the neutral wire isn't insulated. It doesn't need to be, because the current it carries is at zero volts, or nearly so. You could push a ladder against this wire all day long and not worry about getting shocked (assuming that you could do this without bothering the hot wires, which are typically wrapped around it).

The service wires that serve my house are connected way up near my roof, at a point known as the service entrance. From there they travel down a metal conduit and into a gray metal box on the wall in my basement. This box is known as the service panel. Inside it, each of the hot wires is attached to a metal bar known as a hot bus bar. All the 120-volt branch circuits in my house originate at one or the other of these bus bars; all of the 240-volt branch circuits (which serve such major machinery as the drier, the well pump, and the electric range) originate at both, with one wire attached to each.

All these branch circuits also end inside the service panel, at another metal bar, called the neutral bus bar. The neutral bus bar is connected both to the neutral service wire (which leads back out to the utility pole and, from it, to the utility company) and to a so-called grounding conductor. At my house the grounding conductor is a cold-water pipe that runs from my house out into the earth. The grounding conductor at your house may also be a cold-water pipe, or it may be a metal rod driven into the ground near your foundation, a metal gas line, a concrete-reinforcing rod in your foundation, or some combination of these. Whatever it is, this grounding conductor gives household current a secondary return path (through the earth) and ensures that the house and the neutral service wire are always at the same (zero) voltage with respect to the earth nearby.

Inside my house, the branch circuits that begin and end at the service panel behave pretty much exactly like the larger circuit that begins and ends at the power company. Most of the branch circuits in my house are supplied by cables containing three separate wires. The first of these wires, which is usually covered with black insulation, is called the hot wire. It is attached to the hot bus bar, and its function is to carry current at 120 volts to any power-consuming devices (known in the trade as "loads") attached to it. The second wire, which is usually covered with white insulation, is the neutral wire. Like the neutral service wire, its function is to carry "used" current back to the service panel. The third wire, which is usually either uninsulated or covered with green insulation, is the grounding wire. Like the neutral wire, it is attached to the neutral bus bar. Its purpose is to provide an alternate route back to the service panel for current that, as a result of some malfunction, is diverted from the normal circuit created by the hot and neutral wires.

TROUBLE

In any properly wired electric circuit, the hot wire is not attached directly to the hot bus bar. It is attached instead to either a fuse or a circuit breaker, which in turn is attached to the hot bus bar. Fuses and circuit breakers are known as over-current protection devices. They serve as bridges between the hot bus bar and individual circuits. Their purpose is to shut down circuits that, for one reason or another, suddenly begin to draw more current than they are able to handle.

No wire can carry an unlimited amount of electric current. As the current on a wire increases, the wire's resistance converts electrical energy to heat at a geometrically increasing rate. If the current is great enough, the wire can become so hot that it melts or starts a fire in combustible materials near it. Fuses and circuit breakers prevent this from happening by interrupting the circuit once a certain threshold of current has been crossed. For example, fourteen-gauge electrical wire—which is commonly used in simple household lighting circuits—is intended to handle no more than fifteen amps. For this reason, a properly installed fourteen-gauge circuit will be protected by a fifteen-amp fuse or circuit breaker. If the current on the circuit ever exceeds fifteen amps, the fuse or circuit breaker will shut it down. This is what happens when a fuse "blows" or a circuit breaker "trips." Fuses are a bit faster than circuit breakers at shutting down an overloaded circuit, but blown fuses have to be replaced while circuit breakers can simply be reset. Virtually all new installations use circuit breakers.

Overloads occur when too many power-using devices are plugged into a circuit and turned on. Every device that uses electricity requires a specific amount of current in order to function properly. A hundred-watt light bulb, for example, draws a little over eight-tenths of an amp at 120 volts. (Wattage—named for James Watt, a Scottish inventor who died in 1819—is a way of expressing an electric current's capacity for doing work. It is derived simply by multiplying amps times volts. If you know how many watts an electrical device uses, you can calculate its appetite for amperage by dividing the number of watts by the number of volts on the circuit. One hundred watts divided by 120 volts is .83333 amp.) A circuit protected by a fifteen-amp fuse or circuit breaker can thus handle roughly eighteen hundred-watt light bulbs all operating at the same time, because their total current requirement is just under fifteen amps. If more fixtures are added to the circuit and turned on, the fifteen-amp ceiling will be exceeded and the fuse or circuit breaker will fail, interrupting the circuit and halting the flow of electricity.

If the fuse or circuit breaker weren't there, the overloaded circuit would draw more current than its wires could handle, and the wires would overheat. This is why it is foolish to use a twenty-amp fuse on a circuit whose wiring is intended to carry only fifteen amps, or to bypass a fuse altogether by inserting a penny or some other conductor in its place. These classic handyman solutions to circuit overloading are extremely dangerous. The safe and responsible way to deal with an overloaded circuit is to eliminate the overload—perhaps by plugging the vacuum cleaner into an outlet in the hall.

Fuses and circuit breakers also provide protection from another kind of current overload—one caused by a short circuit. A short circuit exists whenever current is allowed to flow through a complete circuit without passing through a load. You could create a short circuit by removing the light bulb from a lamp, spitting into the empty socket, and turning on the lamp. Current from the socket's hot terminal would pass through your saliva (an excellent conductor) to its neutral terminal. With no light-bulb filament to resist the passage of electricity, the current would flow unchecked, creating an overload that would blow the fuse or circuit breaker and interrupt the circuit.

Fuses and ordinary circuit breakers are intended to protect wires and appliances, not people. Several years ago, acting on my vague instructions (we were getting ready to install some wallboard), my brother used a screwdriver to poke around inside an electrical outlet box containing a live outlet. The screwdriver I had given him for this chore not only had a metal blade, like all screwdrivers, but also had a metal handle. Soon after my brother began to poke around, the screwdriver's blade simultaneously touched the outlet's hot terminal and the side of the grounded metal outlet box. This gave my brother a shock and caused him to question the instructions I had given him. It also created a short circuit that burned a small crater in the side of the screwdriver's blade and tripped a circuit breaker.

The circuit breaker tripped not because my brother had been shocked but because his screwdriver had become part of a circuit that, because there was no load on it, drew more current than the circuit breaker could handle. The circuit breaker protected the wires, not my brother. What protected my brother was the fact that human skin is a poor conductor (except when it's wet) and that an electric current always follows the proverbial path of least resistance—in this case, from the hot terminal to the grounded box by way of the screwdriver blade. A small amount of current took a side trip through my brother, but it was negligible in comparison with what went through the screwdriver that he was holding. My brother felt a shock, but he didn't feel anything like a full fifteen amps, which would have been enough to kill him.

The Walls Around Us

When people are killed by household electricity (as happens approximately 150 times each year) it is usually because current has passed through their chests. The human nervous system is a miniature electrical network. A heart beats because it receives repeated electrical jolts measuring about .006 amp. If an outside current stronger than .006 amp is allowed to pass through or near the heart, the nervous system can be overwhelmed, causing the heart to stop beating. Touching a hot wire with one hand is thus far less dangerous than touching a hot wire with one hand and a neutral wire or other grounded object with the other. A current that runs from one hand to the other necessarily passes through the heart. For this reason, electricians often keep one hand in a pocket while working near hot wires.

There is one kind of circuit breaker that does protect people from being dangerously shocked in certain situations. This special type of breaker is known as a ground fault circuit interrupter (GFCI), or simply as a ground fault interrupter (GFI). GFCIs are manufactured in several versions: some are installed in place of ordinary breakers in the service panel, some are installed in place of regular outlets, and some are plugged into existing outlets. The National Electric Code now requires that GFCIs be used to protect certain circuits in bathrooms, kitchens, basements, and other places (such as outdoors) where the presence of moisture increases the risk of shock.

A GFCI protects an outlet or circuit by monitoring the current passing through it and shutting it down if an imbalance appears. In a normally functioning circuit, the current flowing out of an outlet has exactly the same amperage as the current flowing back in. Suppose, for example, that you go into your bathroom and turn on a fifteen-hundred-watt portable electric heater, which uses 12.5 amps of electricity at 120 volts. As long as the heater is on, 12.5 amps will flow into it from the hot side of the outlet and 12.5 amps will flow out of it into the neutral side. These two values are the same, so the GFCI does nothing. (The voltage on the two sides is different—120 on the hot side and zero on the neutral side—but that's another matter.)

Now suppose that you fill the bathtub with water, climb into it, pick up the heater, and drop it into the water with you. The water creates a short circuit. Current continues to flow into the heater from the hot side of the outlet, and some of this current continues to flow out into the neutral side. But some of the current flows away by a different path—for example, through the water, through you, through the tub, through the pipes, and into the ground. Because not all of the incoming current is flowing out over the neutral wire, an imbalance exists. The GFCI senses this (it can sense imbalances as small as 0.005 amp) and breaks the circuit within about a fortieth of a second. Any outlet within a cord's length of a sink, bathtub, or shower should be protected by a GFCI. So should outlets installed outdoors, in the garage, or in the basement. Installing GFCI outlets in vulnerable outlets is a truly valuable handyman activity in any house too old to have them already. Wiring them is easy, and the outlets themselves look pretty cool.

Another type of protection from shock is provided by the third wire—the grounding wire—in a standard electric cable. This wire is a little like a safety valve. Its function is to give misdirected current an alternate return path to the neutral bus bar.

When I first started to learn about wiring, I felt a little skeptical about grounding wires. When I looked inside my service panel, for example, I saw that the grounding wires were just attached to the same thing (the neutral bus bar) that all the white wires were attached to. They were not, in other words, attached to anything special of their own. This made me suspect that grounding wires were just a big hoax.

But they're not. In fact, they're very important. An electric current always follows the easiest return path. In a properly functioning circuit, this path is always the neutral wire. But sometimes mistakes happen. Suppose, for example, that the hot wire serving an electrical outlet in your kitchen somehow works loose from its terminal and comes into contact with the decorative brass plate that covers the outlet. Suppose also that this outlet is ungrounded—that is, that it isn't attached, directly or indirectly, to a grounding wire. When you now reach down to plug in your coffee maker and, in doing so, touch the brass cover plate, your body suddenly completes a circuit. Current from the loosened hot wire flows through the plate, through you, through the floor, though your house, and into the earth. In the process of doing so, it shocks you, since you are part of the circuit along which the current is flowing.

If that faulty outlet had been grounded, you wouldn't have been shocked. The current would have flowed from the hot wire, through the plate, through the metal screw attaching the plate to the outlet, through a conductor inside the outlet, through the grounding wire attached to the outlet, and back to the neutral bus bar in the service panel. This would have created a short circuit over which current would have surged without the resistance of a load. The circuit's amperage limit would have been exceeded, and the fuse or breaker would have blown. Your repeated efforts to get this circuit back into operation (by either changing the fuse or resetting the breaker) would have failed, causing you to call an electrician, who would have found the problem and repaired it.

Grounding wires don't provide protection only in outlets, wiring boxes, and built-in fixtures. They also provide protection in any appliance or device with a three-prong plug. The third prong is attached to a grounding conductor inside the tool. It fits into the third hole, known as the grounding slot, in a 120-volt electrical receptacle. The grounding slot is connected in turn to the grounding conductor in the circuit serving that outlet. If a wiring flaw develops inside the device, the "leaking" electricity will flow back to the neutral bus bar along the continuous grounding path established between the device and the service panel. This will blow the fuse or circuit breaker and prevent you from being shocked when you touch the device.

Like many old houses, my house is something of a wiring museum. The newest circuits are wired with modern vinyl-sheathed cable. This stuff, known in the trade as NM (for non-metallic) or Romex (a popular trade name), contains a hot wire, a neutral wire, and a ground. The bulk of the circuits, which date from just after the house was moved, in 1970, are wired with flexible armored cable, which is commonly called BX. A few circuits, which date from who knows when, are wired with an earlier version of armored cable. None of the armored cable contains a separate ground wire; the metal covering itself serves as the grounding conductor and is connected, inside the service panel, to the neutral bus bar. (Modern BX does contain a grounding wire.)

Nowadays many power tools and other electrical devices are "double-insulated." My electric drill is an example. The plug on my drill doesn't have a grounding prong, but the drill still provides protection from shock. It does this because any possible source of current inside the drill is isolated from the exterior surface of the drill by insulating materials (primarily the drill's plastic body). If a hot wire inside the drill becomes detached, I'll still be able to touch the drill without being shocked.

SMARTER HOUSES

The first widely used electric appliance, other than the light bulb, was the iron. Electric companies promoted the use of irons because irons had something going for them that light bulbs didn't: people used them during the day. In the very early years, generating stations didn't have much to do before evening. The power stream trickled all day long, surged as the sun went down, then pinched to a trickle again when people went to bed. The power companies got their big break, in the 1920s, with the proliferation of the refrigerator. Refrigerators operated around the clock and, then as now, were hungry consumers of household power.

Most of the truly dramatic changes since those days have had to do with growth in consumption. The last big technological news was grounded outlets, which were introduced in the 1950s and 1960s. People use vastly more power now than they did in the 1920s, and they use it for many more purposes (operating fax machines, for example), but the power they use is delivered around the house in pretty much the same old way.

This may now be on the verge of changing. For several years now, a number of competing groups have been working on new ways of wiring houses and making use of electricity in the home. The best-known, and in many ways the most ambitious, of these is the so-called Smart House system, which is being developed by a consortium of manufacturers, utilities, builders, and others organized by the National Association of Homebuilders. Smart House, in the words of its developers, is "a revolutionary energy distribution, communications, and control system that enables whole-house automation."

Every reasonably up-to-date house contains a hodgepodge of current-carrying wires. In addition to the basic grid of electrical branch circuits, my house is strung with wires or cables serving telephone, thermostats, stereo loudspeakers, doorbells, television sets, computer peripherals, and other devices. Installing each new type of device has involved installing a new set of wires or cables and making a new expedition into the walls or under the floors. Subscribing to cable television in my house involved drilling holes through siding, floors, and the insides of cabinets. Likewise with adding new telephones. When I installed a set of stereo speakers near the kitchen, I had to run wires under the floor along a path that was virtually (but not precisely) identical to the path along which I had earlier run a cable to feed a TV.

In the Smart House system this hodgepodge of wires is replaced by a single cable (which itself contains a hodgepodge of wires) that can be run in something like the same way that ordinary household cable is wired now. The main difference is in the outlets. Each one is capable of serving not just electric lights and appliances but also telephones, TVs, stereos, computers, security systems, intercoms, smoke detectors, and so on. In addition, each outlet contains its own computer chip, which is capable of communicating both with appliances and with other outlets. A device plugged into one outlet can interact with devices plugged into other outlets, or with devices wired into the system itself.

If you had talked to me twenty-five years ago, I would have told you that everyone would be getting around in personal minicopters by now. So I hesitate to speculate about the prospects of Smart House. Will I ever really feel like calling my oven from a pay phone and asking it to start cooking my dinner?

Probably not. (I didn't even think Crock-Pots were all that great an idea.) I'll also probably never care whether or not my house's wiring system is able "to display a message on the television screen when the washing machine has completed its cycle," something the Smart House people have told us we can look forward to being able to do.

On the other hand, I wouldn't mind being able to turn off all the lights in my house from my bed, or being able to call my house in a snowstorm and ask it to turn up the heat a couple of degrees. Nor would I mind being able to find out what my house is up to while I'm on vacation, or to communicate easily between the computers that are on the verge of outnumbering the people in my house. Smart House has fallen far behind the optimistic timetable originally announced by its originators, but it nonetheless has a feeling of inevitability. Someday it or something like it will be the standard for new wiring.

One of Smart House's most attractive features is safety. Electric current doesn't flow in a Smart House circuit unless a properly functioning appliance is plugged into it and asking for power. This means that children (and grown-ups) won't be able to electrocute themselves (or their friends) by poking car keys into outlets. Circuits won't be allowed to overheat. Frayed extension cords will be detected and their circuits shut down automatically. Vastly improved security and fire-detection systems, with centrally controlled detectors in every room, will be a snap.

One major problem with Smart House, as with other semibold schemes, is that everybody has to decide it's a good idea at pretty much exactly the same time. If nobody wants to make Smart House coffee makers, having a Smart House wiring system won't make a very dramatic change in your morning. (A regular coffee maker would still work, but it wouldn't be as clever.) Smart House is also intended mainly for brand-new construction. Consolidating a hodgepodge of different wires into a single cable is no help at all if the hodgepodge is already neatly concealed inside the walls. On the other hand, how could anyone be against a plan that would make it possible to own a houseful of snazzy new gadgets?

Chapter 7

The Roof

A contractor in my town once built a house whose roof had a persistent leak. The contractor tried every solution he could think of. He replaced shingles, he replaced flashing, he stood in the attic and brooded, but he couldn't figure out where the water was coming from. Finally, in desperation, he hauled an old bathtub up the stairs, put it under the drip, and walled it up with Sheetrock.

When the owners of the house moved in a couple of months later, they didn't know about the bathtub hidden inside the walls. Time went by. The bathtub collected water when it rained and permitted the water to evaporate when the weather was dry. It might have continued to do so forever, except that an abnormally wet spring came along and the hidden bathtub overflowed. When a carpenter was called in to repair the leak, the bathtub was discovered and the contractor's secret was exposed, to his continuing embarrassment.

Fighting a leak with a bathtub was a dumb idea, but it's easy

175

to sympathize with the contractor. Roof leaks can be very frustrating. Water that enters through a hole in the flashing can run for many feet over sheathing, down rafters, and along joists before it drips into the insulation, pools on top of the ceiling, and pours down on the living space below. Tracing a path from the damp spot on the ceiling back to a hole in the roof can be extremely difficult. Nearly every time it rains, my friend Ken goes up into his attic to worry about a small, chronic leak the source of which he has never been able to find. Standing in his attic and staring at the water on his rafters never does any good. Occasionally it does harm. During one such expedition, he slipped from the joist on which he was standing and put his foot through the ceiling of a hallway below. (You can still see where he poked through; he hasn't gotten around to repairing it yet.) Being the victim of a leak is like being the victim of a robbery—you feel violated. There's also something nightmarish about dripping walls. I still shudder when I think of the morning on which I looked up from the newspaper to see a vast brown water stain slowly consuming the kitchen ceiling.

Roofing problems are at or near the top of most homeowners' lists of complaints about their houses. This is true not only of people who live in old houses but also of people who live in brand-new ones. In the days when my roof's main function seemed to be channeling rainwater into particular rooms, I used to envy my sister, who lived in a house that at the time was less than a year old. New roofs typically last twenty years or more. Imagine not having to think about leaks for twenty years! Then one day my sister walked into her living room to find water streaming down the wall above her fireplace. It turned out that the builders had (astonishingly) forgotten to put flashing around the chimney. An entire wall and a room's worth of carpeting had to be replaced.

When my wife and I moved into our house, the roof was in terrible shape. The asphalt shingles on the main roof were buckled and worn. The asphalt roll roofing on the relatively flat roof of the one-story addition in the back of the house was badly eroded. Almost immediately after we bought the house, I spent two days trying to buy some time for the low roof by covering it with asphalt roof coating, a thick, sticky, tarlike gunk that comes in five-gallon cans and is pretty much like the thick, sticky, tarlike gunk that people sometimes use to seal their asphalt driveways. The instructions printed on the cans said that the coating could be applied with a brush or a roller, among other things, but the stuff was much too thick for that. I had trouble spreading it even with the long-handled squeegee that the guy at the hardware store had talked me into buying for that purpose. I ended up spreading a fair amount of the coating with an eight-inch wallboard-taping knife. By the time I had finished, the squeegee, the knife, my shoes, and my clothes were ruined, there was roof coating on the seat of my car (I was able to remove it with paint thinner), and my roof was very little better off than it had been before.

Then the winter came. One day I opened the door of a closet and noticed that water was trickling down the rear wall. The closet was directly below one of the roof's more problematic sections. Using a large serrated bread knife I cut a hole in the closet's ceiling. As I cut, cold water streamed into my armpit. When the torrent had slowed to a trickle, I reached into the hole and pulled down handful after handful of sopping insulation. Feeling panicky and helpless, I grabbed one of my daughter's ultra-absorbent disposable diapers and stuffed it into the hole.

BACK TO THOSE POOR, MISERABLE PILGRIMS

In the very earliest American houses, roofs were made of thatch. Slender members called thatch poles were secured horizontally across the rafters, and thick bundles of reeds were lashed to them in overlapping rows, like the scales on a fish. Thatch had a long history in Europe (and it remains the preferred form of roofing in many parts of the world today). But like the wattle and daub first used as siding, it wasn't well suited to American weather. Builders soon gave up on bundles of reeds and turned to shingles.

Early shingles were sometimes made of oak, but cedar rapidly became the raw material of choice. A log was stood on end and riven, or split, into thin slabs with a froe, the same tool used in making clapboards and barrel staves. Each slab was tapered, as modern shingles are. To keep the log's dimensions uniform, the shingle-maker would flip it end over end between slabs. He would then place each slab on a stand called a shaving horse and plane it smooth with a drawknife.

Cedar is an ideal wood for making shingles. It splits easily and cleanly, and it is naturally (though not permanently) resistant to bugs and rot. In the seventeenth and eighteenth centuries, parts of what is now New Jersey consisted of vast swamps filled with old-growth cedar trees. These massive trees were logged relentlessly, and the great stands were depleted. Then, in the early 1800s, as the last of the big trees were disappearing, it was discovered that the bottoms of the swamps were covered with a thick carpet of old logs and fallen tree trunks, most of which had been submerged for centuries. These logs, which were still in perfect condition, were brought to the surface and turned into high-quality shingles and clapboards. The resurrection of these old logs, which was known as cedar mining, remained a profitable industry in New Jersey for more than fifty years.

Old roofs were almost always very steep. A steep roof sheds water more readily than a relatively flat roof does, and it's better at resisting large loads, such as heavy accumulations of snow. A steep roof also permits the use of roofing materials that would tend to leak if used on gentler slopes. Wood shingles, ceramic tiles, and slate, for example, all require relatively severe pitches in order to be weathertight. If the slope is too low, water doesn't run off rapidly enough and makes its way into the house.

People will sometimes look at a modern version of a "colonial" house and wonder why it doesn't really look very much like an original. Is it the placement of the windows? The size of the door? Very often a major reason is the slope of the roof. The steep, massive roof of a typical eighteenth-century New England house has a powerful visual impact that is usually missing from contemporary interpretations. Flatten the roof, and the structure's proportions seem out of whack.

One reason why modern versions of traditional roofs tend to be less steep than the originals is that modern roofing materials usually don't require severe slopes. Asphalt shingles don't need to hang at a forty-five-degree angle to keep out water. Another reason is that architects and builders are increasingly using prefabricated trusses in place of traditional rafters in roof framing. The most common kind of roof truss is made of two-by-fours and looks like a squat triangle with a W inscribed in it. Viewed from the side, each truss is a full cross-section of the roof. Usually the slope of this cross-section comes well short of the slippery inclines favored by the old builders.

Trusses are usually delivered to a building site on the back of a big truck and lifted into place with a crane. A couple of carpenters can install an entire roof's worth in a fraction of the time it would take to measure, cut, fit, and join the members for a traditional roof frame. Because of the exacting way in which they are engineered, trusses can be made from lumber whose relatively meager dimensions would otherwise be inadequate for the load that rafters have to carry. All of this saves a lot of money. As a result, trusses are becoming increasingly popular in new construction.

But roof trusses have several drawbacks, in addition to the aesthetic one. In most versions, the bracing eliminates usable attic space. Some trusses are designed so that a small storage area can be created in the center of the attic, but these spaces are far from cavernous. Because most people view storage space as some of the most valuable space in a house, any saving achieved by using trusses also carries a big cost. Replacing storage space lost through the use of trusses (by, for example, adding a couple of hundred square feet of closets on the lower floors) can be substantially more expensive than not using trusses in the first place.

Trusses are also prone to misuse by carpenters and others

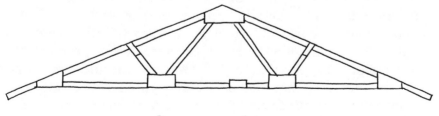

Common roof truss

who don't understand that tinkering with them—by cutting through a brace to make room for an air-conditioning duct, for example—can render them worthless or even dangerous. Trusses have to be designed and specified carefully for particular applications, and they have to be installed exactly as intended. This isn't always done.

REROOFING

After a period of hemming and hawing that lasted approximately two years, my wife and I finally got around to hiring a contractor to reroof our house. Primarily for aesthetic reasons, we decided to use cedar shingles. The existing asphalt shingles made our house look old and tired, we felt; cedar would make it look historic. Indeed, cedar shingles can give an almost sculptural quality to an otherwise featureless roof. Even viewed from far away, a wood roof has a visual character that is lacking in a roof paved with petroleum distillates.

There are two kinds of wood roofing materials: shingles and shakes. Shingles are always smooth on both sides. They're almost always sawn nowadays, rather than split by hand as in the old days. Shakes are thicker than shingles, and they last a bit longer as a result. They usually have one smooth surface (which is sawn) and one rough surface (which is split), although there are several possible configurations. Shakes look cruder than shingles and are often assumed to be more "old-fashioned," but they're not. Colonial builders almost always planed their shingles smooth.

Unfortunately, cedar shingles and shakes are both hellishly expensive. Roofing with cedar typically costs two, three, or four times as much as roofing with asphalt (an expense that is seldom even partially recovered at resale in most parts of the country). Still, wood roofing materials can be quite durable, even rivaling asphalt, assuming that they are properly installed and carefully maintained. They also have certain practical advantages. Wood is a far better insulator than asphalt, which means that a wood roof transmits less heat. In fact, switching from asphalt to wood can reduce summertime attic temperature by as much as thirty degrees, depending on how the attic is constructed and insulated. This in return can cut air-conditioning costs. We decided to use the highest grade of red cedar shingles.

The first order of business was to strip away the old shingles, of which there were quite a few: three layers of asphalt shingles and one layer of cedar. The cedar shingles, which were at the bottom of the pile, weren't the house's original shingles, but they were plenty old. All of this old roofing material had to be removed before new shingles could be installed. (Cedar shakes are occasionally installed over existing roofing, although they work better and last longer if they're not. Asphalt shingles can usually be installed over a single layer of existing wood or asphalt shingles, although people frequently go overboard. I once saw a house in Los Angeles that had seven layers of asphalt shingles—not a good idea.)

Stripping a roof is ugly, hot, filthy, dangerous, horrible work. On an ordinary summer day, the temperature on the surface of an asphalt roof can reach more than 150 degrees. Over the decades, old cedar shingles deteriorate into a sort of fine black mulch that clogs pores and coats eyelids. Like the fighting of wars, the stripping of roofs is work best done by young men in late adolescence. The contractor I hired sent several helpers of draft age to do the dirty work at my house. By the end of the day they looked like coal miners.

Before they began stripping, the young men used long two-by-fours and sheets of quarter-inch plywood to erect a protective skirt across the entire front of the house. This skirt served as a sort of ramp down which chunks of old shingles could slide. It kept the mess reasonably contained, although I still find nails and pieces of shingles in the pachysandra. The next time I buy a new roof, I'm going to lay down some sort of ground cloth before stripping begins. I'm also going to be sure to close all the storm windows, to keep the screens from becoming clogged with dust.

Stripping the old shingles produced an almost unbelievable volume of trash—enough to fill a dump truck several times. It also revealed a few secrets. When they were stripping the flat roof on the back of the house, the roofers found a metal funnel with several feet of plastic tubing attached to it. The funnel had been positioned under an old, persistent leak that had actually originated in some damaged flashing near a place where an old apartment door had been cut into the second story. The plastic tubing dangled inside an interior wall. Water from the leak was supposed to drip into the funnel and then be channeled into the wall cavity. From there, I guess, it was supposed to percolate into the basement. My wife and I have preserved this desperate device as a souvenir.

Stripping all those shingles revealed a solid roof deck made of wide chestnut boards attached horizontally across the rafters. These boards are a little over an inch thick, and some of them are nearly three feet wide. Eighteenth-century builders made their roof decking out of boards that had too many knots and splits to be suitable in more refined applications, such as flooring or paneling. The old roof boards on my house were still in good condition, so the contractor was able to attach the new shingles directly to them.

In new construction, wood shingles are installed on decks made of narrower boards. These boards (usually one-by fours) are nailed across the rafters with horizontal gaps between them,

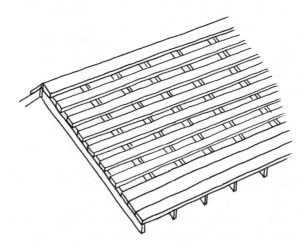

Open roof deck

a technique known as open decking or spaced sheathing. The spaces between the boards permit air to circulate beneath the shingles, extending the life of the roof by preventing moisture from becoming trapped in contact with the shingles. In the case of my roof, the numerous cracks, holes, and gaps in the old roofing boards served the same function.

Builders sometimes install wood shingles on solid decks made of plywood, usually with an intervening layer of asphalt-saturated felt (popularly known as tar paper). This practice, which is standard for asphalt shingles, is not recommended for wood. The plywood and the felt block the flow of air and can shorten the life of the roof by several years. Contrary to what you might think, a wood-shingle roof installed on an open deck is actually tighter than one installed on roofing felt and ply-wood. In areas where plywood decks and roofing felt are required by building codes, the shingles can be installed on furring strips attached to the top of the felt-covered plywood, creating an air space beneath them. (This is a practice that is worth considering even in areas where it isn't necessitated by code restrictions.)

Wood shingles are applied in overlapping courses in such a way that roughly one-third of their length is exposed. (The exact exposure for a given roof is determined by the slope of the roof in combination with the length and quality of the shingles.) This means that at almost any point on the roof the cedar covering is three shingles thick, which usually works out to three-quarters of an inch or so. That's quite a thick skin—thicker than many people imagine when they think of a wood-shingle roof. Nails are driven just flush with, but not below, the surface of the shingle. Driving the nails too hard creates a depression that can trap water and promote rot later on.

Shakes are installed somewhat differently from shingles. Trapped moisture is much less of a consideration, because the rough surface of the shake gives water easy avenues of escape. In addition, the extra thickness of the wood makes shakes much more resistant to moisture-related deformities, such as cupping and curling. As a result, shakes can be installed on either spaced or solid decks. Either way, roofing felt is always used with shakes, although not in the same way that it is used with asphalt

183

Cedar shingles, three shingles thick

shingles. Rather than being stapled to the deck before the finish roof is applied, the felt is interleaved between shake courses. Careful application of the felt is extremely important, because the felt accounts for most of the protection provided by a shake roof.

Many people worry that wood roofs pose a fire hazard. Well, they *are* made of wood. On the other hand, only a small minority of house fires ever start as a result of burning material landing on and igniting a wood roof. Most fires start inside. Even in areas where wind-driven brush fires are common, roofing material is often beside the point. Houses involved in such fires often burn from the inside out, as heat radiated through windows causes the interiors to burn first.

There are some experts who say that a wood roof can actually be an advantage in a fire. The reason is that a fire that reaches an attic will quickly burn through a wood roof, creating a "chimney" that clears deadly smoke and combustible fumes from inside the house. (Firefighters do the same thing with axes.) In contrast, an asphalt roof on a solid deck will trap smoke and fumes and force a fire back down into the house, especially if the asphalt is more than one layer thick.

Where fire is a worry or where codes require them, it is possible to buy shingles and shakes that have been pressure-treated with a fire-retardant chemical. The treatment is permanent and doesn't degrade significantly over the life of the roof. It can also give wood shingles and shakes the same fire-resistance rating as top-quality fiberglass-based asphalt shingles. Even so, a few local building codes prohibit wood roofs of any kind. In 1989, for example, the city of Los Angeles banned the use of wood shingles and shakes in new roofs and in renovations involving more than 10 percent of existing material. In most areas, though, limitations on building materials are based on fire-resistance rating alone.

Cedar roofs can be used successfully in most parts of the country, although they are extremely difficult to maintain in areas that suffer extended periods of high humidity. In the Gulf states, for example, the service life for cedar roofs is typically a third of what it is elsewhere. The high humidity encourages fungus growth, and the consistently warm weather provides a twelve-month growing season. Shingles and shakes in this sort of environment can be consumed by decay in as little as five or ten years.

In all areas, cedar roofs require more care and upkeep than asphalt roofs do. One of the major enemies is overhanging trees. Leaves, pine needles, seed pods, and other organic matter can accumulate in valleys and in the gaps between shingles. All this stuff traps water, which promotes the growth of fungus, moss, and something that looks for all the world like tiny red mushrooms on green-gray stalks. Oak trees are especially nasty: they drip resins that encourage lichen growth. Some people will tell you that moss and lichen growth are good for a wood roof, because they plug holes and gaps, but this is not true. They just trap water.

Getting rid of this stuff is difficult. Shake roofs can be cleaned with the same sort of pressure washer that painters use to clean exterior siding (see Chapter Two), but it's crucial not to let the pressure get out of hand. The person handling the sprayer should work from top to bottom, so that the water isn't forced up under the shakes and into the house. The water will remove not only foreign growth but also the top layer of wood fibers, leaving the shakes roughly the same color they were when they were new. (Pressure washing isn't recommended for shingle roofs, which aren't as thick as shake roofs and—if properly installed—aren't backed up by a felt underlayment.)

After smothering trees, the worst enemy of a wood roof is the sun. Like any untreated wood surface, an unprotected cedar roof will ultimately succumb to ultraviolet light. The sun destroys wood cells on the surface of the shingles and hastens the formation of striations and cracks, which permit water to penetrate the surface. Since a roof typically receives more direct sunlight than any other part of a house's exterior, this damage can occur rapidly. Cedar contains an oil that makes it naturally resistant to deterioration, but this oil doesn't last forever. Sun and rain combine to deplete much of it after just a few years. To keep this from happening, or to protect the wood after the oil has weathered away, a cedar roof should be treated every four or five years with a preservative especially formulated for the purpose. (The first treatment should be given about a year after installation.) Regular use of the proper preservative can extend the life of a new cedar roof almost indefinitely. It can also squeeze extra years out of an old roof, although it won't plug existing leaks.

Finding a good preservative is difficult. Virtually any preservative carried by hardware stores and home centers is likely to be too weak. To get good results from these preparations one would need to apply them every year or two, which in the long run would be more expensive than letting the roof fall apart at its own rate. The Forest Products Laboratory of the Texas Forest Service, which has done extensive research into wood shingles and shakes, recommends several more potent preservatives. One of them is TWP Roof and Deck Sealant, which is manufactured by a company called Amteco, Inc. TWP is sold in two finishes, Clear and Cedartone. The Clear finish doesn't alter the natural, weathered appearance of shingles or shakes; the Cedartone finish has a tan cast that some people prefer, although it looks fake to me.

I have used TWP on two cedar roofs: the roof of a small cabin in Massachusetts and the roof of my own house. I applied TWP to the cabin roof with a hand-pumped garden sprayer at the Forest Products Laboratory's recommended coverage rate of one gallon per hundred square feet. This worked fine, although the method would be too slow for a large roof. On my own house, the TWP was applied by a professional painter, who used a commercial airless sprayer. Only a couple of years have passed since both these roofs were treated, so I'm not in a position to offer any judgments based on personal experience. But the Forest Products Laboratory has assembled a great deal of convincing data, including some very compelling photographs of treated and untreated shingles that were allowed to weather side by side. The untreated shingles had deteriorated visibly after just a few years in the Texas sun; the treated shingles still looked great.

ASPHALT AND FIBERGLASS

The most popular residential roofing material by far is not cedar but asphalt. I happen to think that wood shingles look better on certain kinds of houses, but it's difficult to think of many other serious objections to asphalt. Modern fiberglass-based asphalt shingles can last for twenty-five years or more with a minimum of upkeep. For most people, they are really the only choice.

There are two types of asphalt shingles. The first, known as organic-based asphalt shingles, dates back to the late nineteenth century. These shingles consist of a paperlike core of felted organic fibers (nowadays usually made from sawmill scraps and recycled newspaper) that has been saturated with asphalt, covered with more asphalt, and coated with tiny granules that reflect sunlight and provide color.

The second type of asphalt shingles is known as fiberglass-based asphalt shingles, or simply as fiberglass shingles. These are essentially the same as organic shingles, except that in place of the saturated-felt core they have a core of fiberglass. Introduced by Owens-Corning in 1958, fiberglass shingles now account for around 80 percent of the market for asphalt shingles. They usually last longer than their organic counterparts, and they are substantially more fire-resistant. They are also less likely to be damaged by moisture, since the fiberglass core, unlike an organic core, can't absorb water.

Whatever the type, asphalt shingles are usually sold in strips measuring twelve inches by thirty-six inches, or thereabouts. For this reason they are often referred to as strip shingles. The strips are installed horizontally in staggered, overlapping courses in such a way that the top half of each strip is covered by the bottom half of the strip above it. This leaves anywhere from four to six inches of the strip exposed. In the most common configuration, the lower portion of each strip is notched, dividing it into three equal-sized tabs. When the strips are installed in overlapping courses, the tabs look like individual foot-wide shingles.

One of the most important recent trends in shingledom has been a growing preference (at the high end of the market) for so-called laminated shingles. These are strip shingles that have been beefed up through the addition of an extra layer of material. This extra material is intended to suggest something of the hearty three-dimensionality of wood shingles. Many versions actually do look quite good, even if they don't really look like wood. The extra thickness, in combination with variation in tab width and sometimes in color, can keep the roof covering from

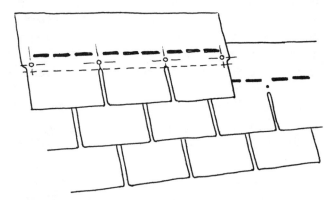

Three-tab asphalt shingles

looking monotonously smooth and thin in the way that most asphalt roofs do. Thickness also improves durability. Laminated shingles can usually be expected to last several years longer than single-layer varieties, and they typically have longer warranty periods. Naturally they also cost more.

Some manufacturers try to create the appearance of extra thickness by adding dark "shadow lines" to the surface of their shingles. These are bands of black granules that are intended to resemble long shadows cast by the lower edge of the course above. Actually, though, these shadow lines tend to look pretty dumb—like too much eye makeup. This is especially true on houses whose roofs sweep to within ten or fifteen feet of the ground, making it easy for a passerby to see that the "shadows" are fake.

Asphalt shingles are sold in a nearly stupefying assortment of colors, including black, red, white, blue, and shades with names like Heather Blend and Evening Mist. Some styles are offered in more than a dozen different tones and combinations of tones. Choosing a color is mostly a matter of personal taste (or lack of it), although there are other considerations. Light-colored shingles tend to last somewhat longer than dark-colored ones, because they reflect more sunlight. (They also keep the inside of the house cooler.) On the other hand, light-colored shingles tend to look mangy sooner than dark-colored shingles do, in part because there's such a stark contrast between the color of the surface granules, which erode over time, and the color of the underlying asphalt. My own favorites are the dark grays and brownish grays, which to my eye look the most like weathered cedar. (The bright tans that are billed as looking just like cedar usually don't look anything like it, in the same way that wood-grained vinyl siding doesn't look anything like real wood.) I also like plain old black.

Asphalt roofs usually require minimal maintenance. The best protection is to remove overhanging tree branches or keep them trimmed back as far as possible. Every so often it's a good idea to sweep away fallen leaves and pine needles, which can accumulate and trap water. There's a barn not far from my house that has a seven-foot maple tree growing on its roof in a pile of litter that had accumulated behind a chimney over a period of years. A roof with a tree growing on it is not a healthy roof.

LOW-SLOPE ROOFS

Not all roofing materials can be used on all roofs. The main consideration is usually steepness. In the roofing world, steepness is described using the terms *rise, run, slope,* and *pitch*.

The rise of a roof is its height—the vertical distance between the top of the house frame and the ridge. The run of a roof is the horizontal distance between the outside edge of the roof and a point directly below the ridge. On a symmetrical gable roof— the kind of open-book roof that children usually draw—the run is equal to half of the roof's total width.* The relationship between a roof's rise and run is called its slope, which is expressed as the number of feet of rise for each twelve feet of run. A roof that has a rise of four feet and a run of twelve feet has a slope of four-in-twelve. A roof that rises at a forty-five-degree angle—

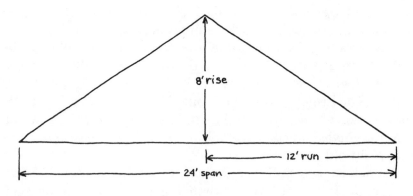

Rise, run, and span

*On a shed roof, which is basically half of a gable roof, the run is equal to the total width. On asymmetrical roofs, such as the roofs on some saltbox houses, the slope has to be calculated separately on each side of the ridge.

190

very steep for a roof, especially nowadays—has a slope of twelve-in-twelve. The slope of the main roof on my house is ten-in-twelve.

Pitch is similar to slope. It is expressed as a fraction representing the ratio between a roof's rise and twice its run. Thus, a roof with a slope of four-in-twelve would have a pitch of $4/24$, or $1/6$. Yikes! Unfortunately (or fortunately) roofers aren't very careful about using these terms precisely.

Asphalt shingles can't be applied to roofs whose slopes are less than two-in-twelve. The reason is that on relatively flat roofs, melting snow tends to back up under the shingle tabs and, frequently, seep into the house. (For more on this problem, see the section on ice dams later in this chapter.) Until recent years, the most practical choice for covering residential roofs with slopes lower than two-in-twelve was usually a material known as asphalt roll roofing. This is essentially the same stuff that asphalt strip shingles are made of, except that it is thinner, has no tabs, and comes in long, thirty-six-inch-wide rolls. The most durable roll roofing is so-called double-coverage, which is installed so that the courses overlap each other by nineteen inches, leaving seventeen inches exposed. Nails are used to attach roll roofing to the deck, and roofing cement is used to bond the parts that overlap. Nails are usually driven only on the part of each strip that will be covered by the succeeding course, a technique known as blind nailing.

Roll roofing is popular because it is relatively inexpensive and fairly easy to install. The contractor I hired to deal with my roof chose it for the nearly flat roof on the back of my house. As it turns out, this probably wasn't a great idea. The life expectancy of roll roofing is often as little as four or five years, and seldom more than ten or fifteen. The reasons for this have to do both with the nature of the material, which isn't as heavy as shingle stock, and with the low slopes of the roofs on which it is usually installed.

Roll roofing is also subject to a number of life-shortening installation errors. For example, using too much roofing cement, or failing to let the cement "flash off" briefly before covering it with roofing material, can cause blisters or bubbles to form later in the finished surface. This happens because roofing cements contain volatile solvents that can push their way through the roofing material, dissolving it as they do. Once formed, the blisters become the weakest parts of the roof and, in time, turn into leaks. My roof now has quite a few blisters on it. They break when I walk out onto the roof to stare at them and worry.

When I finally do have to replace my roll roofing, I'll probably use one of a class of roofing products known as membranes. The most commonly used membranes at the moment are those made of a material called modified bitumen. Modified bitumen resembles asphalt roll roofing, to which it is related, but it lasts much longer and can be used on roofs with no pitch at all. Modified bitumen consists of a fiberglass or polyester base that has been coated with a kind of chemically altered asphalt. The alterations make the asphalt last longer and retain a certain amount of flexibility.

There are several types of modified-bitumen membranes, and several methods of installation. The most common method involves using a blowtorch to soften the back of the membrane, which is then pressed into place either on a bare deck or on existing asphalt-based roofing. Like any building technique involving continuous use of an open flame, this method can be quite dangerous (houses occasionally burn down), but it is otherwise extremely forgiving. Mistakes and loose spots can simply be retorched and pressed back into place.

Some kinds of modified-bitumen roofing materials are self-sticking. (The backs of the strips are covered with an adhesive.) Other kinds are applied in a layer of hot asphalt that is mopped onto the deck. Still others are glued down with "cold" asphalt cements. Whatever the application method, a properly installed modified-bitumen roof can offer close to the sort of service life that one would expect from asphalt strip shingles applied to a steeper surface.

One popular brand of modified-bitumen roofing in my area is made by a company called Tarmac. *Tarmac* has always been one of my favorite words. I especially like movies in which people refer to things that are happening "out on the tarmac." But until recently I wasn't quite sure what the word meant.

Then, while reading some of Tarmac's roofing literature, I found out. It seems that a man named E. Purnell Hooley was taking a walk in Denby, England, one day around the turn of the twentieth century. Hooley passed a place where a barrel of tar had fallen off the back of a wagon and spilled onto the road. In an attempt to cover up the spill, some ironworkers had shoveled slag onto it. Hooley, according to the pamphlet I was reading, "noticed that the resulting composite had properties far superior to the road surfaces of the day." He went back to his laboratory, made a few refinements, and applied for a patent. Hooley called his invention Tarmac, a trade name he had coined from the words *tar* and *macadam*. (Macadam is a paving material made of compacted small stones. It was named for its inventor, a Scottish engineer named John L. McAdam.) Hooley's company, which was called the TarMacadam Syndicate Limited when it was founded in 1903, is known today as Tarmac PLC.

Newer and in many ways more promising than modified-bitumen roofing materials are the so-called elastomeric membranes. These are made of synthetic rubber and are commonly referred to as rubber roofs. Elastomeric membranes (like modified-bitumen membranes) are used primarily on commercial flat roofs, but they are beginning to find a place on residential flat roofs as well. They last longer than modified bitumen, and they stand up better to sunlight and other environmental forces.

The most widely used elastomeric membrane is ethylene propylene diene monomer, which is referred to as EPDM. Roofs made of EPDM may last as long as fifty years. The membrane is usually manufactured in sheets that are up to twenty feet wide and a hundred feet long and anywhere from forty millimeters to sixty millimeters thick. The sheets are usually bonded to the roof deck with contact cement, although some systems use screws and special washers. Seams are sealed with adhesives or with special tapes.

EPDM is incompatible with asphalt roofing and other petroleum products, contact with which can cause the membrane to deteriorate. Because of this, EPDM membranes are ideally installed on bare wood decks. Where this is impossible, a special liner can be installed between the EPDM and the old asphalt roof. Using a liner is not an ideal solution, however, since the integrity of the roof may depend on the care with which the liner is installed. Homeowners also need to be careful not to patch worn spots with asphalt roofing cement: it can eat right through the membrane.

OTHER ROOFING MATERIALS

When the contractor's crew stripped the low roof on the back of my house, they found an old metal roof under the deteriorated roll roofing. This was made of a material called terneplate, which typically consisted of an iron substrate to which a coating of tin and lead had been applied. With proper upkeep, terneplate roofs held up extremely well, and many are still in service today. In fact, terneplate roofing materials are still being manufactured, often with a backing of aluminum rather than of iron or steel.

Metal roofs have a long history. In the early 1800s, Thomas Jefferson roofed the main part of Monticello with sheet lead, which had been a popular roofing material in Europe for some time. At various other times, parts of Monticello were covered with tin, sheet iron, and other materials. Jefferson also used metal roofs in his design of the University of Virginia, for which he devised an innovative system of folded terneplate shingles. Jefferson believed his new shingles would last a hundred years or more. As it turned out, they leaked profusely and had to be replaced (with slate) in little more than a decade.

Jefferson's difficulties notwithstanding, metal roofs remained popular even for relatively humble structures until asphalt roofing materials displaced them in the early part of this century. In recent years, metal roofs have made something of a comeback. Modern metal roofs are expensive, but when properly installed they can last several times as long as asphalt shingles. For houses whose designs can accommodate them, metal roofs offer several advantages, not the least of which, in some cases, is historical accuracy.

The most popular variety of metal roof is the so-called standing-seam roof, which consists of long metal panels whose edges have been folded and bent in a complicated way and then crimped together to form a continuous surface. The panels are attached to the decking in such a way that no fasteners penetrate the surface of the metal. The standing seams keep out water but accommodate the sometimes considerable expansion and contraction of the metal.

Standing-seam metal roofs are available in a variety of materials. The most popular is galvanized steel with a durable baked-on finish. Another popular, though more expensive, choice is aluminum, which, like aluminum siding, is always coated. An architect friend of mine recently covered his own house with an aluminum standing-seam roof that he had had custom-made. My friend expects his roof to last well into the second half of the next century. The coating on the roof is a light green color that is very attractive and is, in fact, reminiscent of aged copper.

Copper is also a possibility, though its cost renders it out of the question for virtually everyone. Copper roofs are also especially vulnerable to acid rain, which can leave the same kind of blue-green stains on siding that a dripping faucet leaves on a sink. Nowadays copper roofs are seldom used for anything larger than a portico or a bay window, and even in those relatively modest applications they are the choice primarily of people who don't feel comfortable spending less than too much.

When most people think of luxurious roofing, they think of slate. Not all houses can live up to a slate roof, but on the ones that can, slate has a sort of rugged grandeur that other roofing materials don't. Indeed, a roof made of top-quality slate can also last for a very long time. The twelve-hundred-year-old Saxon Chapel in Stratford-on-Avon still has its original slate roof. Today, a slate roof can sometimes be expected to last a century or more, a comforting thought if you're thinking of leaving your house to your great-grandchildren.

Not all roofing slates are top-quality. The American Society of Testing and Materials (ASTM), a nonprofit group that establishes standards for just about everything (including gasoline and cardboard boxes), has established three grades for roofing slates. Slates rated S-1 can be expected to last between seventy-five and one hundred years; slates rated S-2 should last between forty and seventy-five years; slates rated S-3 should last twenty to forty years. Some slates available today don't even qualify for an S-3 rating, which means that the buyer must beware. There is no sense in paying slate prices for a roof that won't last as long as asphalt.

It's also possible to buy convincing-looking artificial slates made of fiberglass-reinforced portland cement or concrete. The cost is substantially less than that of slate, and the life expectancies are very good. As with many artificial materials, the principal aesthetic flaw in fake slates is their uniformity. This can be overcome to some extent by mixing colors or varying sizes.

In some parts of the country, the most common roofing material, even in tract housing, is tile. Clay tile has been a popular roofing material all over the world since its invention by the ancient Egyptians. Recent technological advances have made it even more versatile and durable. Modern clay tile roofs can be expected to last a hundred years or more. Excellent results can also be expected from concrete tiles, a much more recent (and somewhat less expensive) invention whose share of the roofing market is growing. Modern clay and concrete tiles come in a broad range of colors, finishes, and styles. Purists say that the coloring of concrete tiles is less subtle than that of clay tiles, but most people can't tell the difference. Tiles are available not only in the familiar vaulted profiles, but also in styles suggestive of shakes, slates, and other roofing materials.

The most exotic roofing material I've seen is the Prestige Copper Shingle, an Italian product that consists of a standard asphalt shingle to which a thin layer of copper foil has been laminated. The manufacturer—a company called Tegola Canadese—says a Prestige roof may last two hundred years. On the other hand, the manufacturer's warranty lasts only ten.

TROUBLE

The most trouble-prone parts of any roof, no matter what it is covered with, are the places where it is interrupted by other things. Chimneys, attic vents, plumbing vents, skylights, dormers (which have their own little roofs), and valleys formed by intersecting minor roofs all create seams that provide entry paths for water. To keep the water out, all such seams must be protected with flashing, which consists of sheets or strips of protective material, ideally metal, that bridge the trouble spots and divert water. When a roof leaks, the source of the leak is very often in the flashing.

Flashing problems also cause paint problems. When flashing fails, water can work its way behind siding and push off paint from the exterior as it tries to escape. When you see paint peeling from the siding directly above the flat roof of a porch, the problem can usually be traced to failed or improper flashing in the seam where the roof meets the wall. The more complicated a roof is, the more flashing it requires and the more likely it is to fail. The most durable and economical roofs are usually the very simplest ones: steep, unbroken, no-frills roofs like the ones built by our eighteenth-century ancestors.

Architects nowadays have a tendency to get carried away with roofs. Award-winning house designs often feature roofs with multiple slopes, elaborate dormers, and complicated valleys. These features are often visually striking, but they can also be very expensive, not only in terms of construction cost but also in terms of maintenance later on. Sticking a few dormers in a simple gable roof can double the roofing cost, because each dormer requires a prodigious amount of flashing. When the time comes for reroofing, the dormers may need to be stripped of their siding so that the old flashing can be replaced. In the meantime, all those tricky joints and intersections are invitations to leaks.

During the 1990 Builders' Show, *Family Circle* magazine unveiled what it called the Busy Woman's Dream House. The magazine's editors said that the house (which is located in a suburb of Atlanta) had been designed in accordance with the results of a survey of readers and is meant to reflect what women in the 1990s are looking for in a house. One thing they are looking for, apparently, is a huge expanse of complicated roofing. The Busy Woman's Dream House has considerably more roof area than floor space. The multi-hipped and -gabled roof lies on more than a dozen different planes and is sprinkled with corners, angles, overhangs, valleys, seams, and indentations. (But no gutters, even at the place where three separate slopes join to funnel rainwater onto the front steps.) Busy though she is, the woman of the 1990s apparently has plenty of time for cascading water, peeling paint, rotting trim, and leaks.

Simplicity is by no means the only virtue in home design. But complexity in a roof almost always carries with it a substantial cost, especially in areas that receive a lot of snow. The little gratuitous flourishes that make you gasp the first time you see a house may make you gasp again when the time comes to reroof or when water begins to trickle through the ceiling of the family room.

The most devastating roofing problems are caused by ice. When I was a lad I used to love seeing the enormous icicles that formed along the edges of the roof of my grandmother's house. They looked like something out of Carlsbad Caverns. Occasionally they would become so heavy that they would fall, making a tremendous noise and impaling the snow-covered bushes below.

Now that I am a grown-up and have icicles of my own, I take a less romantic view of them. I think of them not as natural wonders but as symptoms of a roofing problem known as ice damming. An ice dam is a thick accumulation of ice that forms along the lower edges of a roof, creating a barrier that traps melted snow and causes it to back up under the shingles and leak into the house. The trapped water can also refreeze and, as it expands, break shingles or push them away from the roof. Ice dams shorten the lives of most roofing materials. They can also cause ruinous damage to framing, siding, exterior paint, interior paint, wallboard, and just about every other part of a house.

Ice dams form when heat from the inside of a structure escapes through the roof and begins to melt the roof's snow covering from underneath. As this snow melts, water trickles down the roof. The trickling water is protected from refreezing by both the heat from below and the insulating blanket of snow above. But when the water reaches the colder lower portions of the roof—either the very edge of the roof or the cold area directly above the eaves—it refreezes. As more and more water flows down from above, a glacierlike mass of ice gradually forms. When this mass achieves sufficient size, runoff water backs up behind it. Because virtually all roofing materials are designed to shed only water flowing downhill, not water flowing up, the dammed water typically works its way up under the shingles and causes trouble.

Ice dams don't form on all roofs. I have never seen an ice dam on, for example, the roof on my garage or the roof of my screened-in porch. The reason is that both of these structures are unheated. The temperature on the underside of their roofs is the same as the temperature of the outside air. When the snow on these roofs does melt (after the air temperature has risen above freezing), it disappears gradually and uniformly. No ice dams form, and no water is forced back under the shingles. Sometimes a row of small icicles will appear along the eaves (the same thing sometimes happens on my mailbox), but they are nothing like the natural wonders I used to see on my grandmother's house.

Ice dams also don't form on the roofs of structures that are properly insulated and ventilated. If a house doesn't leak significant amounts of heat through its roof, snow on the roof will melt the way it does on my garage: it will just sort of gradually disappear. But before this can happen, two conditions must be met. First, the insulation must be adequate. Second, outside air (which in the winter means cold air) must be allowed to circulate freely under the entire roof deck. When both these conditions are met, the outer surface of the roof remains as cold as the roof of my garage, and ice dams don't form.

There are several ways to maintain a steady flow of cold air under a roof deck. The best way is to place vents both in the soffits under the eaves and along the ridge of the roof. Differences in air pressure caused by breezes blowing over the house will cause air to flow constantly between these two sets of vents, cooling the roof as it does. To do a good job, the ridge and soffit vents should both run the entire length of the roof; if invididual soffit vents are used, one should be placed between every pair of rafters. Care must be taken to ensure that the soffit vents are not blocked by insulation, a common construction flaw. If the attic is finished, an unobstructed air channel connecting the soffit and ridge vents must be left between the top of the insulation and the bottom of the roof deck. In addition, the ridge vent must be equipped with a baffle designed to prevent the infiltration of wind-driven rain and snow.

Proper insulation and ventilation are the only truly effective remedies for ice dams; there are many ineffective ones. If you live in a part of the country that receives an appreciable amount of snow, you have probably seen houses with resistance-type heating cables attached in a zigzag pattern to the first few courses of shingles, just over the eaves. In theory, these cables—which are switched on as the snow begins to fall—melt ice dams before they can form. In practice, they simply don't work. As a matter of fact, they can actually make ice dams worse. They also act as a trap for dirt, leaves, and pine needles.

All that heating cables really do is change the shape of the heated portion of a roof. Ice dams still form. Often they form both directly above and directly below the cables. There's a house near the village green in my town that has a brand-new set of heating cables. After a big snowstorm last year, the cables gradually melted their distinctive zigzag pattern through the snow along the edge of the roof. As they did so, icicles began to form at the apex of each V. Meanwhile, a large, ragged ice dam formed just above the cable, and a series of mini-dams built up in the small, triangular areas just below it. The resulting problem was in all likelihood worse than it would have been had the homeowner not installed those expensive cables in the first place.

A roofer told me that I could overcome the shortcomings of heating cables by installing them not only on the edge of my roof but also in my gutters and downspouts. But he was wrong.

For cables to be effective, they would have to cover the entire house and run all the way to the ground. Short of that, the cables don't eliminate ice formation. They just shift it around.

Since large ice dams often engulf gutters, people sometimes assume that gutters are the cause of the problem. They aren't. Remove the gutters and the ice dams will still form. They'll just look a little different. It is true, however, that ice dams can harm gutters. The first winter that we lived in our house, my wife and I decided to escape the snow for a while by taking our daughter to Florida for a week. Just as we were about to leave, I ran back upstairs to get something we had forgotten. I paused at a window for a moment to gaze out on the snow-covered hill beyond the road. Suddenly there was a tremendous noise. Two feet in front of my face, a twenty-foot section of ice-packed gutter tore loose from its anchors and swung like a pendulum past the window and across the front of the house. We were already late in leaving for the airport. There was nothing to do except run back downstairs and out to the car. Throughout the entire vacation, I thought of little but that gutter.

Yet even on houses where ice dams are common occurrences, good gutters solve more problems than they cause. When some people I know reroofed their old house a few years ago, they removed the existing gutters and didn't replace them. They did this partly for aesthetic reasons and partly because they believed that the gutters had been causing ice dams. Almost immediately afterward, water began to leak into the basement. Then, in the winter, the ice dams returned. In the spring, the gutters went back up.

Because ice dams typically form on overhangs, people sometimes assume that they could eliminate the problem by eliminating the overhangs. In fact, roofs on new houses are occasionally designed with this in mind. But leaving out the overhangs is not a solution. Ice dams still form at the edge of the roof and, because there's no overhang, often spill over onto the siding as well. Instead of dangling from the eaves, large iciclelike accumulations may form on the sides of the house, not to mention on or even inside upper-story windows.

This kind of ice dam often does more damage than the kind

that forms on overhangs. When water backs up behind an ice dam on an overhang, it usually leaks into the overhang rather than into the house. If the overhang is ventilated and not stuffed with insulation, the water will dry up or drip out fairly rapidly. On a house without overhangs, however, the water has nowhere to go but into the house. It may leak through a ceiling, or it may seep into the wall cavity. If the cavity is insulated, this can create an enormous mess, the first sign of which may be peeling paint on the siding.

In some parts of the country, people try to solve ice-dam problems by installing a wide metal band in place of the first few courses of shingles over the eaves. Commonly known as ice belts, these sheet-metal bands are usually several feet wide. They usually do prevent ice dams from gaining a purchase on the lower edge of the roof, because they are so slippery that snow and ice slide off, but they also cause *other* ice dams to form along their upper edges. Because these other ice dams are located higher on the roof, the leaks they produce tend to be more troublesome.

Several manufacturers sell self-adhering waterproof membranes that can be installed between roof deck and shingles in leak-prone areas, such as eaves and valleys. The membranes, which come in three-foot-wide rolls, are designed to seal around punctures, which means that they remain waterproof when roofing nails (or the nails used to hang gutters) are driven through them. The barriers don't prevent ice dams from forming but they do prevent backed-up water from leaking through the deck and into the house. On eaves the barriers should be applied so that they extend two or more feet beyond the outermost edge of the heated space in the house. Usually this requires the installation of at least two overlapping strips.

Waterproof barriers aren't a solution to ice dams. They just provide additional protection from some of the consequences. Using the barriers is no substitute for proper insulation and ventilation, although they can prevent water damage in houses that aren't (or can't be) properly insulated and vented.

A few years ago I bought an aluminum roof rake. It has a large, flat blade and a twenty-foot handle made up of four snap-together extensions. With it I can stand in my front yard and clear snow from the bottom three or four feet of my roof. The first time I used the rake I figured that my ice-dam problems were over for good.

But they weren't. Ice dams still formed—at the uppermost edge of the area I had cleared with my snow rake. Why? Because now that the insulating blanket of snow was gone from the bottom of the roof, the top of the cleared area was the cold edge. Water from the melting snow above trickled down that far and froze solid. Like the installation of a snow belt, this made my ice-dam problem worse, because it moved the dam—and the potential for leaks—away from the overhang and onto the part of the roof above the living section of the house.

In most cases, a snow rake is useful only if you can use it to clear snow from the entire roof. On small houses with accessible roofs this may be possible and worth the trouble. On large, multistory houses it's probably not. There's also the danger of doing more damage to a roof by raking it than by leaving it alone. Dragging a rake across asphalt shingles or roll roofing can scrape away the ceramic-coated granules that protect the asphalt from the sun.

I now use my snow rake only to clear snow from the top of a shed-style dormer on the back of my house. This dormer has a roof with a fairly gentle slope and no overhang. Once or twice each winter, an ice dam on this roof used to cause water to leak into the dormer's three windows and, on one occasion, through the ceiling of a room two floors below. The leaking also pushed paint off the window trim and once caused monstrous icicles to form between the storm window and the double-hung sash.

Now I am able to control this problem by using my snow rake to remove heavy snow accumulations not only from the dormer's roof but also from the part of the main roof that drains onto it. To do this I have to stand on a ladder on top of the flattish roof below and run the snow rake all the way up to the ridge of the main roof. Of course, my solution to this problem is in many ways more troublesome than the ice-dam problem itself. I resort to it only after the one or two snowfalls each year that seem most likely to cause a problem.

203

What I really need to do with the roof of that dormer (and with the rest of the roof on my house) is take the time to beef up my insulation and improve the circulation of outside air. The easiest time to do this would have been when the new roof was put on a few years ago. But I didn't know about ice dams then.

Chapter 8

Kitchens, Bathrooms, and Plumbing

There is a house a little over a million dollars up the road from mine that has been undergoing a major renovation for nearly as long as I have lived where I live. The renovation began five or six years ago, when the house was bought by a couple who planned to fix it up and sell it. The fixing up went on for more than two years. During this period a day seldom passed when there weren't three or four pickup trucks in the driveway. On some days there were seven or eight. The guys who arrived in these pickup trucks stripped off all the old stucco, put up new cedar clapboard siding, gutted and rebuilt much of the interior of the house, excavated the entire foundation in order to waterproof it, and added a two-story wing with a three-car garage underneath it, among other things.

One of the biggest and most expensive parts of the entire project was the construction of a magnificent new kitchen. This kitchen was designed and installed by a local company that has designed and installed a number of very nice kitchens in my area. For several days I watched this company's trucks come and go, and I watched new appliances being unloaded and carried inside. The name of the company was Ducci Kitchens, Inc.

Shortly after the new kitchen was finished, the house was sold. Although the paint had scarcely had time to dry, the new owners immediately began a major renovation of their own. The pickup-truck population of the driveway returned to historic levels. Some of the new renovation work involved removing and redoing parts of the old renovation work. A landscaping crew hired by the previous owners had planted a row of shrubs and small trees along the front edge of the property. The new owners now hired their own landscaping crew, which removed these shrubs and trees. They also brought in an electrician to replace some expensive new outdoor light fixtures that an electrician hired by the previous owners had installed, and they hired some carpenters to tear down and replace a fancy new porch railing that the previous owners' carpenters had built. In addition, they called in a local company to remodel the freshly remodeled kitchen. The name of this company was Ducci Kitchens, Inc.

The way many people feel about their kitchens borders on the nutty. I know a couple with grown children who recently bought and remodeled a luxury apartment. The most expensive part of the job was the construction of a new kitchen packed with top-of-the-line appliances (three ovens, two refrigerators, two dishwashers, three sinks, etc.). You could run a restaurant out of that kitchen. Everything in it is the world's most expensive version of whatever it happens to be. And yet this couple essentially never cooks. They live in the apartment just half the year, and when they are in residence they almost always eat out. The only gadgets they use with any regularity are the coffee maker and the microwave. The rest of the kitchen gets a real workout only during parties, when it is used not by the couple but by people they have hired.

This couple did not build a drop-dead kitchen because they wanted to create a pleasant working environment for servants and caterers. They did it because they wanted to send the world a message about themselves. Their kitchen is not so much a place to cook as it is an affirmation of their wealth and good taste.

Of course, fancy kitchens aren't solely status symbols. For reasons that aren't symbolic at all, the American kitchen has evolved over the last few decades into the focus of family activity. The living room and dining room have diminished in size and importance in new construction, while the kitchen—almost always with a large connecting family room—has grown. Many new houses don't even have separate dining rooms. Some don't have living rooms. The kitchen, in combination with the family room, has largely taken the place of both.

This isn't entirely new. The kitchen has long functioned partly as a family room. Even back in the days when virtually everyone's kitchen was hot, cramped, and uncomfortable, families tended to be drawn there. It may simply be that, like cockroaches, human beings have some powerful natural need to be hot, cramped, and uncomfortable. But in the last couple of decades, the kitchen's function as gathering place has become more explicit, and kitchen design has changed to accommodate it. A vacationing college freshman doesn't have to sit on the counter anymore to explain to his mother and father why their way of life is corrupt. Nowadays, quite often, he can sit on the couch by the fireplace.

My own feelings about fancy kitchens are somewhat complicated. On the one hand, I think that ostentatiously elaborate kitchens are wasteful, exhibitionistic, and dumb. On the other hand, I want one for myself. And I don't even like to cook.

Building a kitchen requires better planning and more foresight than does building any other room in a house. In order to learn about how this is done, and also in the hope of reaching some sort of philosophical accommodation with my conflicted feelings about expensive appliances, I made an appointment to visit the showroom of Ducci Kitchens, Inc., the company whose trucks I had seen in the driveway of that big house up the road from my own. Any company that would be called on to install two kitchens in the same room in the space of just a few months had to be on to something.

DREAM KITCHENS

Like almost everybody, I spend a lot of my time wishing that I had a lot more money than I currently have (none). Usually it is the thought of owning a particular house, car, electronic gadget, or power tool that makes me feel this. But sometimes it is the thought of owning kitchen counters made of various expensive materials. I had this feeling very powerfully when I walked into the Ducci showroom. Seeing those model kitchens made me feel poor and ashamed.

After I had looked around a little and pulled myself together, I sat down to talk with Gail Olsen, the office manager of Ducci Kitchens. Her husband, Charles Olsen, is the company's president. Gail and Charles are in their forties. Gail has blondish hair and a voice that she says she doesn't like but that sounded fine to me. Charles has a beard and wears an earring. They work together in designing the kitchens that their company builds. (Installation is handled by a full-time crew consisting of five installers and one helper.) I told Gail that I was interested in finding out how new kitchens are designed and in knowing what goes through people's minds when they decide to remodel.

Gail said that the first thing she and her husband do with potential customers is interview them. They ask how big their families are, what kind of meals they usually cook, how many people take part in cooking them, how they entertain, where they eat, what they do with their garbage, whether they like to talk on the telephone while they wash dishes, and what kind of appliances they're interested in. If they were interviewing my wife and me, they might also want to ask, "How many bottles of dog medicine do you keep on top of your good china?" Gail and Charles used to use a written questionnaire in these sessions, but they found that people are more helpful when they are allowed, in effect, to free-associate. Also, a questionnaire seems too much like a test, in some people's opinion.

After the initial interview, Gail and Charles visit the site (if the job is a remodel) to measure the existing space and get a feel for the clients' tastes and life-style. Sometimes you can tell a lot

about what kind of kitchen cabinets a person will like by looking at the person's living-room couch. If the clients are unusu-
ally tall or short, Gail and Charles may also measure the
clients—specifically, the distance between their elbows and the
floor—to get an idea of whether cabinets and appliances should
be installed at nonstandard heights. In most houses, counters
are installed at a height of thirty-six inches, a standard that dates
from the days when the average cook was a bit under five and
a half feet tall. Taller cooks sometimes feel more comfortable
with work surfaces that are somewhat higher, especially for
tasks like rolling dough (which is easier if the elbows are bent)
and washing dishes (the bottom of a sink is six or eight inches
lower than the surface of the counter around it). Still, straying
too far from the norm can lead to problems, since appliances
and factory-made cabinets are usually sold in standard heights
as well. Unusual counter heights can also make a house harder
to sell to people who are not themselves unusual.

While taking measurements, Gail and Charles usually ask the
clients what they like and dislike about their current kitchen. In
new construction, they like to be involved in the design of the
kitchen before the architect's plans are final. They have found
that architects are not always very good at designing kitchens,
and that their kitchen layouts are sometimes something of an
afterthought. Gail told me that architects don't always allow
enough room for all the features their clients want, and that
they sometimes place doors in inconvenient places. (Doors
should be located so that people who are merely passing
through the kitchen on the way to somewhere else won't have
to elbow their way past the cook.) These and other problems are
obviously easier to deal with before concrete has been poured.

After visiting the site, Gail and Charles make a floor plan
based on the measurements they took, then draw two or three
possible designs on tracing-paper overlays. These rough designs
are presented to the clients at a second meeting in the showroom. At this meeting, options in cabinetry, counters, back-
splashes, appliances, and sinks are discussed. When everything
is settled, Gail and Charles prepare a final proposal consisting
of a finished floor plan, a finished elevation, and a price. The

finished design usually ends up incorporating features from all of the initial drawings.

One thing that most people have trouble with, when they begin to think about remodeling any part of their house, is visualizing how much space they have and how much junk can reasonably be crammed into it. Most people simply do not have a very good sense of, for example, how wide a thirty-six-inch counter is. If you ask them to hold their hands thirty-six inches apart, they will often be fairly far off. When people sketch out ideas for new kitchens, furthermore, they tend to be somewhat flexible about scale. If you built a kitchen directly from one of these sketches you might end up with, for example, a fifteen-inch-wide refrigerator and a four-foot-wide dishwasher. And even if they get the width of the dishwasher right (virtually all dishwashers are two feet wide and thus physically interchangeable) they often forget that a dishwasher's door, when open, extends twenty-four inches into a room. That means that at least twenty-five inches (and preferably thirty-six or more) must be left between a dishwasher and any permanent obstruction, such as an island. Dishwashers should also be positioned so that their doors don't get in the way of cabinet doors. There are quite a few people in America who have to close the door of their dishwasher before they can open the door of the cabinet in which they wish to put their nice clean dishes.

Another thing that people have trouble visualizing is what the sleek, wide, empty counters in a kitchen showroom will look like when they are installed in their home and buried beneath toaster ovens, mixers, coffee makers, drying racks, bags of groceries, baseball gloves, and all the other stuff that people inevitably pile onto any flat, elevated surface in their home. A counter that looks ample when it is empty will look substantially less so when it is not. It is probably true that no amount of storage space is enough, and that junk inevitably expands until it occupies a volume at least 10 percent greater than that available to contain it. But people should still try to be sensible. This is possible even in small kitchens, since most people use only a relatively tiny fraction of their kitchen stuff on a daily basis. It took ten years, but my wife and I finally moved roughly a cubic yard of essentially untouched wedding presents out of our kitchen and into the basement, where they now serve as a sort of dust-collection system in my workshop. Doing this created a momentary storage vacuum that unfortunately was filled almost immediately by a lot of other stuff we never use.

Because of this tendency of one's possessions to exercise tyrannical control over one's life, kitchen storage should be planned carefully with a view to how it will be used. Quite simply, where and how one stores things should reduce one's labor rather than increase it. For several years my wife and I stored everyday plates and glasses in a bank of cabinets on the wall opposite the main work area. Unloading the dishwasher involved making repeated trips across the kitchen (and around the table in the middle of it). Now we store our plates and glasses in a cabinet directly above the dishwasher. This means that we can unload the dishwasher without taking a step. We had no good reason for doing it the other way for so long. The original arrangement was determined by nothing more than the order in which we had unpacked boxes after moving.

Many aspects of sound kitchen design are governed by fairly standardized formulas and rules of thumb. For example, it is usually recommended that there be at least eighteen inches of countertop "landing space" on either side of a cooktop or range. This gives the cook a handy surface on which to set down a hot or overflowing pot. It also makes it possible for the cook to position pots so that their handles don't protrude over the front edge of the cooking surface, where children can reach up and grab them or grown-ups can bang into them as they walk past while making unhelpful comments about the proper way to cook linguine. Sinks and refrigerators should also have landing areas. This is not for safety but for convenience. Loading or unloading a refrigerator is vastly easier if there is a nearby surface on which a bag of groceries can be placed.*

The most widely used formula used in kitchen design is one

---

*In Japan, refrigerators are often placed not in kitchens but in living rooms, where they serve a status-enhancing function that is impossible for Americans to understand.

based on the so-called work triangle, a concept that grew out of time-and-motion studies performed at Cornell University in the 1950s. In its most basic version this formula states that the sink, refrigerator, and primary cooking surface should be positioned at the vertices of an imaginary triangle whose perimeter measures not less than twelve feet and not more than twenty-two. The Cornell researchers found that most cooks spend most of their time shuttling back and forth among these three positions. Placing the vertices too close together severely restricts the amount of usable counter space. Placing them too far apart exhausts the cook. (In many ways, kitchens that are too large are less convenient than kitchens that are too small. Our old kitchen in New York was dinky and cramped, but it had one very nice feature: you could stand in the middle of it and reach virtually everything in it. Some new kitchens are so absurdly large that the people who work in them virtually need roller skates.)

The easiest way to create a work triangle is to install the main appliances and cabinets in a U-shaped configuration—for example, by running them around three of a room's four walls. This is the most common kitchen design. An extremely popular variation involves placing the cooking surface or a work area on an island in the middle of the U, separate from the main work counters. One of the worst arrangements is the one my wife and I have in our house, where the refrigerator, sink, and stove are all lined up on one wall. This leads to lots of shuffling back and forth and much wasted motion.

Work triangles were easier to design twenty or thirty years ago, when most cooking really did involve just the sink, the fridge, and the stove. Nowadays there are other appliances to consider, including microwave ovens, trash compactors, stand-alone ovens, freezers, and so forth, and many of them cry out to be crammed into the triangle. In addition, a traditional work triangle is too cramped for a kitchen in which two people frequently cook at the same time. Such kitchens should ideally have two work triangles, with one shared leg.

Despite these and other complications, the work triangle is still sound and still very much a part of good kitchen design. In fact, the basic idea can be extended to the design of any area in which people move from task to task, such as an office or a workshop. The point is to design any space so that it will help rather than hinder the people who will use it.

KITCHEN STUFF

After we had talked for a while, Gail showed me around the Ducci Kitchens showroom. Like most such showrooms, it resembled a series of mini-kitchens, each intended to show off a particular style of cabinetry or some other feature. The first one we looked at had been fitted with some fancy cherry cabinets made by a company called Wood-Mode Cabinetry. They looked like something you would be more likely to find in a fancy library than in a kitchen. As a matter of fact, high-quality kitchen cabinetry can be converted to use in other rooms, a fact that has not been lost on a number of manufacturers, including Wood-Mode. Buying cabinetry from a company like this and having it built into a room is often less expensive than having similar cabinets built from scratch.

Cabinet manufacturers have become quite ingenious at devising accessories for kitchens. There are double-layer cutlery trays, built-in spice racks, knife-block drawer inserts, tilt-out sponge holders, swinging and sliding contraptions that make efficient use of otherwise unusable corner space, drawers with adjustable dividers, drawerlike sliding shelves for large pots and pans, and countertop cupboards called appliance garages, which are used for storing toaster ovens, food processors, mixers, and other midget-sized appliances. If I were building a new kitchen right now, I would want all of these things. I would also want a built-in, carpet-lined, under-the-counter hideaway for my dog. Ducci didn't have one of these when I visited, but I've wanted one ever since I saw one in a picture in a decorating magazine.

"Believe it or not," Gail said, "the biggest hit right now is waste receptacles." She pulled on a drawer handle near the sink. Out slid a frame holding two full-sized wastebaskets. This accessory is especially popular with people who recycle. You can put paper in one wastebasket and plastic or metal in the other. You can also buy a third slide-out receptacle, with a lid that opens and closes automatically, for garbage. Other manufacturers make other kinds of bins for separating wastes.

One of my favorite kitchen accessories is the pantry cabinet. Years ago, even small houses often had a separate room devoted solely to the storage of nonperishable food and food-related accessories. Nowadays, though, very few houses have separate pantries. The pantry cabinet is an attempt to achieve some of the same storage capacity inside the kitchen itself. The best ones are floor-to-ceiling mini-closets that unfold as ingeniously as old steamer trunks. They have nesting shelves and overlapping racks that make extremely efficient use of limited space. Other models are short, so that they can fit under a counter, or very thin, so that they can be tucked beside a refrigerator.

For the cabinetry itself, there are two main competing types: traditional face-frame cabinetry, and the newer frameless cabinetry. In both types the cabinets are simple boxes made from plywood, particleboard, medium-density fiberboard (MDF), or some other engineered material. (All these materials are well suited to cabinet construction, because they are strong and dimensionally stable. Their only real drawback is that they are prone to water damage, which one should be careful to prevent.) In face-frame cabinetry, the ugly forward edges of raw cabinets are covered with a frame made of solid wood. The frame not only hides the plywood or particleboard but also strengthens the cabinets and provides a solid surface to which doors can be attached. Sometimes the face frame for an entire bank of cabinets is built as a single unit, with the joints doweled or tenoned together; sometimes the frame is built piece by piece after the cabinet boxes are installed. Doors and drawers are designed either to close flush with the surface of the frame or to overlap it slightly, with the help of a small lip tooled into their edges with a router or a shaper. Flush doors (also known as inset doors) look better, I think, but they are harder to hang and are more likely to bind as the weather changes or the house shifts. Lipped doors and drawer fronts can be mounted successfully in

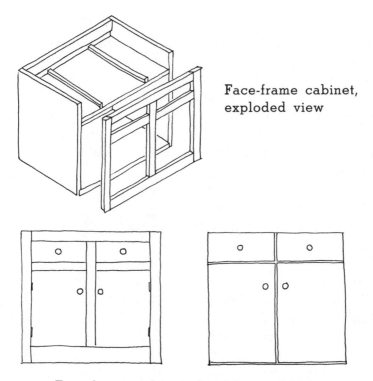

Face-frame cabinet,
exploded view

Face-frame cabinet, frameless cabinet

face frames that are slightly out of square. Lipped doors usually cost much less, because less labor is required to install them.

In frameless cabinetry, which is also known as European or Eurostyle cabinetry, the forward edges of the raw boxes are not finished with solid-wood frames. Instead they are masked with thin pieces of veneer or laminate, and the cabinet doors are mounted with special hinges that attach to the backs of the doors and the insides of the boxes. When the door of a frameless cabinet is closed, you see only the door, whose raw edges are also hidden behind veneer or laminate. This style of construction originated in Germany in the 1930s and has become popular in this country in recent years. A lot of people think that it looks slicker and more modern than face-frame cabinetry.

One of the main advantages of frameless cabinetry is that the fabrication of its components is easy to automate and standardize for high-volume production. One of the main advantages of face-frame cabinetry is that it provides a liberal margin of error for both the cabinetmaker and the installer, since the frame can be adjusted to hide small discrepancies in the size or alignment of the raw cabinets. As a result, face-frame cabinets are easier to build for someone who doesn't have access to a full-blown European-style cabinet-making factory. They also have (for most Americans) the sort of timeless look that arises from long familiarity.

Whatever the construction style, cabinets vary greatly in quality. Less expensive ones tend to have thinner finishes, cheaper raw materials, flimsier drawer slides, fewer and less convenient accessories, fewer door and drawer-front styles, and more disquieting details, such as warped doors, stapled joints, and loose veneers. As with most things in life, price provides a general indication of quality. Really good cabinets are never cheap.

Gail and I moved on to a mini-kitchen that had a countertop made of a fairly new material called Avonite, which is a "homogeneous blend of polyester alloys and fillers," according to its manufacturer. Avonite is one of several polymer-based materials (which are known generically as solid surfacing materials) that look pretty much like polished stone but that can be cut and shaped with ordinary woodworking tools. Another advantage of such materials is that their colors extend uniformly through them. This means that nicks, scratches, chips, and burns can be sanded away or patched more or less invisibly.

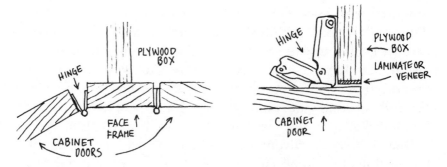

Hardware details: face-frame cabinet, frameless cabinet

The first of the solid surfacing materials was Corian, which is still the most popular. Corian was introduced, by DuPont, in the early 1970s. Corian doesn't really look all that much like real stone, but, like most solid surfacing materials, it has a striking beauty of its own. I began yearning for Corian the instant I first saw it. It looks smooth and cool and dignified. Gail and Charles have a chessboard in their home that was made out of Corian scraps by the foreman of their installation crew.

The first Corian counter that Gail showed me had a rounded edge. This detail was created by bonding an extra strip of Corian to the bottom of the counter's forward edge and then shaping both with a router. I tried to detect the seam between the two pieces of Corian but was unable to. Indeed, this is one of the great advantages of all the solid surfacing materials. If the installers know what they're doing (Ducci's have all taken special courses sponsored by DuPont and the other manufacturers), and if they're careful about matching dye lots, they can create large, curving, elaborately tooled surfaces that appear to have been formed from a single piece. This is a practical advantage as well as an aesthetic one, since open seams are the most vulnerable part of any surface that comes into frequent contact with water. Special sinks made of the same material can be bonded directly to the countertop, leaving no visible joint.

Ducci Kitchens installs so much Corian that DuPont has extended it the equivalent of most-favored-nation status. Along with a handful of other major outlets, it sees some DuPont products before other people do. The floor in the front of the showroom, near the entrance, is covered with Corian floor tiles, a DuPont product that is still in the experimental stage. Actually, the only experimental thing about the tiles, which look great and have all the maintenance advantages of Corian countertops, is their price. Corian and the other polymer materials are not cheap. Covering an entire floor with one of them would run up a big bill in a hurry.

Up toward the front of the showroom was the real thing: a countertop made of polished granite. Granite looks very sharp and lasts forever, but it's hellishly expensive. It's also very hard, which means you have to be a little careful when you slam down your wineglass on top of it. Slate and marble are also used sometimes for countertops, but both are more vulnerable to moisture and stains.

One way to get most of the look of a granite counter is to use granite tiles. These are less expensive than granite slabs, and they can be installed by do-it-yourselfers. (See the discussion of bathroom tile later in this chapter.) The only trouble with granite-tile countertops is that the joints between tiles are substantially less dependable than the tiles themselves. This is true of ceramic-tile countertops as well. The grout gets dirty and can deteriorate or crack. Deterioration is especially likely near the edges, where the stresses are strongest. Staining can be minimized by using an epoxy-based grout or by treating the seams frequently with a sealer. (Avoiding light-colored grouts can also help.) But tight, permanent joints are harder to achieve in tile than they are in various synthetic materials. The joint between a tile countertop and a sink is especially tricky. Eternal vigilance is required to keep water from working its way under the tiles and making a mess of the substrate beneath them.

The limitations of grout notwithstanding, ceramic-tile countertops are quite popular, and they are relatively inexpensive. They also come in a huge variety of styles, sizes, and colors. Still, you can't roll dough on them, and glasses wobble on the heftier varieties. One way to get the look of tile without the inconvenience is to use tile not on countertops but on the wall area between the surface of the counters and the bottoms of the overhead cabinets. One of the model kitchens at Ducci was set up in this way.

The most popular countertop material by far is plastic laminate, which consists of many layers of kraft paper (the stuff that grocery bags are made of) that have been impregnated with phenolic resin and squished together. The outer surface is made of a higher-quality, colored paper that is coated with melamine resin. All the layers are bonded together under great heat and pressure. This process creates a thin, tough sheet that can be attached with contact cement to plywood, particleboard, MDF, or some similar material. The edges are trimmed flush with a small router known as a laminate trimmer.

The first plastic laminate was Formica. It was introduced in

1913 as an electrical insulator (in which capacity it was a replacement "for mica"). It became popular as a countertop material some twenty years later, and it and its numerous imitators have been popular ever since. They have remained popular because they are tough, attractive, and available in a huge variety of colors and patterns. They also cost much less than other countertop materials and can be installed by a moderately ambitious amateur. In fact, installing plastic laminate is one of those satisfying handyman activities that, once mastered, sometimes threaten to take on a life of their own, to the point where one may decide that there is no surface in one's house that wouldn't be better off with a rugged resin-impregnated coating. (Soldering copper pipe is another of these activities. When I learned how to do it—see later in this chapter—I found myself wondering, Gee, wouldn't it be nice to have running water in the living room?)

There are two main problems with plastic laminates. One is that the resinous surface erodes with use, especially if the countertop is used as a cutting board or cleaned with an abrasive cleanser. It's not at all unusual to see older laminate countertops that have unattractive whitish or brownish areas where the color has worn away. This can happen after just a few years. The other problem with laminates is that most of them have begun to look a bit old-fashioned in comparison with Corian and other more expensive materials.

Even so, laminates are still extremely popular, and installers and manufacturers have found a number of ways to make them look more up-to-date. One way to do this is to apply wood trim, such as a rounded oak nosing, to the forward edge of a laminate counter, or around the edges of laminated cabinet doors and drawer fronts. Doing this eliminates the telltale brown line that is visible at the edges of ordinary laminate counters. (The brown line is the kraft-paper core of the laminate, which is made visible when the edges are trimmed.)

Another way to eliminate the brown line is to use the newer color-through laminates, which are more expensive than ordinary laminates but are a uniform color throughout. In one popular treatment, three or four strips of laminate, each in a

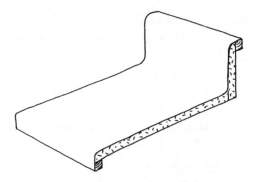

Section, post-formed plastic-laminate counter

different color, are built up along the edge of a countertop and then beveled with a router. This creates a tiny rainbow of color that runs around the entire counter. Very often this is done in combination with a wood molding. It's even possible to use color-through laminate to create a pretty good imitation of Corian and other surfacing materials. Whatever the edge treatment, color-through laminates have a longer service life than ordinary laminates, because erosion of the surface layer is less conspicuous.

REPLACING A KITCHEN COUNTER
AND SINK

At the time of my visit to Ducci Kitchens, the countertop in the kitchen of my house was made of butcher block—strips of maple glued together to form a slab roughly two inches thick. Butcher block looks great when it's in good condition, but it requires careful maintenance, and it's a poor choice for any part of a kitchen that gets wet on a regular basis. Over the course of many years, the counter and backsplash near our sink had deteriorated in a very unattractive way. In fact, they had begun to rot.

My wife and I, like a lot of people, hope to have a really great kitchen someday. We'll tear out all the cheap stuff we have now and knock down a few walls and put in a lot of expensive appliances that will make all our friends hate us. But we're not ready to do that yet. So we decided to see if we could replace the rotting counter with something nice but inexpensive that would last until we're ready for a full-scale remodeling, five or ten years from now.

What we settled on was a factory-made countertop manufactured from something called post-formed plastic laminate. This is ordinary plastic laminate that has been shaped under pressure in a way that is easier to do if you have a factory than if you don't. The type I bought had a curved forward edge and a curved, built-in backsplash. The laminate had been applied in a single piece, so there was no seam between the backsplash and the countertop. I ordered the countertop through the kitchen department at my hardware store, paying ninety dollars for a ten-foot-long blank. (That's roughly what you might expect to pay for one or two square feet of Corian.)

The counter I wanted to replace was a bit less than ten feet long, so I had to trim the blank. I did this with my portable circular saw, turning the countertop upside down and cutting from underneath to keep the blade from chipping the brittle surface. Then I cut a hole for the sink (also new, and made of stainless steel). To lay out my cut, I carefully traced around a hole-sized cardboard template that had come with the sink.* Then I used my handheld jigsaw to cut just inside the pencil line. If I had been planning to reuse the old sink, I could have made my own template by tracing the cutout in the old countertop. Making the cut took longer and required more concentration than I had thought it would: plastic laminate is tough stuff.

Like most new drop-in sinks, the one I bought is held in place

---

*Before using a template of any kind, even one supplied by the manufacturer, it's a good idea to check it carefully to make sure it really is the right size. When my friend Ken and I installed some canister-type light fixtures in the ceiling of my kitchen, we didn't check the supplied templates before making our cutouts. To our great surprise, we ended up with holes that were a quarter of an inch too big. This made the supplied mounting brackets useless, which meant that we had to improvise our own brackets. Everything worked out fine in the end—the brackets we improvised worked better than the supplied ones would have—but the overall experience was pretty annoying. Sheesh!

with small metal clips that hook into a slot beneath the rim of the sink and bite into the underside of the counter. Tightening these clips with an electric screwdriver pulled the rim snug against the counter's surface. Tightening the clips also compressed a tubular rubber gasket attached to the underside of the rim and intended to keep water from seeping underneath. (Installing some sinks requires the application of a caulklike sealant before seating the sink and tightening the clips.) To make sure the seal would remain tight, I bought a couple of extra clips and installed them on the side of the sink where a permanently wet dish drainer would sit.

Before I could install the new countertop, I had to get rid of the old one. It was held down, from underneath, by four or five L-shaped metal brackets that were screwed both to the bottom of the countertop and to the insides of the cabinets. To get at the brackets, I had to remove the drawers and a couple of big pots and pans. Then I reached in with my electric screwdriver and removed the screws from the bottom of the countertop. I left the other screws where they were, because I wanted to reuse the brackets. Then I slid the new countertop into place, jiggled it to make sure it was snug, and put back the old screws. Making the switch took all of fifteen minutes. I lugged the old countertop down to my basement and flipped it over on top of a couple of sawhorses, creating an instant workbench. Because maple workbenches are quite expensive, I actually turned a profit on this project—an excellent rationalization.

I hired a plumber to help me hook up the sink and install a new faucet. I had been tempted to do these chores myself, but at the last minute I decided it would be safer to call in a pro. This turned out to be a good idea. The plumber made quick work of the hookup, and when he was finished I didn't have to call a plumber to come fix all the leaks, the way I usually have to do when I do the work myself.

Actually, I probably could have made that hookup without incident. I had done similar chores in the past. Indeed, there are many useful plumbing skills that are well within the reach of a moderately ambitious homeowner. Possessing a few of these skills can not only save on a fair amount of money, but can also spare one a great deal of nuisance. If you know how to repair a burst pipe or a broken fixture, you don't have to pace around your flooded kitchen in a panic until the plumber arrives next week.

I learned most of my rudimentary plumbing skills at the feet of a couple of plumbers who did some work in my house a few years ago. The plumbers were interested in buying an old wood-burning furnace that the previous owners of my house had installed as a backup to the oil-burning furnace, but that I had never used. I told the plumbers that I wouldn't sell them the furnace but that I would trade it to them for a plumbing lesson. A few days later they came over after work, disconnected the old furnace, and showed me how to work with copper tubing.

Most of the water-supply pipes in most people's houses are made of copper. So are most of the pipes in hot-water heating systems. Copper tubing is a durable, versatile material that is relatively easy to cut and join. Its chief drawbacks are that it is expensive (vandals in New York City rip copper wires out of streetlights and sell them for scrap) and that it is easily etched by acids. The blue stain in the bottoms of my sinks and bathtubs is copper that used to be part of my pipes: acid in the water etched it out. A very slight degree of.acidity usually isn't a problem, but highly acidic water—which is what we now have in my part of the country, where acid rain is prevalent—can eat its way through pipes and fixtures over a period of years.

I never thought about the acidity of my water supply until I noticed a pinhole leak in one of the hot-water pipes in my basement. This leak turned out to be not an isolated mini-disaster but a symptom of a general crisis. I ended up buying a water treatment system that maintains my water in a roughly neutral state by injecting an alkaline solution into it. I also ended up having to replace a couple of hundred feet of copper pipe whose inside walls had been deeply grooved, over the course of twenty years, by the flow of nasty, untreated water. The plumbers who installed the new pipes were the ones who carted off my old furnace and gave me my plumbing lessons.

The main skill that I had wanted to learn from these plumbers was how to make "sweat" joints, the soldered connections that are used to link pieces of copper pipe and to attach many kinds of fixtures. Like most activities involving molten metal and a blowtorch, this one appealed to me. And yet, it also looked scary. I began to wish that I had studied it in college in place of some of the things I actually did study, such as the essays of Ralph Waldo Emerson. That was when I thought of having real plumbers teach me.

The first practice joint I made was a ninety-degree one. I used two foot-long scraps of copper pipe that were a half inch in diameter, and an elbow-shaped copper fitting whose inside diameter was a hair larger than the outside diameter of the pipes. The basic idea was to stick the pipes into the elbow-shaped fitting and then solder the whole thing together. Okay! The basic skills used in doing this are the same ones used in making all sweat joints.

My first step was to square off the ends of the pipes. I did this with a tubing cutter, which is a hand tool that looks a little like a C-clamp (known in England as a G-cramp, incidentally). Mounted on the inside of the C is a sharp cutting wheel, like the one in a can opener. You fit the tool around the pipe, adjust a knob until the cutting wheel is pressed snugly against the copper, and then turn the cutter around and around, tightening the knob slightly after each turn. Copper is a very soft metal. Cutting through a pipe doesn't require much muscle. (It's also possible to cut copper pipes with a hacksaw, although it's easier to get a clean cut with a tubing cutter.)

I have two tubing cutters. One is teeny (for making cuts in tight places) and the other is fairly large. The fairly large one has a bladelike attachment called a reamer, which is used to remove burrs from inside the cut ends of pipes. If the burrs aren't removed, they can promote the plumbing equivalent of atherosclerosis, by providing little nubs on which mineral deposits can accrete. I used my reamer to remove the burrs from the ends of both of my pipes.

Solder won't stick to copper that is dirty or oxidized. For this reason, all surfaces that will be touched by the solder must be carefully cleaned until they are as shiny as new pennies. This is probably the most important step in making a sweat joint. The cleaning is usually done with narrow strips of aluminum-oxide sandpaper, also known as emery cloth or plumber's cloth, or with steel wool. I tore off a piece of plumber's cloth six or eight inches long and pulled it back and forth around the pipe with the same two-handed buffing motion I would use to shine my shoes if I ever got around to shining my shoes. The idea is to rub the metal briskly enough to leave it uniformly shiny but not so briskly as to deform it. Proper cleaning is extremely important. A single greasy fingerprint can prevent the solder from sticking and cause a leak.

I also had to clean the inside surfaces of the elbow-shaped fitting into which I would insert the clean end of each pipe. This can be done with a rolled-up tube of plumber's cloth, but it's easier to do with a small wire brush made especially for that purpose. There are different sizes of brushes for different sizes of fittings.

Once all the surfaces were clean and shiny, I slathered them with flux, an acidic paste that facilitates the flow of solder and keeps the copper from oxidizing when heat is applied. I stuck the fluxed ends of the pipes into the fluxed openings of the fitting and twisted them around a little to make sure that the flux was evenly distributed. Then I lit my propane torch (a handyman model, available at any hardware store, also useful in making *crème brûlée*) and aimed the blue part of the flame at the back of the fitting, near the tip of the elbow. In making a sweat joint you heat the fitting, not the solder. The idea is to get the fitting hot enough to melt the solder, which is then drawn into the joint, toward the source of the heat, by capillary action.

As I heated the fitting, I dabbed at the joints periodically with a length of solder, to test the temperature. As soon as solder liquefied, I removed the torch and ran the solder all around. It flowed up into (and around) each joint, sealing it tight. Then I wiped the soldered area with a wet rag to clean away excess solder and flux and to speed the hardening of the joint. (If you are soldering a new joint near an existing joint and don't want to risk ruining the existing joint, you can wrap a wet rag around it to keep it cool.) If you need to disassemble a joint for some reason, you do it the same way, but backward: you heat the fitting with your torch to loosen the solder, then you knock it apart with a hammer or a piece of wood.

Making sweat joints on pipes that are already in place—as you do when, for example, you add a branch to an existing water pipe—is more difficult. The first step is to turn off the water and drain the pipe. Since the torch will vaporize water left in the pipe, creating a potentially dangerous pocket of steam, it is very important to make sure that the pipes adjacent to the spot where you will be working are dry. You should also open a tap on the drained line, to give any steam an escape route. In instances where completely halting the flow of water is impossible (because a shutoff valve has become worn, for example), plumbers will sometimes stuff a wad of white bread into the dripping pipe. The bread holds back the water for a while, giving the plumber time to solder the joints. Then it gradually dissolves. It is crucial while doing all of this to protect wood framing from the heat of the torch. Plumbers sometimes forget about this, and house fires occasionally result.

Until fairly recently, the solder used in virtually all plumbing of this sort was made largely of lead. Lead is—well, we all know the problem with lead. Acidic water can sometimes leach it out of soldered joints. It is generally recommended that people whose water-supply lines are soldered with lead (that is, the great majority of us) let the water run for three minutes each morning, to flush out toxic concentrations that may have accumulated in the pipes overnight. (We should also have our water tested.) This precaution usually isn't necessary in houses that have brand-new plumbing. Lead-free solder has been required in most parts of the country for several years. In addition, the water pipes in many new houses are made of plastic. These pipes are cemented together rather than soldered.

The relationship between plumbing and lead is not an incidental one. The Latin word for lead is *plumbum.* A *plumber* was originally simply someone who worked with lead. The word began to assume its modern meaning when it turned out that lead was a swell material for making pipes and fixtures: it was easy to melt, easy to shape, easy to bend. There are still houses today that have lead water-supply pipes. Quite obviously pipes like this pose an extraordinary health hazard and should be replaced immediately.

THE PIPES IN A HOUSE

The water in most people's houses comes from a public water supply of some kind. It's brought to the house by a pipe that branches off from a main supply line that runs along the street. The water is under pressure when it enters the house, and it is this pressure that moves the water to the washing machine on the first floor, the toilet on the second floor, and the shower on the third floor. The more fixtures that are in use at one time, the less pressure is available to move water to each one. There's always a main cutoff valve inside the house (or, occasionally, just outside), usually right next to the water meter. Knowing the location of this valve is essential. If you suddenly discovered water pouring through your ceiling, you would want to be able to shut down the entire system in a hurry so that you could look for the source of the problem in a relaxed state of mind. It's a good idea to put a big, colorful tag on the valve, so that other people will be able to find it, too.

The water in my house is not from a public utility but from a well. This is usually the case in rural areas. My well is in my yard, next to the path that leads from the driveway to the back door. It is 350 feet deep and a few inches in diameter. Suspended near the bottom of it is a torpedo-shaped electric pump. The pump is connected to a flexible plastic pipe that runs all the way up the well and into a tank in my basement. Inside the tank is a rubber bladder. When water is pumped from the well, it presses against the bladder, compressing a pocket of air above it. It is this compressed pocket of air that provides my water pressure. Older water tanks have no bladder, and need to be recharged periodically with compressed air.

When it leaves the pressure tank, the water at my house passes through a smaller tank, where measured amounts of alkaline solution are injected into it. Then it passes through a dirt-and-rust filter, which removes crud from my water and which I have to change every couple of months. (I can tell that the filter is becoming clogged when the water pressure in the shower begins to fall.) Then it divides into two separate branches. One of these branches leads to the hot-water heater

227

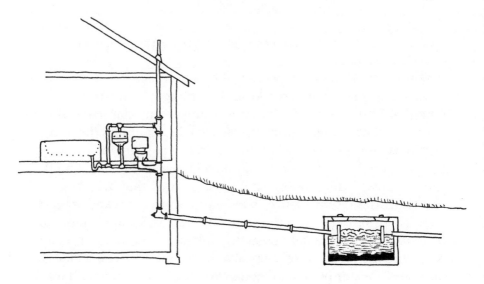

Simple plumbing layout showing vents, drains, and septic tank

and, beyond it, to all the fixtures that use hot water. The other branch carries cold water. The main hot and cold branches are further divided into secondary branches, which carry water to individual bathrooms, the kitchen, the laundry room, and so on. Ideally every secondary branch should have its own shutoff valve, preferably in the basement near the point where it branches off from the main line. This can make it possible to, for example, shut down the water to a single bathroom or to the laundry room without cutting off the entire house. In addition, most fixtures have their own shutoff valves. The knob on the small pipe leading from the floor to the tank of a toilet is such a valve. If a toilet tank springs a leak, you can stop it by closing this valve and flushing the toilet to empty the tank.

Getting water to fixtures is just half the battle. The other half is carrying waste water (and other wastes) away. The pipes that do this are known collectively as the drain-waste-vent (or DWV) system. These pipes are not pressurized. Wastes move through them by the force of gravity, with periodic nudges from flushing toilets or draining bathtubs.

When you flush a toilet, the contents of the bowl are pushed (by the force of the water released from the tank) into a short, slightly sloping drainpipe that empties into a big, vertical pipe called a soil stack. The soil stack carries waste from toilets and other fixtures down to a big, slightly sloping waste pipe known as the main drain. The main drain, which occupies the lowest stratum in the plumbing system of a house, leads either to a public sewer line or to a private sewage system, such as a septic tank. My house has a septic tank.

Every soil stack leads not only down to the main drain but also up through the roof, where it looks like a small round chimney. This upper portion of a soil stack is known as a stack vent. It has two functions. One is to provide an escape route for noxious fumes formed by the decomposition of wastes. The other is to equalize the air pressure within the DWV system. If the system weren't vented, wastes would move through the pipes only sluggishly, if at all, for the same reason that you have difficulty swallowing when you have a stuffed-up nose, or that you have trouble pouring tomato juice out of a can in which you have made only one small hole with a church key. In the early days of indoor bathrooms, plumbers sometimes connected the soil stack to the chimney flue rather than punching a separate hole through the roof. This was not a terrific idea. A spark in the flue could ignite methane in the soil stack, making the chimney look like a rocket blasting off in the wrong direction.

Some fixtures are vented directly by a stack vent. Others are vented by branch vents, which are pipes that connect the fixtures' drain lines with a stack vent. My house has just one stack vent, and all the plumbing fixtures in my house are tied into it in one way or another. Many other houses have more than one stack vent. You can tell how many you have by going out into your yard and counting the pipes that poke through your roof.

The elementary school in my town had some terrible plumbing problems a few years ago. Toilets overflowed, bad smells filled the bathrooms, sinks wouldn't drain. There was talk of hellishly expensive repairs to the septic system. Then a custodian thought of going up on the roof and shining a flashlight down the stack vent. He discovered—and removed—a big rock, a tennis ball, some old leaves, a dead bird, some other things. After that, the bathrooms worked fine. (It is possible to buy a small wire "cage" that fits into the vent opening and keeps things from falling in.)

To keep sewer gas from backing up into a house under normal circumstances, every fixture is isolated from the heart of the DWV system by a curved pipe known as a trap. The easiest place to see a trap is under a sink. If you look you will notice that a pipe connected to the sink's drain heads straight down, turns back up, and then either turns down again or bends back into the wall. This bending section of pipe is the trap. It is shaped either sort of like a P lying on its side, in which case it is called a P-trap, or sort of like an S lying on its side, in which case it is called an S-trap. Whatever its shape, its function is to maintain a constant plug of water in the drain line. If this plug weren't there, a big gust of sewer gas from the soil stack would knock you off your feet when you bent over the sink to look for your contact lens. (The trap for a toilet is similar to the trap under a sink but is built into the toilet itself.)

Traps are very important. In fact, it was the invention of the trap, in 1840 or so, that made indoor plumbing possible. Early designs were often ingenious but were substantially less reliable than modern ones, and gas leaks were common. One way to test for such leaks, or for breaks in the waste pipes themselves, was to climb onto the roof, pour oil of peppermint into the stack vent, stuff the vent with paper, then walk through the house

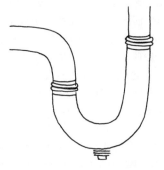

P-trap with cleanout

230

sniffing. At the turn of the century, druggists sold sealed two-ounce vials of peppermint oil specifically for this purpose.

In addition to trapping water, traps often trap hair, grease, and other solids that are rinsed down drains or flushed down toilets. Every year or two I have to remove the trap from the sink in our bathroom and ream out the plug of sediment (mostly toothpaste, hair, and a mysterious kind of slime) that has occluded the pipe and made drainage sluggish. Often the obstruction is not in the trap itself but in the short length of vertical pipe directly above it. Clearing away a blockage like this is easy. Some traps have a clean-out valve (usually at the elbow) specifically for this purpose, although if the blockage is substantial it is usually easier to remove the entire trap (by using a large wrench to loosen the fittings) and poke at the glop from both ends. This is also a good way to look for lost contact lenses and diamond rings. (My wife washed both her contact lenses down the sink one morning several years ago about an hour before we were supposed to leave for the airport. I found them buried in toothpaste in the trap.) A bad way to clean out slow drains is with caustic chemical drain cleaners, which are horrible pollutants.

When a toilet clogs or flushes very, very slowly, the blockage is almost always in the trap and not twenty feet away, at the

Toilet-bowl cross section, showing trap

bottom of the soil stack. The best way to remove one of these blockages is with a plunger, also known as a plumber's helper. Almost everybody already has one of these. A few strong pumps will usually push the blockage past the bend in the trap and into the more spacious drainpipe to which the toilet is attached.

Sometimes the problem is more dire. The brother of my brother-in-law once had a toilet that had become hopelessly clogged. What had happened was that his dog had put a chicken bone in the toilet, and then someone had flushed. The chicken bone had become lodged sideways in the trap. My brother-in-law's brother's solution was to take the toilet out into his back-yard and ask my wife, who had the smallest hands among those present, to reach in from underneath and pull it out. Surprisingly, she did this.

Sometimes the blockage is farther down the line. A couple of years ago, all the toilets and drains in my house became sluggish over the course of about a week. When any of these toilets was flushed, the drain in the sink of the first-floor bathroom would make a gurgling noise. This is the sort of hellish symptom that causes many people to contemplate putting their house on the market. But quiet reflection indicated that the range of possible problems was fairly small. The fact that all the toilets and drains were affected meant that the problem could not be a blockage in any one of them. It also suggested that the problem had to lie somewhere *below* the last fixture on the line—that is, it had to lie somewhere between the first-floor toilet and the septic tank. It was also possible that the trouble lay in the vent, but this seemed unlikely.

Checking the most accessible possible trouble spot first, I opened the inlet cover on my septic tank, which is under my patio. The inlet cover is hidden by a large, decorative stone, which I removed. Sure enough, the mouth of the drainpipe feeding into the tank was clogged with a huge mass of what appeared to be mainly toilet paper. A few jabs with the longest pry bar I could find and, presto, a torrent of waste was released. This immediately eliminated all the symptoms noted earlier.

If my poking around in my septic tank had not solved the problem, I would have turned over the investigation to a plumber. Very possibly the plumber would have begun at the septic tank as well, by feeding a long metal cable (known as an auger) into the sewer line and twisting it around, probably with the aid of an electric motor. Some augers are fitted with a sharp, propellerlike cutting head that can chew through tree roots (which can work their way through joints and cracks in sewer lines) and other solid obstructions. Other augers have less fearsome heads that look more like uncoiled springs. The plumber might also have fed the auger into the main drain's cleanout valve (which is in my basement) or through the drain beneath the first-floor toilet.

My wife, my children, and I spend part of each summer with several other families at an old farm on Martha's Vineyard, in Massachusetts. The plumbing at this place is quite rustic. Roughly every other summer the main drain becomes clogged. One year we were able to clean it out by removing a toilet and feeding a rented auger into the floor drain. Two years later the line clogged again, and, with the memory of that auger still fresh in our minds, we called a plumber.

The plumbing system at the place on Martha's Vineyard feeds into a vast hundred-year-old brick cesspool. Some water seeps out between the bricks, but for the most part that cesspool is like a great big bucket in the ground that stores waste until someone comes with a big truck and pumps it out. My septic tank, in contrast, is part of an ingenious waste-processing system in which tiny organisms break down wastes naturally, permitting relatively clean water to be returned to the ground. While a cesspool is a mostly closed container, a septic tank has an outlet that feeds treated water into a network of perforated drainage pipes known as a leaching field or seepage field.

Septic-tank purists often claim that a septic tank can be maintained in such a way that it will never need servicing. This isn't true. Even a perfectly functioning tank develops a layer of irreducible sludge that has to be removed periodically. Furthermore, bleach, cleansers, caustic chemical drain cleaners, and other household poisons can decimate the crud-digesting flora in the tank, reducing its effectiveness at processing waste. Almost any tank should be pumped out every year or two. Doing

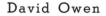

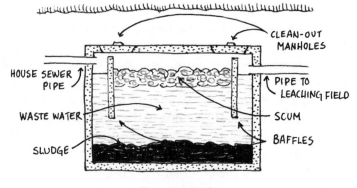

Septic tank

this greatly reduces the possibility that solid wastes will over-flow into the seepage field, clogging the perforations in the drainage pipes and necessitating a monstrously expensive exca-vation and reconstruction.

The motto of the man who pumps my septic tank is "It may be waste to you, but it's my bread and butter." When he pumps a tank he crouches over the opening, gazes down into the cham-ber, and guides his big green suction hose into promising sec-tors. He has a shovel with a ten-foot-handle which he uses to stir up sludge. When he moves the hose, it sometimes makes a hor-rific slurping sound and jerks sideways, like an angry python. While he works, he comments critically on what he sees. ("Don't you people ever do anything except go to the bathroom?") No man is a hero in the eyes of his septic-tank pumper. To prove that I am not squeamish, I stand near him and ask him about the septic arrangements of various people I know. I have some friends who share a septic tank with the Episcopal Church on the village green. I have some other friends whose sewage trav-els through crumbling old pipes down a long hill to the waste-treatment system of a local school. The last time he came to my house I asked him whether the inside of my tank looked the way it was supposed to. "Yup," he said, "only more so." As we talk I often wonder what I would do if the man were suddenly to fall into my tank, as he frequently appears to be in danger of doing. "Don't worry!" I would probably shout. "I'll run inside and call your wife!"

MORE TROUBLE

The principal bathroom in my house is the one on the second floor. Like the fancy bathrooms in rich people's houses, it is very big (it used to be a good-sized bedroom). Unlike rich people's bathrooms, however, it has ugly, upside-down wallpaper and light-blue fake-tile vinyl-sheet flooring that usually reminds people of *The Flintstones.* It also has (in addition to a tub, a toilet, and a double sink) a couch, a bookcase, a broken refrigerator without a door (in which we store extra towels, books, magazines, toilet paper, and toys), a table next to the toilet (for current periodicals), and a whatnot shelf that used to belong to my grandmother. We put all these items in there either because we felt bad about sending them to the dump (the refrigerator*) or because they weren't nice enough to go in any other room (everything else).

Houses often seem to deteriorate from the bathrooms out. This is not surprising. A bathroom's function is to move water, and water is the primary agent of ruin for most building materials. It promotes rot, loosens tiles, corrodes nails, softens adhesives, and destroys paint. In sum, it dissolves money. A neglected bathroom can metastasize far into a house, carrying destruction with it.

Our Flintstones bathroom is nearing the terminal stage of its disintegration. Tiles are falling off the sides of the tub enclosure.

---

*The coolant used in virtually all refrigerators (not to mention air conditioners) is Freon, a trade name for any of several gaseous compounds of chlorine, fluorine, and other substances. These compounds are among the notorious chlorofluorocarbons that are playing a major role in the ruination of the earth's atmosphere. The Freon in a refrigerator usually remains inside the refrigerator until the refrigerator is pitched onto a landfill and crushed by other junk. One way to prevent this from happening is to have the Freon removed before the fridge is junked, but this is expensive and is seldom done. Still, one can indefinitely postpone the impact (and ease the strain on the landfill) by putting an old refrigerator to work doing something else, such as holding towels and toilet paper. Eventually I will move our bathroom refrigerator into either the basement or the garage, where I will use it as a storage cabinet for junk. (In some areas, utilities offer free pick-up service for old refrigerators. Some offer bonuses or discounts on new equipment.)

Only one of the two sinks works. Wood trim near the tub is rotting. The ceiling is splotched with mildew. The vinyl sheet flooring is coming loose. Setting foot in this room would fill me with shame if my wife and I were not planning to transform it soon into two entirely new (and normal-sized) bathrooms, one for us and one for our kids.

The most alarmingly deteriorated surfaces in this bathroom are the tiled walls that enclose the combination shower and bathtub. About a dozen large tiles just below the built-in soap holder have come loose and are now held in place by long strips of duct tape, which I applied over a broad area in overlapping layers, like clapboards. Duct tape is a phenomenally versatile and durable material; my patch has already held up for several months. But of course what these tiles really need is major surgery.

The source of my tiles' predicament is, naturally, water from the shower and the bath. This water worked its way behind the tiles and destroyed the surface to which they had been applied. The water entered along two routes. First, it penetrated small cracks and crumbly areas in the grout between tiles. I could have prevented this by keeping a watchful eye on the grout lines and by sealing them periodically with a silicone-based grout sealer. Second, the water worked its way up through the joint between the rim of the tub and the bottom row of tiles. A joint like this is hard to seal well, because it can open and close as the tub is filled and emptied and as people climb in and out. A joint in this location should be caulked rather than simply grouted, because a properly applied bead of caulk will stretch and contract as the tub moves. Even if the caulk is applied carefully, though, this joint requires scrupulous maintenance. Several manufacturers make an adhesive-backed vinyl tape that is meant to be used to seal this joint, but my experience with these products has been that they don't last very long.

The problems in my tub enclosure are compounded by the fact that the tiles were applied to ordinary gypsum wallboard, which deteriorates when exposed to water. Even so-called water-resistant wallboard—which contains asphalt and other moisture-antagonistic additives and which is easily identified by its green facing paper—falls apart if it is allowed to become truly wet. Many builders use water-resistant wallboard as a backing for tiles, and it does a pretty good job (except on ceilings, where it is too brittle to be used, with or without tiles). But a far better choice is cement backer board, a relatively new product that usually consists of portland cement mixed with a light weight filler and reinforced with fiberglass mesh. USG's cement board is called Durock; National Gypsum's is called Wonder Board. At trade shows, both manufacturers demonstrate the virtues of these products by sticking samples in tubs of water and leaving them there for days and days. They don't deteriorate, become soggy, swell, or fall apart. The panels are smaller, harder, and denser than regular wallboard panels, but they are installed in pretty much the same way and can be managed easily by amateurs.

Some builders (especially on the West Coast) prefer to install virtually all tiles over inch-thick beds of cement-based mortar. Tile installations like this are known as "mud jobs." The floors in my laundry room and first-floor bathroom are mud jobs that probably date from the 1940s or 1950s. A good mud job provides a terrific base for tiles. It's essentially waterproof, and it can last virtually forever. But cement boards work almost as well in most applications and require substantially less labor. Besides, bathrooms are the most frequently remodeled rooms in many houses. There's not much point in building a room for the eons if you or someone else is going to strip it to the studs in a decade. (Of course, if your house is built on a concrete slab rather than over a basement, you can lay your floor tiles right on the slab.)

One way to avoid the maintenance requirements of tile is to buy a tub or shower with an integral enclosure. These units, which have no seams and are typically molded from fiberglass-reinforced plastic, can usually be used only in new construction: they're so big that they can't be squeezed through windows or doorways. But it's possible to get many of their benefits by buying modular enclosures that are assembled from three or four big pieces. You still have joints to worry about, but you don't have as many. Of course, plastic and fiberglass don't have the reassuring heft of cast iron and concrete. But they have a lot of compensating advantages.

In bathrooms (and other rooms) where tile is used, it's important to make sure that the framing is stiff enough to support it. The problem is not the weight of the tile but rather its inflexibility: rigid tiles don't stay put when they're laid on springy surfaces. This difficulty is most often encountered in very old construction (where framing members are likely to have been weakened by age and decay) and in very new construction (where the builders may have trimmed costs by using the widest permissible spacings for joists and the thinnest permissible underlayments). The previous owners of my house put slate tiles on the floor of the kitchen. The tiles look okay, but the floor in this room is so bouncy that the windows sometimes rattle when the dog walks through. As a result of all that movement, many of the grouted joints have deteriorated, and some of the tiles are loose. The floor should have been beefed up before any sort of covering was put down.

Another important source of bathroom-plumbing trouble is the toilet. Like all machines with moving parts, toilets require periodic maintenance. Fortunately, the inner workings of most toilets are less mysterious than they seem. When a toilet begins to misbehave, the problem can usually be eliminated with a fairly simple repair. When my wife and I moved into our house, for example, the tanks of two of the toilets took many minutes to refill after flushing. A properly functioning toilet should refill its tank in sixty to ninety seconds. I was able to eliminate the problem by replacing a small washerlike gizmo that controls the flow of water into the tank. I arrived at this solution by removing the lid of the tank and poking around inside for ten or fifteen minutes while I repeatedly flushed. I didn't know anything about toilets when I began; by the time I finished, I knew everything I needed to know about mine. If my repair had not worked, I would have been able to replace the guts of the tank with an off-the-shelf assembly from my hardware store or from a plumbing supply store, another project that is well within the reach of an amateur.

People often think that toilet tanks are leaking when in fact they are merely sweating. What happens is that the water in the tank cools the tank's vitreous-china shell, creating a cold surface on which water vapor from the air will condense. Droplets form and run down the sides of the tank, creating puddles on the floor. In humid climates these puddles can be quite large. The water can work its way into the floor, loosening tiles and promoting decay in the subfloor and the framing.

There are several ways to cure this problem. The most foolproof is to buy a toilet with an insulated tank. The outer surface of an insulated tank remains at roughly the same temperature as the air in the room, eliminating the possibility of condensation. A somewhat trickier and less satisfactory solution is to line the tank of an existing toilet with half-inch-thick foam, such as carpet padding. This is hard to do well, however. The foam doesn't want to stay put, and minerals in the water can turn it grungy and horrible in a short time. Still another solution is to have a plumber add a hot-water feed to the cold-water line that supplies the toilet. This warms the water in the tank, eliminating the cold outer surface and thus the condensation. But anyone willing to do something this drastic and expensive would be better off simply buying a new toilet.

Toilet buying used to be very simple: almost all toilets were almost exactly the same. Now it's complicated. The most obvious differences among toilets are the cosmetic ones: toilets are available today in a vast range of colors, shapes, and styles. Even more important are differences that have to do with the capacity of the tank and the volume of water it discharges while flushing. Older toilets often discharge eight gallons or more with every flush. (According to *Garbage* magazine, the average American uses nine thousand gallons of pure water each year to flush away just 130 gallons of feces and urine.) Some new toilets get by with less than a gallon.

Low-flush technology is still being refined, but it has already advanced to the point where one can (and, in some places, must) buy a good, effective toilet that uses just a gallon and a half or so per flush. All such toilets have special features or mechanisms that enable them to squeeze more work from less water. In doing so they can pay for themselves rapidly, in the form of lower water bills (or of reduced strain on a well pump). In a very few years, all new toilets will be of this type.

Replacing an old toilet is relatively easy. Most toilets are simply bolted to a fitting, called a floor flange or a closet flange, that is attached to the top of the floor drain. You close the valve in the water supply line that feeds the tank, drain the tank and bowl by flushing, disconnect the supply line from the tank, and remove the nuts from the bolts. (These nuts are usually concealed beneath decorative caps that can be popped off with a putty knife.) You and a helper can then lift the toilet off the bolts. You should then stuff a wad of newspaper or an old rag into the floor drain, to keep sewer gases from escaping and to keep your glasses from falling in. The guide books always advise removing the tank from the bowl (if the toilet is a two-piece model) before doing any of this, but nobody I've ever watched has bothered. Once you have separated your toilet from the floor, you can put it either in your front-hall closet (as a friend of mine did while he renovated his first-floor bathroom) or in your yard, right next to the back door (as I did while I renovated my first-floor bathroom).

BATHROOM LUNACY

In building houses as in conducting funerals, the profit is in the options. The major cost difference between an expensive house and an inexpensive one is not usually in the framing. It's in the accessories. There's only so much you can do to boost the price tag on a bedroom. But a bathroom (like a kitchen) can be accessorized up to and beyond the point where the client has to go back to the bank to borrow more money. Marble tiles instead of ceramic, bronze faucets instead of chrome, gold-flecked toilets instead of plain, separate tub and shower instead of a shower-equipped tub to do the work of both. The transformation of the bathroom took place in part because manufacturers and builders at some point realized that there was virtually no limit to how much a bathroom could be made to cost. In the funeral business, inflating the final bill in this way is known as "loading the casket."

Articles in decorating magazines make bathrooms sound less

like the places where kings go alone than like Club Med. The modern bathroom, as these magazines describe it, is a "leisure environment" where one can go to become oneself again after a hellish day at the office—a sort of warm, walk-in martini. Master bathrooms in high-end construction not infrequently contain exercise equipment, television sets, sound systems, and other items that people have not always associated with bathrooms. A couple of years ago the magazine *Practical Homeowner* ran pictures of a glass-roofed bathroom that included—in addition to a toilet, a bidet, two sinks, a shower, a bathtub, a linen closet, and two dressing rooms—a private "courtyard" with a hot tub and a place for a guest to sit. "Implicit in the design was the belief that here you can experience nature in privacy, even in reverence," according to the architect who designed it.

At around the same time, an article in the "Home" supplement of the *New York Times Magazine* mentioned a couple in Tenafly, New Jersey, who had just added a new bathroom to their house. This bathroom, according to the *Times,* had lots of marble, "several" sinks, a bathroom-sized shower that was also a steam room, and a two-person whirlpool bathtub, among many other things. A big color picture ran with the story. The bathtub had padded headrests. In one of the marble walls was a marble-lined niche containing a vase. The cost of the bathroom was $300,000.

Twenty-five years ago, people with a third of a million dollars to spend on remodeling wouldn't have spent it on plumbing fixtures. Now, though, luxury bathroom upgrades are near the top of remodeling wish lists. (I once saw an ad in the *Times* for a restored eighteenth-century tavern whose "period details throughout" included not only "exposed hand-hewn beams, wide pine floors, and 8 Rumford fireplaces," but also a "huge master suite w/Jacuzzi and steam room in marble bathroom.") Not many bathrooms are in the multi-hundred-thousand-dollar league, of course. But there are enough at all levels to add up to seven billion dollars' worth of bathroom remodeling every year.

As bathrooms have gotten fancier, they've also gotten bigger. As they have, the size of secondary bedrooms shrank somewhat.

(That extra square footage had to come from somewhere.) In the floor plans of many new houses, the children's bedrooms seem almost like an afterthought. Very often they have been trimmed, sometimes severely, to make room for the hot tub and the bidet. This trade-off—the comfort of one's children for the comfort of oneself while brushing one's teeth—might not have made much sense to an earlier generation. But it is one of the unstated themes of the big-bathroom revolution.

One mistake that architects sometimes make in designing big bathrooms is to design the storage space on the same scale as the bathroom itself—say, a large, pantry-style closet, or a big bank of built-in drawers. The problem with this is that virtually everything stored in a bathroom is teeny: bottles of aspirin, disposable razors, things of dental floss, tampons, rolls of toilet paper, and innumerable other items that can be held in one hand. And yet bathroom storage is usually designed on an entirely different scale. In my own large bathroom, there is a closet with twenty-four-inch-deep shelves and a vanity with two deep cabinets. Putting things away in any of these storage areas is practically the same as throwing them away, because no one can ever find them again. What we really need is lots of tiny drawers, or an entire wall covered with shelves just a few inches deep. Even a small bathroom has space for this kind of storage. (How about a floor-to-ceiling bank of six-inch-deep shelves on the wall behind the door?) The stuff people keep in their bathrooms is smaller than the stuff they keep in other parts of their houses, and it calls for different kinds of storage.

The main point to remember in designing a bathroom is to keep things in perspective. People spend an appallingly large chunk of their lives in bathrooms as it is (seven years, according to one estimate). We should be trying to think of ways to reduce the size of that chunk, not increase it.

Chapter 9

Building Stuff

Shortly after I graduated from college, I worked as a fact checker for a magazine in New York. The job involved calling people on the telephone and asking them whether it was true that, as the magazine was about to claim, they had recently had cosmetic surgery and stolen money from nuns. After about six months of this I decided that I had had enough of facts, and I quit to become a free-lance writer.

My work as a free-lance writer was not, initially, very demanding. During the first few months it consisted mainly of smoking cigarettes and reading the newspaper while eating candy and listening to records. Still, I needed a place to sit while I was doing this. I staked out a corner of our apartment's dining room and furnished it with a small bookcase, the typewriter on which I had pushed forward the frontiers of scholarship in college, a wobbly typewriter table, and one of those lamps that clamp onto things.

As the months and years went by, my job as a free-lance writer began to involve actual writing, and my little office grew.

I bought a computer, a bigger bookcase, a file cabinet, some other items. I bought a new telephone and a little table on which to place it. For several years there was a large plant—the only houseplant my wife and I had ever owned—whose small pot I kept inside an enormous copper bowl. Then my daughter was born. My wife and I walled off our dining room and turned it into a bedroom, and I moved my office into a corner of the living room, which was now also the dining room. Our apartment began to seem a little like a yacht, in the sense that if you wanted to go from one part of it to another you had to shuffle sideways.

Then we moved to our house and I was able to claim an entire room for my writing. This was an improvement, but not as much of one as I had hoped. Although I now had my own room, I felt imprisoned by the dinky, pathetic stuff that constituted my office equipment. My desk, for example, consisted of three tables that I had pushed together. The tables were of different heights. If I tried to lay an open book across the faultlike junction of two of these tables, the book would snap shut, and, often, various papers would slide to the floor.

In the evenings, while watching MTV and consuming an alcoholic beverage, I would sometimes slip into a reverie in which I would draw page after page of floor plans for the *real* office that I hoped to have one day. As I drew these plans I would be transported in my mind back to the fifth grade, when my twin ambitions were to become an architect and to understand human reproduction. Now, as a technically grown man, I felt that I had finally found an opportunity to achieve, in a limited way, the less elusive of these goals.

The location I had chosen for my office was a former bedroom on the third floor of my house. It measured roughly thirteen feet by seventeen feet, including a closet that ran the width of the room along one end. On graph paper I had bought at the dime store, I drew a rectangle and made it the frame for my ideas.

By the time I began to draw my plans, I had been a free-lance writer for about eight years—long enough to have developed a pretty clear idea of how I liked to work. I wanted my new office to be exactly suited to my habits. For example, I wanted it to have lots and lots of bookcases and cabinets. I wanted it to have a large, wraparound desk and plenty of room for spreading things around. I wanted the desk to be positioned so that while sitting at it I would be able to look through the window and see if there were any delivery trucks in the driveway. (Wondering whether there are any delivery trucks in the driveway is one thing I seem to do quite a bit of during the day.) I wanted there to be a television set that I would be able to watch from anywhere in the room and whose channels I would be able to change with a flick of a remote control kept ever within my reach.

There were also a lot of features that I couldn't make up my mind about. M&M dispenser in the wall? Desk chair that would recline into a bed (for naps)? Secret chamber in which to hide innocent victims from their persecutors? A refrigerator? I toyed with these and other ideas but eventually left them out. Designing, in the end, is a process of elimination. Here is what my final plan looked like:

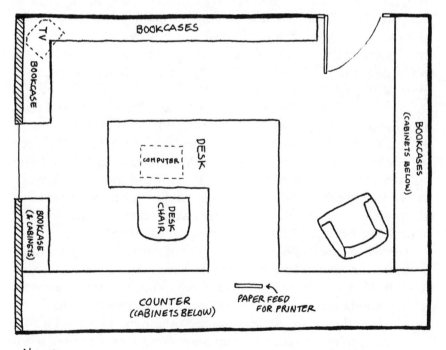

Office floor plan

245

Running the entire length of the eastern wall would be a bank of five low storage cabinets with a countertop above. This countertop would be continuous with the top of the built-in L-shaped desk, creating a wraparound work surface on which I would be able to spread out papers and junk. It would also give me a place to put my photocopier, computer printer, bowling trophies, military decorations, photographs of world leaders, and so on. The closet, which had formerly occupied the northern end of the room, would be eliminated. In its place would be a bank of cabinets with a bank of bookcases above. On the south and west walls would be floor-to-ceiling bookcases. If, while sitting at my desk, I suddenly wondered how to conjugate an irregular French verb, I would need only to thrust my hand to the left and pluck the appropriate reference work from its shelf. The television would sit on the top shelf of the bookcase in the west corner of the south wall. The power supply and cable connection for this television would be wired right inside the cabinet, so that no cords or cables would be visible. In the northeast corner of the room would be a sort of nook where I would be able to sit in a comfortable armchair and engage in the quiet reflection and open-ended television-watching that are such an important part of what I do for a living.

All of a sudden one evening, while watching MTV and consuming an alcoholic beverage, I realized that the time had come for me to stop dreaming and begin building. It was already after ten o'clock, but I figured that I would be able to put in an hour or two before going to bed. Tingling with enthusiasm, I went down into the basement and filled two heavy canvas bags with drop cloths, pry bars, power saws, screwdrivers, chisels, and hammers. I dragged all this stuff up to the third floor.

The room I had chosen for my new office had some furniture in it. Removing the furniture would have taken a lot of time, so I left it. Also to save time, I decided not to remove some recently dry-cleaned clothes that were hanging in the closet. I did, however, close the closet door. I dumped the drop cloths in a pile and began to use a hammer and a pry bar to strip plaster from the outside of the closet wall. I had to do this quietly, because my children were sleeping one floor below. Also, this is the sort of thing that drives my wife out of her mind. All things considered, it would have been smarter to wait until the next day to start working. But I felt that I could wait no longer. My moment had arrived, and I was ready to begin.

The room in which I had decided to build my office is directly under the roof. Roughly three-quarters of the ceiling is flat (and low). The rest of it slants down sharply to a three-foot knee wall that runs the length of the room along the eastern side. This slanting part of the ceiling was in terrible shape (the plaster was cracked and sagging, and a large section was simply missing where a dormer had been removed), so I decided to strip it right down (up?) to the rafters. The knee wall was also in terrible shape, so I decided to strip it, too. For that matter, all the walls were in terrible shape. I decided to strip them as well. Doing all this would allow me to build nice new fresh walls. It would also allow me to install some insulation, a material that at the time was quite a novelty in my house.

Ripping out old plaster, like destroying anything, is a lot of fun, but it is almost unbelievably messy. First, there is the dust. Second, there is the plaster itself. Breaking plaster into pieces somehow causes it to swell to many times its original volume, so that the rubble from a single room can more than fill an entire house. Because I didn't have a dump truck or a dumpster, I had to remove all this rubble by hand, in garbage bags. Doing this involved making dozens and dozens of trips up and down two flights of stairs. On my way down, the bags would leak a Hansel-and-Gretelish trail of lime and sand. On my way back up, I would grind this abrasive spoor into the steps. As I lugged those heavy bags I imagined that my chest and forearms were being transformed into sinuous steel. But when I checked the mirror later I realized that, no, they were still made of the same pale flab.

In addition to all the plaster, I also had to remove the wood lath, the thick oak studs from the demolished closet partition, a lot of junky baseboards and trim pieces, and half a dozen floorboards from the closet, whose floor was inexplicably in terrible shape. I threw all this stuff out the window and onto the snow-covered lawn below, where it looked like debris from an

247

airplane crash. I left it there until spring. Then I salvaged the oak studs for some still unspecified future project and dragged everything else into the garage, where I broke it into pieces small enough for the garbage man to haul away in several installments over the next few weeks in exchange for twenty-dollar bills.

When the last garbage bag was out the door, I swept and vacuumed everything several times. Then I filled in the hole in the floor with plywood (the finished office would be carpeted), insulated the walls and the slanted part of the ceiling, installed a polyethylene vapor retarder, and enclosed the walls with gypsum wallboard. I also used my wallboard screwgun to screw down all the floorboards, which were laid directly over the joists without an intervening subfloor and which were somewhat bouncy and squeaky. These floorboards were not old and they were nothing special to look at. Peppering them with wallboard screws tightened up the floor considerably and eliminated all the squeaks. It was also a lot of fun. When I was finished, the room was a big, clean, empty box in which I would be able to give form to my vision of the perfect work space. This, at any rate, was my plan.

PLYWOOD BOXES

At the time I began work on my new office, I had never built a bookcase or a cabinet. In fact, I had never built much of anything. But I had watched other people build things, and I figured I just about had it licked. A couple of years before, my wife and I had hired some carpenters to turn an ugly old den into a nice sitting room, which we now call the library. This room had originally had red-and-white wallpaper, a wall covered with fake brick, an uneven ceiling, a couple of crummy built-in bookcases, a tacked-on closet that poked out into the adjoining living room, and some drafty, superfluous French doors that opened into the yard. When the carpenters were finished with it, the room had new windows, no French doors, no closet, a new ceiling, a grand new doorway that opened into the living room, handsome built-in bookcases on three walls, and old-looking raised paneling on the fourth wall. This room is now pretty much my favorite thing about our house, and my wife and I spend a lot of time in it.

While the carpenters worked, I hung around and bothered them. One of the things that interested me most was the way they built the bookcases and cabinets. Instead of constructing them in place, as I had naively figured they would do, they did all the rough work in their shop. They built individual bookcase-sized boxes out of plywood and brought them over in the back of their truck. They positioned these boxes around the perimeter of the room, made certain that they were level and plumb, and anchored them in place. Then they covered all the gaps and exposed edges with trim pieces—the so-called face frame—and moldings. These trim pieces and moldings tied all the boxes into a single unit and disguised the fact that they were boxes. (For an explanation of face-frame cabinetry, see Chapter Eight.)

Most of the built-in bookcases and cabinets in most people's houses are built in the same way. They begin as simple plywood boxes, and then other stuff is applied. The parts one sees from the outside are essentially a façade attached to the raw edges of the boxes underneath. No problem!

As a sort of dry run for the cabinetry in my office, I decided to build a small freestanding cabinet for the aquarium in our playroom. Buying this aquarium had been a big mistake on my part. As it turns out, my children and my wife are not interested in looking at small, colorful fish, and I am not interested in cleaning their tank. Still, the aquarium existed, and it needed to sit on something high so that the dog would stop sticking its nose into the water and jumping backward in astonishment.

I decided to make the cabinet roughly two feet tall, two feet deep, and two and a half feet wide, since these would be the approximate dimensions of the boxes from which I would make cabinets in my office. In the middle of the cabinet I decided to place a single fixed shelf on which to store aquarium-maintenance supplies, including the little net that I would use, in the coming months or years, to carry a succession of limp fish to the

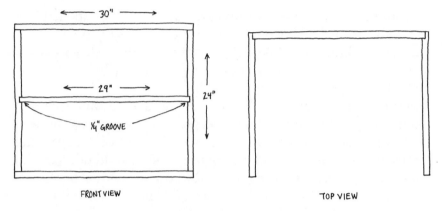

FRONT VIEW   TOP VIEW

Basic cabinet construction

toilet. Clipping a tape measure to my belt—the sign of a serious lumber customer—I went to the lumberyard and bought a sheet of three-quarter-inch A-B plywood. If I had been making a truly serious piece of furniture, I would have used a cabinet-grade hardwood plywood, but I was just fooling around. I had the lumberyard guy rip the panel right down the middle on a big panel-cutting saw that the lumberyard has for this purpose. (Cuts made parallel to the grain of a piece of wood are called rip cuts; cuts made across the grain are called cross cuts. The grain of a sheet of plywood, which is the grain of its face and back plies, runs the length of the sheet.) Doing this turned the four-foot-by-eight-foot sheet of plywood into two two-foot-by-eight-foot sheets of plywood. This made the plywood easier to transport and saved me some cutting later.

If there's anything I love, it's driving around with a load of lumber lashed to the top of my car. So I drove around for a while, waving to people I knew, and then went home and lugged my plywood into the basement. From one of my half-sheets I cut off two thirty-inch pieces (for the top and the bottom) and a twenty-four-inch piece (for one side). From the other half-sheet I cut off two twenty-nine-inch pieces (for the fixed shelf and the back) and one twenty-four-inch piece (for the other side). Then I ripped an inch and a quarter off the fixed shelf, making it twenty-nine inches by twenty-two and three quarters.

If I had been a professional, I probably would have made all these cuts with a table saw, a stationary power tool that consists of a circular saw mounted blade up on the underside of a flat platform. Instead of moving the saw over the wood, you move the wood over the saw. But my table saw, which is designed to be portable, has a platform that is too teeny to handle large pieces of plywood. I once tried to trim a door on my table saw and very nearly destroyed both it and myself. So except for that final one-and-a-quarter-inch rip, which involved a relatively small piece of plywood, I made all my cuts with my hand-held circular saw.

The hand-held circular saw is probably the single most useful cutting tool in a modern carpenter's collection. People who write in handyman publications are always claiming that this or that tool is the single most useful tool in a carpenter's collection, but the circular saw really is. Without it you'd just about have to forget about plywood, because no one in his or her right mind would use plywood if the only way to cut it were by hand. You'd have to forget about a lot of other things, too.

The hand-held circular saw was invented in 1924 by a man named Edmond Michel, who founded the Michel Electric Handsaw Company later in the same year to manufacture and market his invention. The first model (called the Model E, for Edmond) cost $160 and was bought either by a Chicago contractor or by the owner of Atlantic City's boardwalk, depending on which history of hand-held circular sawing you choose to believe. Production was limited initially by the fact that the company had to sell one saw in order to buy the parts to make another.

Perhaps weary of subsistence manufacturing, Michel sold out, in 1926, to two of his original partners, who renamed the company Skilsaw, Inc. In time carpenters appropriated the company's name as a generic term for a circular saw made by any manufacturer—skillsaw. Today the company is known as Skil Corporation. Its second great product was the portable electric hedge trimmer, which it introduced in 1930, just in time for the Great Depression.

I have two skillsaws, neither of them made by Skil: a Black & Decker handyman model that cost thirty or forty dollars and a Makita professional model that cost about $125 from a discount tool dealer. The two look superficially similar, but the Makita outperforms the Black & Decker by a huge margin. One of the most telling differences between the two saws is their base plates—the flat, rectangular pads on which they ride while cutting. The Makita's base plate is made of heavy-gauge aluminum. Its edges are perfectly aligned and straight, which makes it easy to run the saw along a stationary guide. The Black & Decker's base plate, in contrast, is simply an open frame made of lightweight aluminum. The edges are rounded over, which makes them tend to ride up on a guide and throw the cut out of line. I now use my handyman saw only for doing things like cutting through plaster.

When I'm making anything other than a very rough cut with a skillsaw, I set up a guide. I have learned by experience that the time I spend doing this is never wasted in the long run. There are many kinds of cutting guides that can be used with a skillsaw—the simplest one is just a long, straight board—but the one I use most often was made by someone else. Unengagingly called a Clamp 'n Tool Guide, it is a long, straight metal bar with a sliding clamp at either end. I position the bar so that the distance between its edge and the line I wish to cut is exactly the same as the distance between the saw's blade and the edge of its base plate. When I make the cut, I keep the saw in line by pressing it gently but firmly against the bar. This is what I did to cut those pieces of plywood for my fish cabinet (as I now call it). The cuts came out very well, because I spent an agonizingly long time setting up the guide bar, checking my lines with a framing square, and generally being careful.

Useful though they are, hand-held circular saws are also extremely dangerous. In fact, they are responsible for most of the finger-lopping and leg-gashing that goes on in people's basements and garages. Some recent models have electronic blade brakes, which stop the blade almost immediately once the trigger is released. This is a valuable safety feature, and one worth paying extra for, although safety features don't protect people who don't pay attention to what they're doing. Besides, most of the finger-lopping that circular saws do takes place when the trigger is depressed.

BACK TO MY CABINET

When I had cut all my pieces of plywood, I used a tool called a router to cut a three-quarter-inch-wide slot across the middle of each side piece. When the cabinet was assembled, these slots (each of which was a quarter inch deep) would support the fixed shelf, which I would slide into them. Along the rear edge of each side, perpendicular, I cut a three-quarter-inch groove (called a rabbet). These slots would hold the back of the cabinet.

A router is a very versatile tool. It is basically a powerful electric motor with a cutting bit mounted in the bottom of it. It has an adjustable base that provides stability and enables the user to control cutting depth. Routers operate at very high speeds, usually more than twenty thousand revolutions per minute. (Electric drills, in contrast, typically have maximum operating speeds of between five hundred and a thousand revolutions per minute.) The tremendous speed of a router makes it both powerful and dangerous. It also gives it a high-pitched whine that is like the sound of no other hand-held power tool.

The function of a router is determined by the type of bit installed in it. Some bits are used to cut slots or grooves. Some are used to make straight cuts through wood or other materials. Some are used to create clean, crisp edges on pieces of wood.

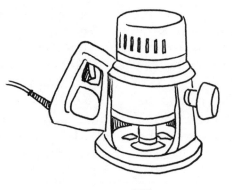

Router

Some are used to create a rounded, beveled, slotted, or sculpted edge. Some are even used to make tricky joints, such as dovetails. Many carpenters and woodworkers find routers to be so useful that they end up buying three or four.

Much of what I know about routers I learned at an all-day router workshop that my friends Rex and Ken and I attended at a crafts center a couple of hours away from where we live. We got up early and drove down together, eating breakfast at Burger King and having many powerful male-bonding experiences during the drive. Then we joined about a dozen other men who were also interested in playing with dangerous tools.

We didn't get down to routing right away. Our instructor, who was a professional cabinetmaker, said that his first concern was with safety, and he spent a half-hour or so imploring us to be careful. We had been told ahead of time to bring ear and eye protection, and all of us had done so. Now our instructor told us that we should never so much as think about using our routers without first making certain that our earplugs and safety goggles were in place. He showed us a special kind of earplug that he said we ought to buy. Woodworkers are as prone to hearing problems as rock stars are, he said. He told us horror stories about people who had been blinded by flying chips, or who had fed their fingers into razor-sharp router bits. He said that when he used a router or any other power tool, he always kept safety first and foremost in his mind.

Finally our routing lesson began. Our instructor described a few standard cuts and then turned on one of his routers to demonstrate. Before he did so, he did not put on his earplugs. He did not put on his safety goggles. To get a better view of what he was doing, he put his face a few inches away from the spinning bit, which was spewing out a blizzard of tiny wood chips. To keep the chips from streaming into his eyes, our instructor sort of squinted, turning his eyelashes into a protective screen. A router is a very loud tool. From where I was sitting, halfway across the room, the high-pitched whine of the motor made my brain area slightly uncomfortable. Still, I didn't put on my earplugs. Like everyone else in the room, I left them lying on the desk in front of me. Also like everyone else, I got out of my chair and moved closer to the whirring router, so that I could get a better view.

I don't think our instructor felt that he was a hypocrite for failing to practice what he had just preached with such passion. In our classroom (as in most people's workshops) safety was an idea to which we paid homage rather than a series of procedures that we actually carried out. We invoked the idea of safety, like a charm, before we turned on our tools. But actually wear our safety goggles? Forget it.

Needless to say, I didn't put on my safety goggles or my earplugs before I used my router to cut the slots for the fixed shelves in my fish cabinet. But I thought about wearing them, and I even spent a little time looking for my earplugs. Then, like most people in the same situation, I simply got down to work. The next time I use my router, though, I'm sure I'll be more careful.

When all my pieces of plywood were ready, I attached the two sides to the bottom with carpenter's glue and eight-penny finishing nails. (Glue is extremely useful in virtually all woodworking and finish-carpentry projects. It is actually stronger than nails, and it helps to keep pieces from wiggling loose later on.) Then I squirted glue into the slots and slid in the back and the fixed shelf. When they seemed about right I tacked them in place with a couple of small nails. Then I laid the top in place and fiddled with everything until all the edges matched up as they were supposed to. Then I nailed the top, the shelf, and the back into place. The slots not only supported the shelf and back but also enabled me to fudge a little in positioning the pieces. Because the slots were a quarter of an inch deep, I could adjust each part slightly without creating gaps. As a result, I ended up with tight seams everywhere, even though the pieces weren't perfect.

When the cabinet was assembled, I made a face frame for the front. This face frame consisted of pieces of one-by-two stock that I applied to the rough forward edges of the plywood sides, top, shelf, and bottom. The face frame gave the entire front of the cabinet a finished look. Because the cabinet was going to fit fairly snugly into a sort of alcove (and because I was really just practicing for the cabinets in my office), I didn't care very much about the appearance of the sides and not at all about the appearance of the back. I sanded the entire box, primed it, painted it a sort of old-fashioned red, and installed it in the playroom.

My fish cabinet is not something that I would care to take to one of those woodworking shows where people display the zebrawood-and-butternut piano they built last year in their garage. But the fish like it well enough, and building it gave me the confidence to continue. Over the next couple of weeks I built five rough cabinets that were pretty much exactly like it, except that their backs were made of half-inch plywood and they didn't have tops or face frames. These five boxes would eventually become the bank of built-in cabinets along the east wall of my new office.

A LEVEL FOUNDATION

People sometimes write letters to newspaper home-repair columns to ask if there is anything that can be done about floors that are not level. "The floor in my dining room seems to dip about a quarter-inch in the direction of the kitchen," these letters say. "What can be done to correct this terrible problem?" Letters like this always make me chuckle nervously, because there are floors in my house that are more steeply pitched than some roofs. In fact, there are several rooms where the difference in elevation between the high and low ends amounts to several inches. Drawing an accurate floor plan of one of these rooms would require the assistance of the United States Geological Survey.

The sagging of my house was arrested twenty years ago, when it was moved onto its new foundation. But the new foundation merely arrested the slump; it did not reverse it. In the room in which I built my office, the floor runs downhill from the southern wall, then rises slightly at the northern end. It also dips somewhat from east to west. The lowest point of the

floor is nearly three inches lower than the highest point. Building cabinets (or anything else) in a room like this is complicated, because there is no level surface to use as a base or even
as a reference point. Because I wanted all the working surfaces to lie on the same level plane, I would have to make
careful adjustments in the installation or construction of each
piece.*

To create a level foundation for the cabinets I had built in my
basement, I made a ladder-shaped supporting framework out of
two-by-fours laid on edge. This frame was about two feet wide
and slightly shorter than the room. It had runglike crosspieces
about every two feet. Setting the cabinets on top of it would raise
their height by the width of the two-by-fours—three and a half
inches. It would also bring them all into the same horizontal
plane, since I would be able to shim up the frame to create a
level base for the cabinets.

I anchored the supporting frame to the floor at the high end
of the room and then leveled it by using plywood and lumber
scraps to raise the other end about three inches. To align it I
used a fancy electronic tool called a SmartLevel. This gadget is
one of the most interesting new tools to come along in several
years. I first encountered it at the 1989 Builders' Show. Smart-
Level was one of the hits of that show. Orders for it ran so far
ahead of production that I had to wait many months for mine
to arrive. Now I keep it in my office, so that I can play with it
when I'm supposed to be working.

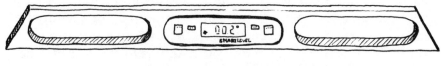

SmartLevel

*Leveling the floor itself—by installing a level plywood surface on top of
the existing floor—was not possible. The door into the room is at the
room's lowest point. Raising that end of the room to the altitude of the
highest point would have created a four- or five-inch step at the entrance,
and it would have reduced the height of the ceiling at that end to somewhat
less than the height of my head.

The heart of a SmartLevel is a battery-powered electronic sensor that detects the angle at which it is being held and conveys this information in any of four different modes on a liquid crystal display. In the first mode, SmartLevel's display projects an electronic imitation of the bubble in a traditional spirit level. (Spirit levels are called spirit levels, incidentally, because the liquid in their bubble vials is alcohol, which is used because it has a lower freezing point than water.) In the second mode, SmartLevel provides a reading in degrees. In the third mode, SmartLevel gives "percent of slope" readings, making it possible, for example, to determine at a glance that one's driveway has a 9.2 percent grade. In the fourth mode, SmartLevel gives its readings in the roofer's traditional rise-and-run form.

SmartLevel has several other intriguing features. The sensor module can be inserted into any of three different rails (measuring two feet, four feet, and six feet); it can also be used alone, as the equivalent of a torpedo level. If I turn my SmartLevel upside down (in order to check the levelness of a ceiling, for example) the electronic display inverts, so that the numbers remain right side up. If I drop my SmartLevel out a window, I can recalibrate it in a few seconds. All I have to do is set it on any surface, press the reset button, turn the SmartLevel 180 degrees, and press the reset button again. The electronic sensor averages the two readings to reestablish its sense of zero degrees.

A SmartLevel is as accurate as most spirit levels, and it's easier to read. I can tell at a glance, for example, that one side of the jamb of my office door is out of plumb by one tenth of a degree. (Carpenters who can't stomach this sort of precision can set their SmartLevels to round off readings to the nearest one-fifth or one-half degree.) A SmartLevel makes it easy to achieve the proper slope in a drainpipe or a gutter. There are a number of landscaping, masonry, and carpentry jobs where it can do the work of a transit.

The best thing about the SmartLevel is that it eradicates level anxiety. This is the mild but gnawing fear that one's spirit level is slightly out of whack. Virtually everyone I know who owns a level feels this fear. With a SmartLevel, you can check. I had always worried that my three-foot aluminum spirit level was a tiny bit off. How else to explain the slightly crooked wobbliness of everything I build? But then I checked it with my SmartLevel and found that it was fine. My SmartLevel gave me the confidence to trust my spirit level, while simultaneously making it obsolete.

When the supporting frame for my cabinets was level in all directions, I inserted more plywood scraps and other shims at intermediate points. Then I anchored the whole thing securely to the floor by using wallboard screws, plywood scraps, and metal framing angles, which I attached, with screws, to both the frame and the floor. Since the entire frame was going to be invisible in the finished office, I didn't care what it looked like. I just wanted to be sure that it was level and sturdy. When I was finished with it, it was.

There was a gap of several inches between the back of the supporting frame and the east wall. I used this gap to conceal some telephone wire that I wanted to run from one end of the room to the other. I also stuffed in a signed copy of one of my books. Then I brought up my cabinet boxes from the basement and arranged them on top of the frame. Since all of these boxes were slightly out of square in one direction or another, I had to fiddle with them a little to get them properly aligned. I didn't have to be perfectly exact, because I knew that the face frame and countertop (both of which I would build later) would conceal small errors and draw everything together. When all the boxes were as good as I could get them, I used wallboard screws to fasten them to one another and to the supporting frame underneath. Because doing this was fun I used way too many screws. Before painting I covered the heads of the screws (which I had countersunk) with spackling compound, so that now they cannot be seen.

One thing I like to do when I am building something is to spend a lot of time staring dreamily at whatever I have done so far. There is almost no limit to the amount of time that I am able to spend doing this. I feel pretty much the same way about reading and rereading things that I have written. My own handiwork! So after I had secured my five cabinet boxes to their supporting frame, I spent a lot of time gazing at them from various angles. The time I spent doing this was in addition to the time I had already spent doing essentially the same thing when the boxes were still in the basement.

During spare hours over the next couple of weeks, I built boxes for the other cabinets and for the bookcases. Some of these I built in the basement. Some of them (the larger ones) I built on the third floor. These boxes weren't the same size as the boxes I had built first, but I built them all in pretty much the same way. The main difference in terms of construction was that the bookcases were designed to have adjustable shelves.

To make all the measurements I needed in the construction of my plywood boxes, I used homemade measuring tools that carpenters call story poles. I made my story poles from six-foot-long pieces of one-by-two pine whose ends I had squared off. I made one for each size of box. Using a measuring tape and a pencil, I made marks on the pole representing all the dimensions that would come into play in constructing each type of box. For example, the boxes from which I would make the bookcases on the north wall were going to be eleven and a half inches deep, so I drew a line across one side of the pole eleven and a half inches from the bottom. (To keep the line perfectly straight, I used a handy tool called a combination square.) I labeled this line *depth.* Those same boxes would all be twenty-eight inches wide, so I drew another line twenty-eight inches from the bottom and labeled it *width.* I then made marks for all the other dimensions I would need, such as the height of the boxes, the length and width of the shelves, and so on.

When I laid out a new piece or set up a cut, I didn't need to consult my measuring tape or my sketches of the various components. I simply transferred the dimensions directly from the story pole. Each time I set up a router cut, for example, the story pole told me exactly where I should place the Clamp 'n Tool Guide. Using the story pole kept me from making careless measurement errors, because I didn't have to remember any numbers and I didn't run the risk of misreading the measuring tape, as often happens. I just looked for the appropriate mark on the pole and transferred it directly to the wood.

When all the rough cabinets and bookcases were in place, I built the desk. I could have built this as a separate unit, the way I had built the cabinets and bookcases, but because of the slope of the floor I decided that it would be easier to build it in place. I first made a skeleton for it out of two-by-fours. This skeleton looked just like the frame of a tiny house, with the equivalent of studs, plates, joists, and so on. The bottom of this skeleton was attached to the floor; one side was attached directly to the inside of the middle cabinet on the east wall. The only tricky part was keeping the sides plumb and the top of the frame perfectly level (and on the same plane as the tops of the cabinets to which it was connected) despite the fact the floor beneath it sloped visibly to the north. But with the help of my SmartLevel I managed to do this. When the skeleton was finished, I sheathed its tops and sides (except for the two bays where I would stick my legs) with half-inch plywood. I did the same thing to the tops of the cabinets on the east wall. The plywood sides of the desk would eventually be turned into decorative paneling. The plywood on the tops of the desk and cabinets would be covered with hardwood plywood, which I would stain.

The rough construction in my office was now completed. The bookcases, cabinets, and desk, though still crude, were all in place. All I needed to do now was to cover all the ugly or uneven surfaces with materials that were attractive and even. In other words, I had to hide almost everything that I had done up until now.

FACE FRAMES

The next thing I did was build face frames for all the rough cabinets and bookcases. Professional cabinetmakers will often build an entire face frame as a single unit, but I think it's easier and less frustrating to build it in place, piece by piece.

David Owen

This is what I did. I started with the two cabinets on the north end of the east wall (the ones immediately opposite the door, between the bookcases on the north wall and the desk), and I worked from the bottom up. The bottoms of those two cabinets were resting on a level frame that raised them about six and a half inches off the floor on the downhill side and six inches on the uphill side. To cover the entire gap between the floor and the bottom of the cabinets, I would have to use a one-by-eight, which would be about seven and a half inches wide. I carefully measured the length of the bank of cabinets, and then cut a piece to fit.

If the floor in my office had been level, the space between the floor and the bottom of the cabinets would have been uniform, and I would have been able to rip this board down to the proper width on my table saw. But the floor was not level, and the space was not uniform. To make the board fit precisely, I would have to cut it in such a way that its bottom edge would match the curve of the floor. Doing this sounds difficult, but it is actually quite straightforward. It involves a carpentry technique known as scribing.

To scribe the board, I first slid it into place along the bottom of the cabinet so that its right end was resting on the high point of the floor. Using shims made from wood scraps, I propped up the left end about half an inch, so that the top of the board was perfectly level. Then I tacked the board in place with two finish nails and used my tape measure to measure the distance between the top of the board and the inside surface of the bottom of the cabinet. This distance was just under an inch and a half. I took a small compass (like the one I used to use in geometry class) and set it so that the distance between the metal point and the tip of the pencil was also just under an inch and a half. I then held the compass perpendicular to the board so that the side of the metal point was touching the floor and the tip of the pencil was touching the face of the board. Slowly I moved the compass along the full length of the board. As I did so, the pencil drew a curving line on the board that precisely matched the contour of the floor. I pulled out my finish nails, removed the board, and

262

Scribing

used my hand-held jigsaw to cut along the line I had drawn with the compass. I returned the trimmed board to the space along the bottom of the cabinets, where it now fit perfectly into place. The bottom of the board rested snugly against the curving floor. The top of the board was level and exactly flush with the inside surface of the bottom of the cabinets. I nailed the board in place with eight-penny finishing nails.

Scribing is an extremely useful technique in an old house like mine, where there are few level surfaces and lots of funny curves and angles. But it can also be useful in brand-new construction, whether to make up for deficiencies in the framing or to compensate for unavoidable irregularities, such as the slight hump above a wallboard joint. I now have a special scribing compass whose arms can be locked into place. Because the walls, floors, and ceilings in my house are so far out of kilter, I end up having to use it almost every time I install a piece of trim.

With the bottom piece in place, I cut and installed the top piece of the face frame for the bank of cabinets. I made this piece out of stock that I had ripped on my table saw to a width of two and one-eighth inches. This piece didn't need to be scribed, because it didn't have to follow the contour of anything except the level top of the bank of cabinets. When the piece was just right, I glued and nailed it into place. Then I cut vertical pieces from the same stock. It was important to make each joint as tight as possible, because seasonal shrinkage would later open up the joints somewhat.

PANELING

A s I mentioned in Chapter Five, interior walls in the very earliest American houses were covered with wood. At first these wood coverings usually consisted of simple wide boards whose edges had been beveled, shaped, or beaded. When my wife and I had our bedroom redone last year, we had the walls and ceiling stripped to the framing and then covered in this way. (Before they were demolished, the crumbling plaster walls had been covered with a bright red patterned wallpaper that looked like Christmas wrap.) The boards are white pine. They range in width from about twelve inches to about sixteen inches, and they are beaded on each edge. They are joined with splines, which are thin wood strips that fit snugly into slots cut into the edges of the boards. The boards are face-nailed with special nails whose heads closely resemble the heads of old wrought nails. We based the room on an original pine-paneled bedroom in an eighteenth-century Massachusetts house owned by my wife's great aunt.

As plaster became widely available, the use of wood as a wall covering declined. Instead of being used to cover all the walls in a house, wood began to be used just on the lower portions of the walls, between the chair rail and the floor, where it served both a decorative and a protective function. In time, this use declined, too. As an architectural historian once pointed out, the modern baseboard is a sort of shrunken remnant of what was once a full-scale wall treatment.

As wood wall coverings became less extensive, they also became more elaborate. Rather than simply butting boards together, carpenters began shaping large pieces of wood into beautiful panels whose edges were beveled with hand planes. These panels are usually called raised panels. In many eighteenth-century houses, entire walls surrounding the main fireplaces were covered with raised paneling. So were staircases and the lower parts of walls.

Old-fashioned raised panels, which were sometimes more than three feet tall and more than four feet wide, were almost always made from single pieces of wood. The wood was usually pine, which was both easy to tool and readily available in widths that today seem unbelievable. To keep these big pieces of wood from splitting as they shrank and expanded in response to changes in humidity, carpenters assembled the paneling in such a way that the individual panels "floated" inside a grid or frame of horizontal and vertical pieces, called rails and stiles. That is, the panels weren't nailed to the wall but were held in place by grooves cut into the edges of the rails and stiles. When the weather changed, the grid permitted the panels to move. (Of course, the grid, which was also made of wood, moved too.)*

This same type of construction was used, for the same reason, in making doors. After the Second World War, the so-called flush door began to replace the paneled door in much residential construction. The face of a flush door consists not of individual panels but of a single featureless piece of plywood, hardboard, or some similar material. The main selling points of flush doors are that they are cheap—the core, which is mostly hollow, is made of inexpensive materials—and that they have a "modern" look. *The Complete Home Handyman's Guide*, published in 1948, contained several pages of detailed instructions for turning old-fashioned paneled doors into up-to-date flush doors by using glue, screws, and nails to attach sheets of

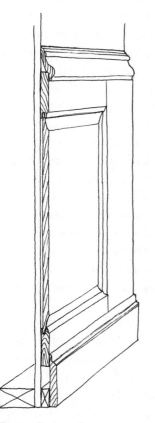

Raised-panel construction, cross section

*Thick layers of paint defeat the purpose of this type of construction, by gluing the panels into their slots, preventing them from moving. This is why one often finds cracks and splits in old wainscoting and in the panels of old doors.

quarter-inch plywood to their faces. Ruining beautiful old doors in this way remained a popular handyman activity until fairly recently, when the trend began to drift in the other direction. Home improvement guides nowadays are as likely to provide instructions for turning ugly modern flush doors into imitation paneled doors by applying moldings to their plywood faces.

Nowadays you can't raise enormous panels from single pieces of wood, for the simple reason that the enormous trees were cut down long ago. When carpenters or cabinetmakers raise large panels today, they have to either use an engineered wood product such as plywood or MDF, or make their own panel stock by gluing narrower pieces of wood together edge to edge. The cutting of the beveled edges is most easily done on a high-powered woodworking tool called a shaper, although it can also be done with other tools, including table saws, radial arm saws, and routers. One common and relatively simple method of making large raised panels is to cut the bevels separately, from pieces of solid wood, and glue them to the edges of a plywood field.

Well, as relatively simple as this method is, I didn't feel up to making raised panels for my office. I had once made a small raised panel on my table saw as a sort of exercise, but the panel hadn't turned out all that well, and making it had been unbelievably dangerous, and I didn't really have the tools to make anything that wouldn't look stupid. So I decided to use a simpler sort of paneling, in which the visual impact is provided not by bevels cut into the edges of the panels but by separate moldings applied along the inside edges of the stiles and rails. This type of paneling has its own distinguished history, and is actually older than raised paneling. It is also a great deal easier to build. I started with my desk.

I had already covered the sides of the desk with half-inch plywood. I would apply the rails, stiles, and moldings directly on top of this. Doing this would leave a rectangular section of plywood exposed in the field of each panel. I decided to divide the north and west sides of the desk into two panels each, and to make a single panel for the south side. To create more shadow lines and to make the design a little more interesting to look at, I decided to use two sets of rails and stiles, one nested inside the other—like a frame within a frame.

Desk-panel details, cross section and head-on

I began with the north side of the desk. First, I cut rails and stiles from five-quarter stock. I ripped the bottom rail to five and a half inches wide, the top rail to two and a half inches wide, and the stiles to three and a quarter inches wide. I scribed the bottom rail to the floor and installed both it and the top rail using glue and finishing nails. Then I trimmed and installed the stiles, one at each end of the desk and another in the middle. This created two panels, each of which was a little under three feet wide. The five-quarter stock stood out from the plywood a little more than an inch.

When this was finished, I cut a new set of rails and stiles from one-by stock. The one-by was three quarters of an inch thick, or a little more than a quarter inch thinner than the five-quarter. All these pieces were two and one eighth inches wide. I installed them inside the two rectangular frames formed by the five-quarter rails and stiles, creating frames within frames.

The next step was to install the molding. The molding I had chosen was one and three eighths inches wide and a little less than three quarters of an inch thick. It looked like this in cross section:

David Owen

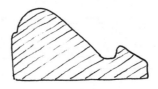

Base-cap molding profile

In the early days, carpenters made their own moldings, using hand planes. Nowadays carpenters typically use hand planes only for a few limited purposes, such as trimming the edge of a sticky door, but in the eighteenth and nineteenth centuries, planes were among the very most important tools a carpenter owned. A typical builder might have made regular use of several dozen planes, including floor planes, plow planes, rabbet planes, cove planes, bead planes, halving planes, and snipe bill planes. (R. A. Salaman's *Dictionary of Woodworking Tools* devotes more than seventy pages to planes.) These versatile tools were used to surface lumber, to cut tongues and grooves, to dress floorboards, to cut grooves and slots, to make raised panels, and to shape elaborate moldings, including the wonderful crown moldings in old houses.

I didn't make my moldings by hand. I bought them at my lumberyard. Like virtually all moldings used in modern residential construction, mine were made in automated mills filled with big, noisy machines called molders. Molders contain whirring blades that rapidly sculpt raw stock into a variety of shapes. The quality of the finished product depends on both the quality of the raw material and on the care of the mill. The moldings carried by my lumberyard are pretty good. The ones carried by most large home centers and discount stores are usually pretty awful.

The type of molding I chose for my office is known as "base cap," because its original use was as a decorative cap on top of baseboards. Nowadays people seldom get that fancy with their baseboards, but base cap has a number of other uses, too, including the one to which I put it. I installed my base cap (with glue and four-penny nails) along the inside edges of the inner rails and stiles—a frame within a frame within a frame.

To make the pieces of molding fit together properly, I had to cut the ends of each one at a forty-five-degree angle. Then I fitted them together in a rectangle, as though they were pieces of a picture frame. The joints formed at the corners are known as miter joints, perhaps because they resemble (vaguely) a bishop's miter. I made all these cuts on my electric miter saw, which has a large circular blade that can be lowered into whatever is being cut, like the arm of a paper cutter. (Because of this chopping motion, these saws are also often called chop saws.) The blade can easily be turned so that it meets the wood at any angle along an arc of a little over ninety degrees. Like most miter saws, mine has positive stops at the most commonly used angles (such as forty-five degrees and twenty-two and a half degrees), which makes it easy to be consistent from one cut to the next.

Electric miter saws are a relatively recent invention. Before they were introduced, trim carpenters made angled cuts with handsaws and guides called miter boxes. A miter box is a sort of open ended trough into whose sides thin slots have been cut. These slots are meant to support the blade of a saw at a particular angle to a piece of wood laid inside the trough. Getting good results with a miter box requires both a top-quality miter box and a top-quality carpenter. Nowadays, though, any idiot with a couple of hundred bucks can make perfect, silky-smooth miter cuts again and again and again.

An electric miter saw can also easily do things that a top-quality miter box can't, such as shave off a hundredth of an inch from the end of a piece of molding that is a hundredth of an inch

Electric miter saw

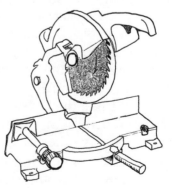

too long. When I use my miter saw, I purposely make my cuts a little bit too long (known as "fat" cuts in the trade) and then shave them down angstrom by angstrom until they are just exactly right.

An electric miter saw is equally useful in rough carpentry. When I framed some partition walls in my basement, I used my miter saw to trim all the two-by-fours. The saw gave each stud two perfectly square ends. This made the entire frame fit together much more snugly than it would have if I had made all those cuts freehand with my skillsaw. My miter saw also enabled me to make minute adjustments in the lengths of studs that had turned out to be a teensy bit too long. (No saw, unfortunately, will enable you to restore wood to lumber that you have cut a teensy bit too short.)

Some people become teary when they think of all the old-fashioned craftsmanship that has been displaced by power-tool technology. I know a man who imported a team of European carpenters to do the finish work in his new American house. He wanted these particular carpenters because he knew that they would make each cut lovingly with Old World hand tools. He also hired some American carpenters, but only to do rough work that wouldn't be visible. The first thing the European carpenters did when they arrived at his house was to put away their miter boxes and ask the American carpenters if they could borrow some of those fancy modern tools.

Those Old World carpenters had discovered something that New World carpenters have known for a long time: power tools are great! Not only do they save labor, they also put professional results within the reach of a reasonably competent amateur. I once watched an old carpenter use a handsaw to make a beautiful forty-five-degree cut in a piece of molding. He lined up his cut visually, by eyeballing the angle formed by the molding and its reflection in the polished blade of his saw. I couldn't make a freehand cut like that to save my life. But I went home and made an even better cut on my electric miter saw, which cost me about $250. My miter saw doesn't make me a good carpenter, of course. But it enables me to do certain things that, just a few short years ago, only a very good carpenter would even have attempted.

MOLDING AND TRIM

M ost houses built nowadays don't have much in the way of interior trim. Casings around doors and windows are minimal. Baseboards are plain and small. Other trim, such as chair rails and crown molding, is usually absent. It isn't hard to understand why. Moldings are expensive, and the skilled labor required to install them can cost many times the price of the materials. Because installing trim is the final step in building a house, money originally budgeted for it often turns out to have been spent on something else. So the crown molding is left out, and the baseboard is streamlined, and the house ends up looking more ordinary than it was meant to.

Nice trimwork is worth planning ahead for. Judiciously chosen moldings can have a dramatic effect on the entire look and feel of a house. Several years ago my friends Jim and Laura transformed their otherwise boxy Manhattan apartment by installing some crown molding in the hall and living room. The molding itself was nothing remarkable, but it made the apartment seem less like the inside of a shoe box and more like the inside of a really distinguished and attractive box. It changed the feel of the entire place.

The most common species of interior trim is the baseboard. Almost every house has at least a rudimentary version. The main reason for this is that installing baseboards can actually save labor, by covering up the otherwise problematic intersections between walls and floors. Hiding this area with baseboards saves everyone a lot of trouble. It also protects the lower portions of walls from kicks, thumps, and vacuum cleaners. And from an aesthetic point of view, baseboards add visual heft to the bottom of a room and (especially in combination with other moldings) lend a sort of sculptural quality to the walls.

In many early American houses, baseboards were plain boards that were installed so that their faces were flush with the finished surface of the plaster above them. As the years went by, baseboards (along with the rest of interior trimwork) often took on a formal grandeur. By the time of the Victorians, baseboards had become wide and elaborate. They were typically built up

271

David Owen

from several pieces, including a "cap" on top and a "shoe" along the bottom. More recently, baseboards have tended to be pretty minimal. In most new houses the baseboards are either simple one-by-something or off-the-shelf baseboard stock with a lightly molded profile.

I didn't really need to install baseboards in my office. The face frames in the desk and cabinetry ran right to the floor. But the bottom part of the face frames looked wide, bare, and unadorned to me. I wanted to dress it up a little, and I wanted to add something to the bottom of the woodwork that would balance the weight of the crown molding I intended to install at the top. I chose a standard one-piece baseboard sold by my lumberyard. It is four inches wide and half an inch thick, and its top edge is molded. In addition, I planned to install a standard half-by-three-quarters base shoe along the bottom. In profile, the combination looks like this:

Baseboard profile

When this standard baseboard is used alone in a regular room, I think it looks skimpy. But as a base for the kind of cabinetry I had installed, I felt it added just the right degree of detail.

Before installing the baseboard, I had to cut the bottom to match the slope of the floor, in the same way I had had to cut the bottoms of the face frames. I began in the same part of the room (the bank of cabinets opposite the door) and used the same scribing technique. The only difference was that I installed the baseboard so that its bottom edge was raised half an inch above the surface of the floor. This half-inch gap would give the carpet installers a small space in which to tuck the edges of the carpet. Tucking in the carpet like this would prevent its edges

272

from working loose. After the carpet had been installed, I would go back and add shoe molding along the bottom edge of the baseboard. The shoe molding would cover any small gaps between the carpet and the baseboard, and it would provide further protection for the edges of the carpet. It would also look nice.

Applying baseboard to a single wall would be easy. All you would have to do would be to cut it to fit. But applying baseboard to an entire room is tricky. The reason is that a room has corners. The ends of each piece have to be cut in such a way that the profile of the baseboard is carried around the room without interruption. There are several ways to do this. Which method is used depends on both the type of baseboard and the type of corner.

When the baseboard is simply a board (such as a one-by-four) and the corners measure ninety degrees, the inside corners can simply be butted. To do this, the first board is run smack into the corner and the second board is run smack into it. This isn't a very elegant joint. Then again, a one-by-four isn't a very elegant baseboard. Why put on airs? Outside corners are also sometimes butted, although this really shouldn't be considered acceptable in any but the most rustic construction. The preferred joint for outside corners is the miter.

Miter joints are also sometimes used for inside corners, although this is usually frowned on. One reason is that inside miter joints tend to pull open when the wood shrinks. Another is that miter joints can be tricky to cut for corners that aren't quite square. If the baseboard has a molded profile (as was true of the baseboard I was using in my office), the preferred joint for inside corners is the so-called coped joint. In a coped joint, the end of the first piece is butted into the corner of the room, and the end of the second piece is cut to match the profile of the first. The second piece is then slid into place against the first. When the coping is done properly, the two pieces fit together like pieces of a puzzle.

Making coped joints is tricky and time-consuming, but with a little practice even an amateur can master it. The first step is to make a forty-five-degree miter cut in the end of the piece that

273

is to be coped. This cut exposes the profile of the molding, as in the drawing below:

Coping

To make the profile line easier to see, many carpenters will darken it by rubbing a pencil against it. The next step is to cut very carefully along the pencil line with a tool called, not surprisingly, a coping saw. A coping saw has a very thin blade that is held taut between the ends of a U-shaped metal frame. Most carpenters back-cut their copes slightly; that is, they hold the saw at an angle to the molding, so that the finished profile edge is sharp. Doing this makes it easier to achieve a tight fit. Imperfect fits can usually be improved by carefully trimming the coped piece with a chisel, a knife, a rasp, or some sandpaper.

Outside corners can't be coped. Instead, they are mitered. An electric miter saw makes this easy and puts professional results within the reach of a reasonably careful amateur. For pieces of

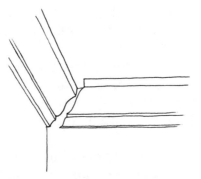

Inside corner, cornice molding. The piece
on the right is coped

trim that have to be coped on one end and mitered on the other—such as the baseboard along the northern end of my desk—the best plan is to get the cope right first and then cut the miter to fit.

When the baseboards were all in place, I installed the crown molding. (The term *crown molding* is commonly used both as a general term for any molding applied to the joints between walls and ceilings and as a specific term for a particular molding profile. Crown molding is also often referred to as cornice molding or ceiling molding.) The crown molding would conceal the small, irregular gaps between the ceiling and the tops of the face frames, and it would give the woodwork a finished look—like a nice hat sitting on the head of a well-dressed person.

Like molded baseboards, crown molding is coped at the inside corners and mitered at the outside corners. Making these cuts in crown molding is trickier than it is with baseboards, because virtually all modern crown moldings are "sprung." That is, they aren't solid. The molding that looks so substantial when installed is actually something of an optical illusion. Its majestic profile is produced by cutting a few shallow troughs in a relatively thin piece of wood. Here's what a typical crown molding looks like in cross section:

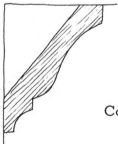

Cornice molding profile

The rear edge rests against the wall; the top edge rests against the ceiling. To make a proper miter cut in a piece of sprung molding, the carpenter must hold the molding in the miter saw at the same angle. If the molding is simply laid flat, the joint won't come together when the molding is installed. In making these cuts (and in making the preliminary miter cuts required for coping), the molding is always held "upside down and backward" in the saw. Doing this permits both the top and rear edges of the molding to be supported in the saw.

COUNTERTOPS

Most serious cabinetmakers stay away from softwood plywood, preferring to use hardwood plywood even for such utilitarian pieces as shelves. Standard softwood plywood tends to be riddled with internal voids, and the faces sometimes require fairly extensive cosmetic work before they can even be painted successfully. Hardwood plywood is less likely to have voids, and it's a better substrate for paint or stain.

Despite all this, I used mostly softwood plywood (with A-graded face veneers) in my office. I did this partly because I didn't know any better and partly because even the relatively pedestrian birch plywood sold by my lumberyard is twice as expensive as plain old fir. As it turned out, this was probably a pretty good decision. Most of the plywood I used was for things that didn't really show, such as the insides of bookcases and cabinets. In the places where it did show, I was able to spackle any defects well enough to make these surfaces look good under a couple of coats of paint.

The one place where I did use hardwood plywood was the top of the desk and counter. I was going to stain these surfaces, so I needed to use a material that, unlike most softwood plywood, would take stain well. I also wanted something that would be strong enough to tolerate having pencils poked into it, coffee cups banged on it, and heavy piles of royalty checks stacked up all over it. So I bought three sheets of three-quarter-inch birch plywood.

To make cuts in the birch plywood, I used my skillsaw and my Clamp 'n Tool Guide. I spent a lot of time setting up these cuts; as a result, the seams where the pieces meet are very inconspicuous. The one mistake I made was in failing to lay out the pieces so that the grain would run in one direction over the entire surface. If I had the top to build again, I would do it that way, although it looks fine the way it is. Besides, the whole thing is almost always entirely covered with junk.

To cover the raw edges of the birch plywood, I used three-quarter-inch half-round molding attached with nails and glue. (Half-round molding has a half-moon cross-section and looks like a dowel that has been sawn down the middle.) I mitered the molding at the outside corners and coped it at the inside ones. The half-round I used was made of pine, but it and the birch veneer stained to the exactly same tone.

I had cut the plywood countertop so that, including the half-round, it overhung the edges of the desk and cabinets by about seven-eighths of an inch. Now I dressed up this overhang a little by applying half-inch cove molding in the angle formed by the bottom of the overhang and the front of the face frames. This cove molding would eventually be painted. Here's what the edge of the desk looked like:

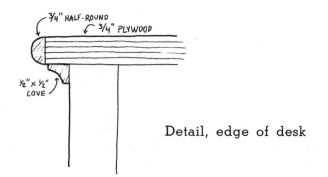

Detail, edge of desk

When the top was finished, I cut two big holes in it. The first, which measured about four inches square, was for computer cables and power cords. To minimize clutter on top of my desk, I had installed two duplex electrical outlets, each on a separate circuit, inside the desk itself. The cords for my copier, a lamp, and one or two other gizmos ran down the hole and plugged into these outlets. Also routed through the hole were the cables from my computer monitor and keyboard. (The computer's central processing unit stands on the floor underneath the desk and is plugged into a surge suppressor that is plugged into one of the outlets.) To make the hole look less holelike, I framed it with a sort of plastic plate that I had bought at an electrical supply store.

The second hole, which measured three inches by fifteen inches, was for my form-feed computer paper. I had designed the desk and cabinets so that I would be able to store three kinds of computer paper in the middle cabinet and feed them up into my printer from below, with the help of a three-way paper-handling device I bought from a computer supply store. (This paper-handling device also neatly covers up the ugly hole.) Doing this lets me keep the computer paper out of sight and leaves more room on top of the counter for junk. I also drilled four small holes through the desktop so that I could install a big mechanical arm to hold up my computer monitor. This arm, which is called a CRT Valet, lets me adjust the angle of the monitor or swing it and the keyboard out of the way when I need more room to spread things out on top of the desk.

A ROOM OF ONE'S OWN

Once the desk was finished, my new office was ready for a seemingly endless series of finishing touches. Moving out all my tools and vacuuming the sawdust took most of a day. Patching, sanding, and painting took more than a week. (Painting the shelves, which I spread out all over my basement, took even longer.) Waiting for the carpet and for some snazzy-looking wooden venetian blinds took several weeks. But eventually I was able to move in and make myself at home.

Back in the days when I could merely dream about the office I wanted to have someday, I figured that actually having that office would make me work harder and enjoy my work more. As it turned out, I was right. Being able to reach out and grab a conveniently located reference work genuinely does fill me with contentment and make me almost eager to buckle down and earn enough money to pay my bills. The fact that I like to be in my office makes it somewhat more likely that I will go to it. And once I am in my office, there is always a chance that I will do some work.

My office is also a good place to go to think about my house. Nearly every permanent part of this room is something I built with my own hands. When I sit at my desk and look around, I see plenty of flaws and mistakes, but I also see things that make me feel proud and fill me with reckless ambitions. Do I have time before dinner to run downstairs and replace the windows in the dining room? How about tearing down the garage? My wife claims that I always begin big projects an hour before company is scheduled to arrive. What she doesn't understand is that there are some forces that are beyond one's power to resist.

My renovation of my house is now, I would guess, halfway complete. Finishing the second half will take another five years or longer, depending on how our lives unfold. Then it will be time to begin again. I've come to view all my current remodeling projects as a sort of dry run for my *real* remodeling projects, in which I will use the experience I am now acquiring to redo everything I've already done. When I go into one of the rooms that's (mostly) finished, I like to think about what I could have done to make that room better.

When my wife, my daughter, and I moved in, this house was the house of strangers. The walls were their walls, the roof was their roof. (Also the leaks.) Now that we have lived here for five years, the house has become partly ours, and the strangers have become familiar. My family and I have decoded part of the record that was left to us, and we have added fragments of our own story to it. And when we finally move on (I mean move on to another house or to a condominium in Florida, not die), the people who follow us will do the same.

Acknowledgments, Sources, and Resources

This book began as an essay on gypsum wallboard that appeared in *The Atlantic* several years ago. After the essay was published, the magazine received a letter from a man in Calcutta named R. P. Banik. "I am very much enlightened with the details of the article," Mr. Banik wrote. "Being an Indian I request you if you kindly give me the address of Mr. Owen as I can cope with him as his vast experience about the building walls (up to date)."

I hope that other readers have been able to cope with me as my vast experience about all the topics I've tried to cover (up to date). Mr. Banik notwithstanding, I can't claim to be an expert on any of them. But I've tried to do my homework and to sift through several mountains of often contradictory advice and information.

Many, many people were helpful along the way. I am especially grateful to my neighbors Ken Daniel, Peter Duncan, Bill Fairbairn, Phil Farmer, Michael Jackson, Dirk Sabin, Todd

David Owen

Staub, Polly Roberts Swain, and Rex Swain, and my fellow
Chilmark Associates; Fred Hammond, William Hardee, Tom
Hearn, Jack Johnson, Joel Johnson, Ron Johnson, Tom Os-
borne, Bill Taff and his crew, Don Wyant, and the staff of the
Washington Supply Company; William Whitworth, Corby Kum-
mer, Eric Haas, and everyone else at *The Atlantic*; Julia Coo-
persmith, my agent, and Diane Reverand, my editor; and
everyone to whom I am related by blood or marriage.

Following is a chapter-by-chapter description of some of the
other sources I used in researching this book, as well as further
information about some of the techniques and products mentioned.

Chapter One: Home Improvement
for Its Own Sake

Thomas Jefferson: I learned about Jefferson's feelings about
working on his house in *Jefferson and Monticello: The Biography
of a Builder*, by Jack McLaughlin (New York: Henry Holt,
1988). This book does a good job of telling the story behind the
greatest home-improvement project in American history.

Homeownership in General: One of the best general guides to
living with a house is the Time-Life *Fix-It-Yourself* series. This
is an updated version of the fine old Time-Life *Home Repair and
Improvement* series. For information about either series you
can contact Time-Life Books, 541 North Fairbanks Court, Chicago, IL 60611. When we moved to the country, I called up
Time-Life and ordered the entire *Home Repair* series, all at
once.

Another good general resource is *Mike McClintock's Home
Sense Care and Repair Almanac*, by Mike McClintock (Blue
Ridge Summit, Pa.: TAB Books, 1989). McClintock writes about
home repair for the *Washington Post*.

The Walls Around Us

Chapter Two:
The Best Paint in the World

Linoleum: If you're interested in tracking down real linoleum, you can contact Bangor Cork Co., Inc., William & D Streets, Pen Argyl, PA 18072. The telephone number is (215) 863-9041. Bangor imports its linoleum from the Netherlands.

Keeler & Long: Keeler & Long is located at Box 460, 856 Echo Lake Rd., Watertown, CT 06795. The telephone number is (203) 274-6701.

Horse Manure: I learned about warming vinegar with rotten horse manure in "Early Exterior Paints" by Gordon Bock, *Old-House Journal,* May/June 1988, pages 33–37. *Old-House Journal* is a good magazine that contains lots of practical advice, some of which would be of use even to people whose houses were built last week. For subscription information you can contact Old-House Journal Corp., 435 Ninth St., Brooklyn, NY 11215. The telephone number is (718) 788-1700. The same outfit publishes *Garbage,* an interesting new magazine that describes itself as "The Practical Journal for the Environment" and would be a useful resource for anyone who would like to be more environmentally responsible.

Painter's Colic: The quote about painter's colic is from *1995 Paint Questions Answered* (New York: The Painters Magazine, 1923).

Lead-Paint Removal: The most thorough (and sobering) study of the lead-based paint problem I have seen is *Lead-Based Paint Testing, Abatement, Cleanup and Disposal Guidelines,* which was prepared by the National Institute of Building Sciences under contract to the U.S. Department of Housing and Urban Development. Before attempting to remove lead paint, you should contact your state's department of health services and ask if it has any lead-abatement guidelines.

Alkyds: The quote from Joseph W. Prane concerning alkyd paints is taken from a paper by Prane called "The Nature of Modern Paints." Prane presented this paper at a symposium called *Paint in America,* presented in 1989 by the Barra Foundation. Prane was kind enough to let me see a draft of his paper. It and the other papers presented at the symposium will be published eventually in book form. The Barra Foundation is located at 8200 Flourtown Ave., Wyndmoor, PA 19118.

White House Restoration: Anyone interested in learning more about the restoration of the White House can do so in "Development of Guide Specifications for the 1980 Exterior Restoration of the White House" (Washington, DC: National Bureau of Standards, October 1980).

Painting: A useful general guide to painting is *Painter's Handbook,* by William McElroy (Carlsbad, CA: Craftsman Book Co., 1987). You can order this book by writing directly to Craftsman at 6058 Corte del Cedro, P.O. Box 6500, Carlsbad, CA 92008. Craftsman publishes a number of other books as well.

An excellent study of decorative interior painting is *Paint Magic,* by Jocasta Innes (New York: Pantheon, 1987). This book gives step-by-step instructions in marbleizing, graining, and other fancy techniques. It also contains some good general information about paint.

Chapter Three: Fear of Lumber

Fear of Hardware: A wonderful confidence-builder for anyone who is afraid to walk into a hardware store is *The Complete Illustrated Guide to Everything Sold in Hardware Stores,* by Tom Philbin and Steve Ettlinger (New York: Macmillan, 1988). If you have been told that you need a Molly bolt but you don't know what one is, owning this book would spare you the shame of having to ask. A similar book is *This Old House Guide to Building and Remodeling Materials,* by Bob Vila (New York: Warner, 1986).

Hewing Wood: For a lively and beautifully illustrated discussion of early techniques of building and working with wood, see *Sketches of America Past,* by Eric Sloane (New York: Promontory Press, 1986). This is a one-volume collection of three of

Sloane's wonderful books, *Diary of an Early American Boy, A Museum of Early American Tools,* and *A Reverence for Wood.* Sloane wrote other wonderful books as well. Another book full of interesting information about old building and woodworking techniques is *Colonial Craftsmen,* by Edward Tunis (New York: Thomas Y. Crowell, 1965).

Wood Science: A pleasant way to give yourself a thorough education in wood science is to read *Understanding Wood: A Craftsman's Guide to Wood Technology,* by R. Bruce Hoadley (Newtown, CT: Taunton Press, 1980). This highly technical but mostly fascinating book would make useful reading for anyone who works with wood, and might even be of interest to people who merely live with wood. Quite a bit of what I know about wood I know as a result of having read this book. Hoadley has also written a new book called *Identifying Wood* (Newton, CT: Taunton Press, 1990).

Hoadley's publisher, Taunton Press, is the publisher of two of my favorite magazines: *Fine Homebuilding* and *Fine Woodworking.* It also produces an excellent series of instructional books and videotapes on woodworking, carpentry, furniture finishing, and related topics. For more information you can contact Taunton Press, 63 S. Main St., P.O. Box 355, Newtown, CT 06470.

Another terrific magazine for ambitious home improvers is *The Journal of Light Construction.* For subscription information you can write to the magazine at P.O. Box 686, Holmes, PA 19043. The telephone number is (800) 345-8112.

Lumber Grading: A good source of information about lumber grading (and other lumber-related topics) is the Western Wood Products Association, Yeon Building, 522 S.W. Fifth Ave., Portland, OR 97204. The WWPA is the nation's largest association of lumber manufacturers.

Hardwood-Lumber Grading: For more information about hardwood-lumber grading, you can contact the National Hardwood Lumber Association, P.O. Box 34518, Memphis, TN 38184.

Plywood: My principal source on the history of plywood was *The Plywood Age: A History of the Fir Plywood Industry's First Fifty Years,* by Robert M. Cour (Portland, OR: Douglas Fir Ply-

285

wood Association, 1955). This book is extremely hard to find, perhaps deservedly so. I am indebted to the American Plywood Association for lending me one of its file copies.

Here's more from the book about the first plywood: "Constant heat had to be applied to the glue. If it dried, the pot would take many hours to clean and be readied for another try. Hand brushes were used to 'paint' the glue on the veneers. A wooden press was improvised. The pressure was applied by putting ordinary house jacks between a backing timber and another timber fixed to the press. The work was slow, tedious; there were failures, many of them, before success. Only one set of panels could be glued up at one time and this took most of one day. The panels were then put in the press and left overnight to set. In March, the first panels were successfully made." These first panels were forty inches wide and were made of spruce, cottonwood, fir, oak, ash, alder, myrtle, and other woods.

The American Plywood Association is a good source for all sorts of information about plywood. The APA's address is P.O. Box 11700, Tacoma, WA 98411. The telephone number is (206) 565-6600.

Hardwood Plywood: For more information about hardwood plywood, you can contact the Hardwood Plywood Manufacturers Association, P.O. Box 2789, Reston, VA 22090. The telephone number is (703) 435-2900.

Masonite: The Masonite Corp. still exists. Today it is a subsidiary of USG Corp., the company that makes Sheetrock gypsum wallboard, among other products.

Formaldehyde Outgassing: A good source of information about environmental hazards within the home is *The Healthy House*, by John Bower (New York: Lyle Stuart, 1989). This book is also where I found the figure on per capita termite poundage.

Enemies of Lumber: I read about the living enemies of lumber primarily in *Insects: Their Ways and Means of Living*, by R. E. Snodgrass (Washington: Smithsonian Institution, 1930); *The Strange Lives of Familiar Insects*, by E. W. Teale (New York: Dodd, Mead, 1962); *The Audubon Society Encyclopedia of Animal Life* (New York: Clarkson N. Potter, 1982); and *Controlling*

Household Pests (San Ramon, Calif.: Ortho Books, 1988). This last book, which is carried in many hardware stores, is an excellent aide in identifying pests and diagnosing bug problems, although it views the application of deadly chemicals as the best solution to nearly every difficulty. This is not surprising, since the publisher is a manufacturer of deadly chemicals. Still, the text is clear and complete, and there are many color photographs.

Treated Lumber: For more information about preservative-treated lumber, including both lumber treated with CCA and lumber treated with borates, contact the American Wood Preservers Association, P.O. Box 849, Stevensville, MD 21666. The telephone number is (301) 643-4163. You might also be interested in a publication called *Guidelines for Protection of Wood Against Decay and Termite Attack.* It is published by the National Institute of Building Sciences, 1015 15th St., NW, Suite 200, Washington, DC 20005. The telephone number is (202) 347-5710.

CCA-Treated Lumber: Among the most important manufacturers of CCA-treated lumber is the Weyerhaeuser Company, Tacoma, WA 98477. Weyerhaeuser's principal pressure-treated product is called LifeWood.

Borate-Treated Lumber: For more information about Bora-Care, you can write to Perma-Chink at 1605 Prosser Rd., Knoxville, TN 37914. The telephone number is (800) 548-3554.

A similar treatment is Tim-Bor, which is sold by U.S. Borax Co. Unlike Bora-Care, Tim-Bor needs to be applied to wood with a relatively high moisture content. The address is 3075 Wilshire Blvd., Los Angeles, CA 90052. The telephone number is (213) 251-5400.

Chapter Four: Bones and Skin

American Architecture: A good (though necessarily superficial) overview of American residential architecture is *A Field*

David Owen

Guide to American Houses, by Virginia and Lee McAlester (New York: Alfred A. Knopf, 1986).

Post-in-Ground: Building on buried posts or poles has a long history throughout the world. The method is still used today. In my part of the country, post-in-ground construction lives on, to some extent, in the modern pole barn and similar structures. A pole barn is a rustic building that can be used not only as a barn but also as a garage or other outbuilding. Like its seventeenth-century ancestor, a modern pole barn is held up by posts that are stuck in the ground. Unlike its seventeenth-century ancestor, its posts are almost always made of wood that has been treated to make it resistant to rot and insects. A pole barn is a simple structure that doesn't cost much to build, primarily because its frame is also its foundation.

Log Cabins: I read about the history of the log cabin in *Wood in American Life,* by W. G. Youngquist and H. O. Fleischer (Madison, WI: Forest Products Research Society, 1977). This book contains a number of other interesting facts about wood and its role in American history.

You can still live in a log cabin today, if you feel like it. Modern log houses don't look all that much like old log houses; they tend to be much larger, much fancier, and much better insulated. Often sold as kits, they are extremely popular in some parts of the country. In my town there's a road where new log houses seem to pop up at a rate of about one every six months. For information on modern log houses, you can scan the advertisements in the back pages of handyman magazines or contact the North American Log Homes Council of the National Association of Home Builders (NAHB), 15th and M Streets, NW, Washington, DC 20005. The telephone number is (800) 368-5242.

Timber Framing: For a good general reference on modern timber framing, see *The Timber Frame Home: Design, Construction, Finishing,* by Tedd Benson (Newtown, Conn.: Taunton Press, 1988). Taunton Press is responsible for much of the renewed interest in this kind of construction. Another source of information is the Timber Framer's Guild, P.O. Box 1046, Keene, NH 03431. For a brief introduction to timber framing, you can look up Philip Langdon's article "Not Log Cabins" in the December 1988 issue of *The Atlantic*. Langdon is also the author of a beautiful and fascinating book called *American Houses* (New York: Stewart, Tabori & Chang, 1987).

Post-and-Girt Framing: An excellent examination of early framing methods is *Early Domestic Architecture of Connecticut*, by J. Frederick Kelly (New Haven, CT: Yale University Press, 1924), now out of print but handsomely reprinted in a paper-back edition (New York: Dover, 1963). This is one of my favorite books in the world.

Balloon Framing: The story of the invention of balloon fram-ing is told in Tracy Kidder's excellent *House* (Boston: Houghton Mifflin, 1985). The invention is sometimes also credited to a Chicago builder named Augustine Taylor, who used two-by-fours to frame a church at around the same time.

Balloon framing is still used, or should be used, in framing two-story walls, such as the end walls of cathedral-style living rooms. When platform framing is used on an unbroken two-story wall, the horizontal joint between the two one-story sec-tions can act as a hinge, permitting the wall to deflect inward in high winds. The danger is increased if, as is usually the case, the two-story wall is filled with windows, which further weaken the structure.

Platform Framing: A good guide to modern framing tech-niques is *Construction Manual: Rough Carpentry*, by T. W. Love (Carlsbad, CA: Craftsman Book Co., 1987).

Wrought Nails: Thomas Jefferson used young slave boys to make the nails for Monticello. According to Jack McLaughlin, author of *Jefferson and Monticello: The Biography of a Builder* (New York: Henry Holt, 1988), Jefferson "kept productivity ta-bles on his adolescent nailers, noting who turned out the most nails and which boys wasted the most nail rod." Jefferson sold his slaves' surplus production to local famers, a business that netted as much as a thousand dollars a year.

Nails for Restorations: It's still possible to buy cut nails and imitation wrought nails for use in restoration work. Probably the best source is the Tremont Nail Co., "America's Oldest Nail Manufacturer," Elm Street at Route 28, P. O. Box 111, Wareham, MA 02571. The telephone number is (508) 295-0038. For a few dollars you can order a sample pack of twenty different nail types, ranging in size from a dinky brad to a three-and-a-half-inch "headless foundry" nail. The company is nearly as old as the cut nail. It was founded in 1819 on the site of an old cotton mill that had been leveled by the British in the War of 1812.

Tyvek: For more information about Tyvek, you can contact DuPont at (800) 44-TYVEK. Tyvek is the same stuff that Federal Express Fedex Pak envelopes are made of.

Cedar Shingles: For more information about cedar shingles, you can contact the Red Cedar Shingle & Handsplit Shake Bureau, Suite 275, 515 116th Ave., NE, Bellevue, WA 98004.

Plywood Siding: One relatively new plywood lap-siding product is Plylap, which has a rabbeted lower edge (which laps over the plank below) and tongue-and-grooved ends. The manufacturer is Laco Lumber, Inc., P. O. Box 1130, Woodland, CA 95695. The telephone number is (916) 661-0812. For general information about plywood siding you can contact the American Plywood Association, P. O. Box 11700, Tacoma, WA 98411. The telephone number is (206) 565-6600.

Hardboard Siding: For more information about hardboard siding you can contact the American Hardboard Association, 520 N. Hicks Rd., Palatine, IL 60067.

Vinyl Siding: One respected manufacturer of good-looking, smooth-finished vinyl siding is Wolverine Technologies, Four Parklane Blvd., Dearborn, MI 48126. The telephone number is (800) 521-9020.

Brick Siding: For more information about brick siding you can contact the National Association of Brick Distributors, 1000 Duke St., Alexandria, VA 22314. The telephone number is (703) 549-2555. The NABD also carries a line of brick-oriented novelty merchandise, including T-shirts that say "You Deserve a Brick Today" and brick-shaped paperweights that say "Think Brick."

Chapter Five:
The Walls Around Us

USG Corp.: USG Corp. is located at 101 S. Wacker Dr., Chicago, IL 60606. The telephone number is (312) 606-4000. USG estimates that 93 percent of the total wall area in new construction is covered with gypsum wallboard.

National Gypsum Company: National Gypsum Company is located at 4500 Lincoln Plaza, Dallas, TX 75201. The telephone number is (214) 740-4500.

Wallboard Information: The best guide to installing wallboard and plaster is USG's *Gypsum Construction Handbook.* The third edition contains more than five hundred pages, costs six dollars, and can be ordered from USG at the address above. This book, which is intended mainly for professionals, is the wallboard bible. Anybody who installs or finishes wallboard should have a copy.

If you're interested in real plaster, you might also want to track down *Plastering Skills,* by F. van den Branden and Thomas L. Harsell (Homewood, IL: American Technical Publishers, Inc., 1984). This book went out of print but was revived by the publishers of *Old-House Journal,* which is where you should write if you would like a copy (Old-House Journal Corp., 435 Ninth St., Brooklyn, NY 11215).

Wallboard Specifications: Wallboard is sold in a variety of lengths and thicknesses. Possible lengths include not only the standard eight feet but also nine, ten, twelve, and fourteen feet. Like many lumberyards, mine stocks mostly eight-foot wallboard, along with a limited quantity of twelve-foot. Other lengths have to be ordered.

Possible thicknesses include not only the standard half-inch but also one-quarter, three-eighths, and five-eighths. Quarter-inch wallboard is used for resurfacing deteriorated walls. Three-eighths-inch is used primarily in double-layer systems. (Quarter-inch is also sometimes used in a double layer, to form curved walls.) Some people try to save money by using a single layer of three-eighths instead of half-inch on the walls, but the difference in price is negligible and the difference in quality is noticeable. Five-eighths-inch is required by some building codes for some applications. It's also sometimes chosen by people who simply want thicker walls.

There are many variations on the standard wallboard panel. Some panels contain additives that make them particularly resistant to fire. These panels are sometimes required by building codes in certain situations. Other panels have an aluminum-foil backing that acts as a vapor retarder. Other panels are intended for use on ceilings that are exposed to weather, such as the ceilings of carports or porches. Still other panels contain additives that make them somewhat water-resistant.

Makita: You can contact Makita USA at 14930 Northam St., La Mirada, CA 90638. The telephone number is (714) 522-8088.

Hot Mud: Durabond comes in several versions, each of which is distinguished by the length of time it takes for it to harden. (Durabond 90 sets in roughly ninety minutes, Durabond 210 sets in roughly 210 minutes, and so on.) You have to mix this stuff yourself, usually in small batches to keep it from hardening before you can apply it.

Plus 3: My hardware store charges roughly twice as much for Plus 3 as it does for All Purpose. This is simply price gouging. A USG spokesman told me that the two products should carry essentially the same price tag. If your supplier doesn't think so, you should complain. (Even at twice the price, though, Plus 3 is worth it.)

Mesh Tape: USG says tests have shown that wallboard joints taped with mesh tape have only about half the strength of joints taped with paper. There is no reason to doubt USG in this matter, since the company makes mesh tape for other purposes (primarily for use with plaster, an application for which it is suitable) and would undoubtedly be happy to sell more of it.

USG does make one type of joint compound that can be used with mesh tape. It is called Durabond LC. (The LC stands for low-consistency.) Durabond LC should not be confused with Durabond 90, Durabond 210, or any of USG's other plasterlike setting joint compounds. Except for the LC version, Durabond joint compounds don't work any better with mesh tape than other joint compounds do. And Durabond LC—which is used primarily in high-volume construction where joint treatment and decoration are to be done in the same day—should probably be considered to be strictly for professionals.

Sheetrock First Coat: First Coat is sold in two versions: pre-mixed (in one- and five-gallon buckets) and powdered (in twelve-and-a-half- and twenty-five-pound bags). The premixed version is vastly easier to use. My hardware store unfortunately carries only the powder. To mix it you need a big bucket and a half-inch electric drill with an enormous mixing-paddle attachment. Most homeowners don't have a half-inch drill or a mixing attachment, but you can pay for both with the money you save on primer. If you mix it yourself, First Coat costs just a few dollars a gallon.

Plaster Washers: The only source I know of for plaster washers is the Charles Street Supply Co., 54 Charles St., Boston, MA 02114; telephone (617) 367-9046.

Chapter Six: Electricity

Amber and Leaves: A negatively charged piece of amber is also capable of *creating* a positive charge in a leaf, through a process known as induction. When the amber is brought close to the leaf, the extra electrons in the amber repel electrons on the part of the leaf closest to the amber and send them scurrying to the leaf's far side. The piece of amber and the positively charged part of the leaf then stick to each other. Similarly, two objects with the same charge will repel each other. You can prove this to yourself by rubbing two balloons against your wool sweater (thus giving both balloons a negative charge) and then dangling them near each other. The balloons will push each other apart.

Edison: I read about Edison's life and work primarily in *Edison: The Man and His Work,* by George S. Bryan (Garden City, NY: Garden City Publishing Co., 1926); *Those Inventive Americans*

(Washington, D.C.: National Geographic Special Publications Division, 1971).

Tesla: I read about Tesla's life and work primarily in *Prodigal Genius: The Life of Nikola Tesla, Inventor Extraordinary,* by John J. O'Neill (Hollywood, CA: Angriff Press, 1981—a reprint of an edition originally published in 1944 or 1945); *Lightning in His Hand,* by Inex Hunt and Wanetta W. Draper (Hawthorne, CA: Omni Publications, 1981—a reprint of an edition originally published in 1964); and *Tesla: Man out of Time,* by Margaret Cheney (New York: Prentice-Hall, 1981).

Alternating Current: Alternating current can be converted to direct current for applications that require it. The control box in my old train set was an AC-to-DC converter that turned powerful household current into a low-voltage direct current that was strong enough to run the simple electric motor in my train but not strong enough to eradicate my enemies. The "power packs" on my telephone-answering machine, laptop computer, portable tape recorder, and Fisher-Price baby monitor do the same thing.

Tesla and Radio: Shortly after Tesla died, the United States Supreme Court ruled that Marconi's radio patents were invalid in the United States because they had all been fully anticipated by Tesla's work. This would have been a great victory for Tesla had it come forty years earlier.

Smart House: For more information about Smart House, you can contact Smart House L.P., 400 Prince George's Blvd., Upper Marlboro, MD 20772. The telephone number is (301) 249-6000.

Chapter Seven: The Roof

General Information: A good general roofing text is the Audel *Complete Roofing Handbook,* by James E. Brumbaugh (New York: Macmillan, 1986). This book isn't entirely up-to-date, and it has nothing to say about membranes, but it's a good place to start.

Cedar Mining: I read about cedar mining in *Sketches of America Past,* by Eric Sloane (New York: Promontory Press, 1986). Here's some of what Sloane had to say:

> It was while a stump was being moved from [New Jersey's cedar swamps] that several sunken logs were loosened and floated to the surface. The logs had been submerged anywhere from a few centuries to a thousand years!
>
> These submerged logs, it was found, were of a superior quality and contained good timber. It was further discovered that a layer of fallen cedar trunks, about twelve feet deep, covered the the swamp bottom. When people learned of the remarkable lightness and durability of this material, there was a great demand for it. With the aid of an iron "progue pin," to probe beneath the surface of the water and locate the sunken logs, *cedar mining* prospered until the Civil War.

The roof on Independence Hall in Philadelphia was made of this material, and many of the three-foot shingles on historic American homes are from cedar that had been buried under water for centuries.

Trusses: Trusses of a different sort are being used increasingly in place of ordinary beams and floor joists. Floor trusses are light in weight but very strong. They simplify the work of plumbers and electricians, who can run their pipes and wires through the open webbing rather than having to drill a lot of potentially joist-weakening holes. In the future, floor trusses will take the place of virtually all solid-wood joists, according to some experts. In the meantime, there are a lot of builders who don't fully understand them. Like roof trusses, floor trusses need to be specified and installed by people who know what they're doing.

Shingles and Shakes: For more information about shingles and shakes, you can contact the Red Cedar Shingle and Handsplit Shake Bureau, Suite 275, 515 116th Ave., NE, Bellevue, WA 98004. A good source of solid information about many aspects of wood roofs is the Texas Forest Service, P.O. Box 310, Lufkin, TX 75902. The telephone number is (409) 639-8180.

Amteco: Amteco, Inc., is located at 815 Cass Ave., St. Louis, MO 63106. The telephone number is (314) 436-4811. TWP is sold in one-gallon and five-gallon containers. It's also sold in a concentrated version, called Radcon. Radcon needs to be diluted 1:4 with a paraffinic oil, which Amteco also sells. Because TWP and Radcon are oil-based finishes, they help to prevent cupping, curling, splitting, and checking, which is something that water-based preservatives don't do.

The Forest Products Laboratory recommends applying TWP at a coverage of about one gallon per hundred square feet. This is heavier than the coverage recommended by the manufacturer. TWP should be applied at a rate that prevents puddling. The best way to do this is to make two or more passes, giving the wood time to absorb the liquid before recoating. (Incidentally, TWP is a swell preservative for decks and other exterior wood.)

The Forest Products Laboratory also recommends Natural Seal X-100, manufactured by American Building Restoration Chemicals, Inc., 9720 S. 60th St., Franklin, WI 53132, telephone (414) 761-2440; and Cunapsol 1, available from Blairstown Distributors, telephone (800) 524-1093. Natural Seal X-100 is oil-based, and Cunapsol 1 is water-based.

Asphalt Shingles: For general information about asphalt roofing materials, you can contact the Asphalt Roofing Manufacturers Association, 6288 Montrose Rd., Rockville, MD 20852. ARMA sells a useful guide called the *Residential Asphalt Roofing Manual.* It also sells a number of other useful publications, including *Algae Discoloration of Roofs.*

Anyone considering installing an asphalt-shingle roof should also order two introductory videotapes from Owens-Corning. The tapes are called "The Fundamentals of Roofing" and "Roofing: Nailing Down the Basics." These tapes, which are intended to serve as training tapes for professionals, constitute a solid introduction to roofing with asphalt shingles. Watching these tapes would even be a good idea if you are planning to hire a contractor. You can order them from Owens-Corning Fiberglas, Roofing Products Operating Division, Fiberglas Tower, Toledo, OH 43659.

Slope and Pitch: There are several methods of determining the slope or pitch of an existing roof, such as the roof on your house. This is something you might need to do before deciding what sort of shockingly expensive roofing material to use in reroofing. One way to find the slope is to measure the rise and run directly, with a tape measure. Especially on tall houses, these measurements are often easier to take inside the attic (rather than outside on a ladder). It doesn't matter if you can't measure the *entire* rise and the *entire* run; all you need to find is the ratio, which is the same for the parts as it is for the whole.

It's also possible to find the slope of a roof with a folding carpenter's rule. To do this you stand a little distance from the house, fold the first segments of the rule so that they form a triangle, hold this triangle at arm's length so that you can see the roof of the house through it, and then fiddle with the folded segments until they match the angle of the roof. There's a standard scale for converting the numbers on the rule into pitch and slope values, but if you don't have a copy of the scale you can always trace the triangle onto a piece of paper and measure it directly.

You can also use a SmartLevel (see Chapter Nine).

Tarmac: Tarmac PLC's American subsidiary, Tarmac Roofing Systems, Inc., is at 1401 Silverside Rd., Wilmington, DE 19810. The phone number is (302) 475-7974. There are a couple of dozen other manufacturers in this country.

EPDM: One source of EPDM roofing materials for residential use is Resource Conservation Technology, Inc., 2633 North Calvert St., Baltimore, MD 21218, telephone (301) 366-1146. RCT's founder and president is Lee Jaslow, who is extremely knowledgeable not only about elastomeric roofs but also about a wide variety of advanced building materials, some of which he imports from Scandinavia. Jaslow says that the installation of elastomeric roofs can be done successfully not only by professionals who specialize in membrane roofs but also by general contractors and careful do-it-yourselfers. The important thing is to follow the manufacturer's instructions.

ASTM: You can write to ASTM at 1916 Race St., Philadelphia, PA 19103. The phone number is (215) 299-5400.

David Owen

Roofing Slates: Manufacturers of natural roofing slates include Evergreen Slate Co., Inc., 68 Potter Ave., Granville, NY 12832, telephone (518) 642-2530; and Hilltop Slate, Inc., P. O. Box 201, Route 22A, Middle Granville, NY 12849. Both of these companies are in the heart of one of America's slate belts. Evergreen has supplied roofing slates for the Baseball Hall of Fame, the Boston Museum of Fine Arts, and the White House.

Fake Slates: Manufacturers of decent-looking fake slates include Eternit, Inc., Village Center Dr., Reading, PA 19607, telephone (800) 233-3155; FibreCem Corp., 7 Woodlawn Green, Suite 121, Charlotte, NC 28217, telephone (704) 527-2727; and Supradur Manufacturing Corp., 411 Theodore Fremd Ave., P.O. Box 908, Rye, NY 10580, telephone (800) 223-1948.

Tile: For more information about tile roofing materials (along with a lengthy list of manufacturers), contact the National Tile Roofing Manufacturers Association, 3127 Los Feliz Blvd., Los Angeles, CA 90039, telephone (800) 248-8453. Major manufacturers include Ludowici-Celadon Co., 4757 Tile Plant Rd., New Lexington, OH 43764, telephone (614) 342-1995; and Gory Roof Tile, Inc., 1100 Park Central Blvd. S., Suite 1800, Pompano Beach, FL 33064, telephone (800) 223-8453. Ludowici-Celadon makes clay tiles, and Gory makes concrete tiles. There are many other manufacturers in many other parts of the country. It is also possible to find tiles and tilelike panels made of perlite, steel, and steel coated with crushed stone, among other materials. These products have distinctive features, but none can be expected to have a service life comparable to that of clay or concrete.

Copper Shingles: For more information about Tegola Canadese's Prestige Copper Shingle, you can contact the company's New York distributor, Decorplast International Ltd., 240 Front St., Hempstead, NY 11550. The telephone number is (800) 872-4263.

Busy Woman's Dream House: The Busy Woman's Dream House is located in Conyers, Georgia. It was designed by Jane Siris and Peter Coombs of Siris/Coombs Architects in New York, and built by Marilyn Turnipseed of CareCraft Homes in

Atlanta. Like most recent show houses, it has a phenomenally high volume-to-area ratio, primarily as a result of a twenty-two-and-a-half-foot vaulted ceiling over the adjoining living and dining rooms.

Self-Adhering Waterproof Membranes: Owens/Corning makes a membrane called Deck-Dri; W. R. Grace makes one called Bituthene Ice and Water Shield. There are several others.

Chapter Eight:
Kitchens, Bathrooms, and Plumbing

Kitchens: A wonderful general discussion of kitchens is *The Kitchen Book,* by Terence Conran (New York: Crown, 1977). The book is out of print but is worth tracking down. Another good book is *Planning the Perfect Kitchen,* by Bo Niles and Juta Ristsoo (New York: Roundtable Press and Stonesong Press, 1988).

Ducci Kitchens: Ducci Kitchens, Inc., is located at 379 Goshen Rd., Torrington, CT 06790. The telephone number is (203) 496-9666.

Storage: A good book filled with interesting ideas about storage in the kitchen and elsewhere is *Sunset Complete Home Storage,* by the editors of Sunset Books and *Sunset* magazine (Menlo Park, CA: Lane, 1984).

Formulas: There are also formulas and rules of thumb governing the placement of individual components in a kitchen. Overhead cabinets, for example, are almost always positioned eighteen inches above the work surface. If the work surface is raised (because the cook is six and a half feet tall), then the overhead cabinets need to be raised, too. This may be tricky in a kitchen whose ceilings are low.

Commercial-Style Ranges: One company that manufactures commercial-style ranges meeting residential building codes is Viking Range Corp., P.O. Box 956, Greenwood, MS 38930. The telephone number is (601) 455-1200.

Energy Efficiency: The American Council for an Energy Efficient Economy publishes a useful pamphlet called *The Most Energy Efficient Appliances.* You can order the pamphlet, which costs three dollars, by writing to the ACEEE at 1001 Connecticut Ave., NW, Suite 535, Washington, DC 20036.

Wood-Mode Cabinetry: You can contact Wood-Mode at 1 Second St., Kreamer, PA 17833. The telephone number is (717) 244-4011.

Avonite: For more information about Avonite, you can contact Avonite, Inc., 12836 Arroyo St., Sylmar, CA 91342. The telephone number is (800) 286-6483.

Corian: For more information about Corian, you can contact E. I. Du Pont de Nemours & Co., Corian Building Products, 1007 Market St., Wilmington, DE 19898. The telephone number is (800) 441-7515.

Other Solid Surfacing Materials: Another major manufacturer of synthetic countertops is Nevamar Corp., 8339 Telegraph Rd., Odenton, MD 21113. The telephone number is (301) 569-5000.

Formica: For more information about Formica, you can contact Formica Corp., One Stanford Rd., P.O. Box 338, Piscataway, NJ 08854. The telephone number is (201) 469-1555.

Backer Board: Durock is sold by USG Corp., 101 S. Wacker Dr., Chicago, IL 60606. The telephone number is (312) 606-4000. Wonderboard is distributed by National Gypsum Company, 4500 Lincoln Plaza, Dallas, TX 75201. The telephone number is (214) 740-4500.

Glass-Roofed Bathroom: The bathroom with the courtyard was featured in the September 1989 issue of *Practical Homeowner.*

Chapter Eight:
Building Stuff

Demolition: Anyone in his or her right mind would rent a dumpster of some kind before undertaking a remodeling project involving more than a teeny amount of demolition. I didn't do it because I was in a hurry, I was lazy, and I intended to do the dirty work a little at a time over the course of several weeks.

Skil Corporation: You can contact Skil Corporation at 4300 W. Peterson, Chicago, IL 60646. The telephone number is (312) 286-7330.

SmartLevel: SmartLevel is manufactured by Wedge Innovations, 532 Mercury Dr., Sunnyvale, CA 94086. The telephone number is (800) 762-7853. The only major flaw in the Smart-Level's design is its shape. The tool has a wedge-shaped profile. This makes the tool "ergonomic," according to the manufacturer. But it also makes it extremely difficult to hold the side of the SmartLevel flush against a wall, as you would want to do, for example, in scribing a level line against which to install a chair rail or a bank of cabinets. So many people complained about this that the company came up with a solution in the form of a pair of vinyl-coated metal clips that attach to the rail and keep it at the proper angle when it's held against a wall. You can supposedly get a free pair of these clips by writing or calling the company, although I called about a year ago, and mine still haven't come.

Flush Doors: I read about turning paneled doors into flush doors in *The Complete Home Handyman's Guide,* edited by Hubbard Cobb (New York: Wm. H. Wise & Co., 1948). The *Reader's Digest Complete Do-It-Yourself Manual* (Pleasantville, NY: Reader's Digest Association, 1973) contains similar instructions.

Dictionary of Woodworking Tools: I looked at pictures of hand planes in *Dictionary of Woodworking Tools,* by R. A. Salaman (Newtown, Conn.: Taunton Press, 1989). This is a reprint of a book first published in England fifteen years before.

Moldings: One way to get around the limited selection at the lumberyard is to have moldings custom-made. A couple of years ago I had some old molding from my house copied at a nearby mill that was willing to take small orders. (I wanted only a hundred feet.) The molding had a profile similar to that of a stock molding carried by my lumberyard, but the old molding was much larger than anything available today. The mill was able to duplicate the old molding, and the cost was roughly what I'm used to paying for many stock pieces (about a dollar and a half a foot). I used the new molding to reproduce some old paneling in my dining room. Because I didn't do a very good job of estimating how much I needed, I still have about fifty feet of it sitting in my basement.

Building Stuff: Some good resources for would-be carpenters: *Carpentry: Some Tricks of the Trade,* by Bob Syvanen (Charlotte, NC: East Woods Press, 1982); *Interior Finish: More Tricks of the Trade,* by Bob Syvanen (Chester, CT: Globe Pequot Press, 1988); *Trim Carpentry Techniques,* by Craig Savage (Newtown, CT: Taunton Press, 1989); *Construction Manual: Finish Carpentry,* by T. W. Love (Carlsbad, CA: Craftsman Book Co., 1974); and the *Fine Homebuilding Builder's Library,* a six-volume collection of reprints from *Fine Homebuilding* (Newtown, CT: Taunton Press, 1988).

Now, go build a wall.

Index

Index

Corian, 217
Corn oil, 30
Cornell University, 212
Corner rollers, 136
Cornice molding, 122, 137, 275
  profile, 274–75 (illus)
Cottonseed oil, 31
Countertops, 276–78
Crown moldings, 268, 271, 275
Cummings, Benjamin, 51
Cupping, 101

Damp-wood termite, 72–73, 77
Davy, Humphry, 152
Dehumidifier, 77
Desks, 261, 276
  details, 277 (illus)
  desk-panel details, 267 (illus)
Dictionary of Woodworking Tools, 268
Dimension lumber, 53
Dimples, 135, 137
Direct current (DC), 153
Dishwashers, 210
  dishwashing detergent, 30
Disodium octaborate tetrahydrate, 83
Dormers, 197
Douglas, David, 61
Douglas fir, 63
Douglas Fir Plywood Association, 61
Dow Chemical, 78
Downspouts, 111–12
Drain-waste-vent (DWV), 228
Drainpipes, 258
  polyvinyl chloride (PVC), 111
Drawknife, 178
Drier, 5–6
Drop-in sinks, 221
Dry rot, 76
Dry-wood termite, 72–73, 78
Drywall, 119
Ducci Kitchens, Inc., 206–8, 213, 217, 220
Duct tape, 236
DuPont, 217
Durabond, 131, 143–44
Durock, 237
Dursban, 78
DWV (drain-waste-vent) system, 230

Early construction techniques, 86
Edison, Thomas, 151–53
Elastomeric membranes, 193
Electric circuit, 166
Electric miter saw, 270
Electric power lines, 162
Electrical:
  energy, 154
  outlets, 4
  wiring, 160
  work, 8
Electricity, 146–74
  history of, 147–51
Electron microscope, 158
Elmer's glue, 33
Emery cloth, 225
Emulsified resin, 31
Emulsion paints, 31
Engineered wood products, 65–68, 103, 266
Environmental Protection Agency, 27
Epoxy glue, 21–22
Epoxy paint, 22, 24–25
Epoxy resin, 21, 36
Ethylene propylene diene monomer
  (EPDM), 193

Exterior paint problems, 23
Exterior stains, disadvantages of, 38

Face frames, 255, 261
  cabinet hardware details, 216 (illus)
  cabinets, cabinetry, 214–16 (illus), 249
Fiberboard, 65
  high-density, 65
Fiberglass mesh tape, 127
Finish nails, 262
Finish paints, 37
Fir, 52
Fire-retardant chemicals, 184
Flashing, 24, 175–76, 197
Flat finishers, 136
Flaxseed, 18
Flexible armored cable (BX), 171
Floors, yellow pine, 12
Flush doors, 265–66
  for kitchen cabinets, 214
Foams, 99
Forest Products Laboratory, 186–87
Formaldehyde, 68
Formica, 218
Formosan termite, 72–73
Frameless (European or Eurostyle)
    cabinetry, 215, 221
  advantages of, 215
  hardware details, 216 (illus)
Franklin, Benjamin, 115, 148
Freon, 235n
Froe, 49, 50 (illus), 96, 116, 178
Fumigants, fumigation, 78
Fungi, 25, 32, 76, 78–80, 87
Fuses, 166–68

Galvani, Luigi, 148
Girts, 89–90
Glossy house paints, 36
Glycerine, 31
Gold Bond wallboard, 119, 131
Gold leaf, 55
Granite counter, 218
Grid, 265
Grooves, 25
Ground fault circuit interrupter (GFCI),
  169–70
Grounding conductor, wire, 165, 170–71
Grounding slot, 171
Grout, 218, 236
Gutters, gutter systems, 109–12, 258
Gypboard, gypsum wallboard, 114, 116,
    119–20, 141, 236, 248
  dimensions of, 95, 123
  installation of, 124
  manufacture of, 123

Hand-held circular saw, 251
Hardboard, 65
  problems with, 103
  siding, 104
Hardwood, 52, 56
  plywood, 63, 276
  properties of, 52
Head rig, 51
Hemlock, 52
"Hewing to the line," 50
Hickory, 52
Holiday House, 12
Homasote, 66
Home improvement, guides, 5, 266
Hooley, E. Purnell, 193
Horizontal lap siding, 103

304

Index

Index

Index

Index

About the Author

DAVID OWEN was born in Kansas City, Missouri, in 1955. He has been an editor of the *Harvard Lampoon*, a fact checker for *New York* magazine, a regular contributor to *Esquire*, a senior writer for *Harper's*, and a contributing editor of *The Atlantic*. He now writes regularly for *The New Yorker*. He lives in Connecticut with his wife and their two children.